Introducing English Syntax

Introducing English Syntax provides a basic introduction to syntax for students studying English as a foreign language at university. Examining English phrase and sentence structure from a descriptive point of view, this book develops the reader's understanding of the characteristic features of English sentence construction and provides the necessary theoretical apparatus for engaging with the language.

Key features include:

- A unique framework combining theoretical and practical approaches to provide an insight into the intricacies of English syntax;
- An accessible and clear style which guides the learner through analysis, application and practical construction of sentences;
- A range of exercises at the end of each chapter and a brand new e-resource housing answers and commentaries to these exercises.

This book requires no previous knowledge of linguistics and is essential reading for students and teachers of applied linguistics and EFL/ESL, as well as those who seek a basic grounding in English sentence structure.

Peter Fenn is a lecturer in English language and linguistics at the Ludwigsburg University of Education, Germany.

Götz Schwab is Professor of Applied Linguistics and EFL teaching methodology at Karlsruhe University of Education, Germany.

Introducing English Syntax
A Basic Guide for Students of English

Peter Fenn and Götz Schwab

LONDON AND NEW YORK

First published 2018
by Routledge
2 Park Square, Milton Park, Abingdon, Oxon OX14 4RN

and by Routledge
711 Third Avenue, New York, NY 10017

Routledge is an imprint of the Taylor & Francis Group, an informa business

© 2018 Peter Fenn and Götz Schwab

The right of Peter Fenn and Götz Schwab to be identified as authors of this work has been asserted by them in accordance with sections 77 and 78 of the Copyright, Designs and Patents Act 1988.

All rights reserved. No part of this book may be reprinted or reproduced or utilised in any form or by any electronic, mechanical, or other means, now known or hereafter invented, including photocopying and recording, or in any information storage or retrieval system, without permission in writing from the publishers.

Trademark notice: Product or corporate names may be trademarks or registered trademarks, and are used only for identification and explanation without intent to infringe.

British Library Cataloguing-in-Publication Data
A catalogue record for this book is available from the British Library

Library of Congress Cataloging-in-Publication Data
Names: Fenn, Peter, author. | Schwab, Götz, author.
Title: Introducing English syntax : a basic guide for students of English / by Peter Fenn and Götz Schwab.
Description: Milton Park, Abingdon, Oxon ; New York, NY : Routledge, [2017] | Includes bibliographical references and index.
Identifiers: LCCN 2017027525| ISBN 9781138037489 (hardback : alk. paper) | ISBN 9781138037496 (pbk. : alk. paper) | ISBN 9781315148434 (e-book)
Subjects: LCSH: English language—Syntax—Study and teaching. | English language—Syntax—Problems, exercises, etc. | English language—Textbooks for foreign speakers.
Classification: LCC PE1375 .F46 2017 | DDC 428.2/4—dc23
LC record available at https://lccn.loc.gov/2017027525

ISBN: 978-1-138-03748-9 (hbk)
ISBN: 978-1-138-03749-6 (pbk)
ISBN: 978-1-315-14843-4 (ebk)

Typeset in Goudy
by Swales & Willis Ltd, Exeter, Devon, UK

Visit the eResource: www.routledge.com/9781138037496

Contents

List of symbols and abbreviations   viii

Introduction   1

0.1 *Who this book is for* 1
0.2 *What this book does* 1
0.3 *What is syntax?* 3
0.4 *The role of meaning* 4
0.5 *The connection to language teaching and training* 5

1 Basic elements of grammatical structure   6

1.0 *Structure* 6
1.1 *What are word-classes or 'parts of speech'?* 6
1.2 *The phrase* 8
1.3 *What word-classes are there, and what are their characteristic features?* 10
1.4 *Phrase, clause and sentence* 28
    Exercises 32

2 The simple sentence and its grammatical functions   34

2.0 *Structure and function* 34
2.1 *Sentence functions explained* 35
2.2 *Verb complementation* 43
2.3 *Functions in the sentence* 44
    Exercises 48

3 Structural variations of the simple sentence and functional consequences   50

3.0 *Basic sentence operations* 50
3.1 *Questions (the interrogative)* 50
3.2 *Voice: active to passive* 54

3.3 Negation 57
3.4 Commands (the imperative) 60
    Exercises 62

4 Phrases and their structure (I) — 64

4.0 Phrases 64
4.1 The noun phrase 64
4.2 The prepositional phrase 79
4.3 The adjective phrase 82
4.4 The adverb phrase 87
    Exercises 94

5 Phrases and their structure (II) — 96

5.1 The verb phrase 96
5.2 Effects of negative, interrogative and passive on the verb phrase 103
5.3 Auxiliary pro-forms 107
5.4 Two- and three-part verbs 108
    Exercises 120

6 The multiple sentence — 122

6.1 Co-ordination 122
6.2 Further aspects of co-ordination 123
6.3 Subordination 127
6.4 Subordination without conjunctions 138
    Exercises 139

7 Non-finite clauses in the complex sentence (I): the infinitive — 141

7.0 Non-finite clauses 141
7.1 The infinitive clause 141
7.2 The infinitive clause as verb complementation 143
7.3 The subject of an infinitive clause 146
7.4 Some special cases in complementation by infinitive clause 149
7.5 The infinitive clause as subject 152
7.6 Semantics: implicative meanings of catenatives with infinitives 154
7.7 Tense and aspect 155
    Exercises 158

8 Non-finite clauses in the complex sentence (II): the gerund — 161

8.0 The gerund 161
8.1 The gerund clause 162

8.2 The semantics of the gerund 167
8.3 The gerund clause as catenative complementation 169
8.4 Questions of tense and aspect 181
8.5 The action nominal 184
Exercises 186

9 Non-finite clauses in the complex sentence (III): the participles 188

9.0 The participles 188
9.1 The present participle and its clause 189
9.2 The past participle and its clause 201
Exercises 207

10 The complex phrase (I): the complex noun phrase 209

10.0 The complex phrase 209
10.1 Postmodifiers: the relative clause 211
10.2 Postmodifiers: other structures as reduced relative clauses 221
10.3 Postmodifiers: apposition 224
Exercises 228

11 The complex phrase (II): complex prepositional and adjective phrases 231

11.0 Complex prepositional and adjective phrases 231
11.1 The complex prepositional phrase 232
11.2 The complex adjective phrase 234
Exercises 244

12 Selected clause constructions 246

12.0 Return to sentence-level: particular clause constructions 246
12.1 Extraposition 246
12.2 False subject constructions 248
12.3 Existential sentences 251
12.4 Cleft sentences 253
12.5 Nominal relative clauses 255
12.6 Interrogative clauses 258
Exercises 259

Bibliography 261
Index 262

Symbols and abbreviations

Symbols

[ ]	square brackets are used to indicate a subordinate clause at sentence level.
/ /	slants are used to show subordinate clauses inside phrases (i.e. at phrase level).
Ø	indicates omission of a certain element.
△	indicates that the particular unit could be analysed further.
↗ ↙	arrows indicate a general connection between two items (as discussed in the accompanying text).
↰	a kinked left-pointing arrow indicates the relation of a clause inside a phrase to the head of the phrase.
»	indicates a relation of presupposition between two elements.
→	indicates an implicative relation between two elements.
↛	indicates the negation or destruction of a former implicative relation.

Sentence function

- **S** Subject
- **P** Predicator
- **Oi** Indirect object
- **Od** Direct object
- **A** Adverbial
- **Cs** Subject complement
- **Co** Object complement

Other abbreviations

- ELT   English Language Teaching
- EFL   English as a Foreign Language
- ESL   English as a Second Language

Reference abbreviations

- *LGSWE*   Biber, D. *et al.* (1999). *The Longman Grammar of Spoken and Written English*. Harlow: Longman.
- *SAGE*   Fenn, P. (2010). *A Student Advanced Grammar of English*. Tübingen: Narr Francke Attempto.

Introduction

0.1 Who this book is for

This book is intended for both teachers and learners of English. Though primarily aimed at non-native speakers, it will be of interest also to native speakers who are professionally involved in the ELT field or in general linguistics, and to those who simply wish for an overview of the central characteristics of English phrase and sentence structure. It is not a practical grammar, though it does give advice to the learner on various points of difficulty in using the language. The book is oriented to a general international readership within an applied linguistics and ELT framework. The core material was developed within the European context of higher education with special emphasis on language teacher training. Though it deals with many basic issues and concepts 'bottom up', the book is aimed at the intermediate and advanced student in university training, as well as at the practising teacher.

It can be used:

- as a textbook for seminars in syntax and linguistics;
- as a reference work;
- as a self-study course;
- to supplement existing practical courses in English grammar;
- as a first introduction to fields of language dealt with more theoretically in model-based linguistic studies (such as generative grammar);
- for purposes of general reading on the nature and character of English.

No previous knowledge of linguistics is necessary.

0.2 What this book does

The book examines English phrase and sentence structure from a descriptive point of view. The object of study, that is, is the language itself and its central syntactic characteristics, in particular as far as they potentially affect language-learning processes. In other words the treatment here is **applied linguistic** in nature, and is not intended as a contribution (nor indeed as opposition) to any particular theoretical model of syntax (for example, transformational-generative grammar, the Minimalist Program, the Lexical-Functional Approach, Generalised Phrase Structure Grammar, cognitive linguistic approaches, construction grammar, etc.). Nevertheless, the approach does have certain theoretical points of origin and presupposes one or two basic principles that need mentioning briefly. These are set out below, together with other goals we are pursuing and aspects of content that are dealt with.

- The type of analysis used here is what we call **structural-functional**, since it takes as a starting point the two parallel levels of grammar and language function, i.e. the systematic relations between form and meaning within a sentence.
  It is based on concepts that are traditional in talking about language, such as word-classes and functional roles. However, they are more clearly defined and more consistently applied here than in many traditional treatments.
- Essentially, the 'system' is based in its modern form on that used by Quirk, Greenbaum, Leech and Svartvik in their epoch-making descriptive work *A Grammar of Contemporary English* (1972) and its various sequel publications, in particular *A University Grammar of English* (1973). It is further developed, analysed and refined in Fenn, *A Student's Advanced Grammar of English* (SAGE) (2010), but is presented here for the first time in a specific introduction to **syntax**. The latter was used as a reference source whenever it was felt that detailed information might be necessary. Further reference is made in the text to another standard grammar of English based on Quirk *et al.* (1972), *The Longman Grammar of Spoken and Written English (LGSWE)* by Biber *et al.* (1999). Rooted in corpus linguistics, this provides further information on the use and scope of a wide range of grammatical phenomena discussed here.
- The theoretical approach to **sentence functions** is in principle **semantic**. It is rooted in the conception of real-world 'roles' in events, such as **agent, patient, recipient**, etc. and regards these as reflected in functions like **subject** and **object**.
- Besides providing the reader with a solid basis for analysing and categorising sentences and their parts, the book also aims to give both practical and theoretical insight into many of the key structures (e.g. non-finite verb forms) which influence sentence and clause patterns in English. It thereby contributes significantly to the furtherance of high-level language awareness in the learner.
- There is thorough definition and explanation of standard concepts used in talking about syntax, and of the principles of their application. Exercises are provided at the ends of sections or chapters.
- Although we do not distinguish between written and oral codes in detail, we do in places take into account the fact that oral communication has to some extent its own grammatical features (Biber *et al.* 1999, 2002), which can deviate from standard written forms of the language.

- The book has a definite, though flexible, course structure. Chapters 1, 2 and 3 address the basic questions of form and function in grammar, so that the reader can quickly grasp the rudiments of sentence-functional analysis and apply them to simple sentences. Not until after this do we go into the details of phrase structure (Chapters 4 and 5), which we conceive of as a second level of analysis below that of the sentence. The reader now has all the tools required for the analysis of simple sentences and the phrases composing them. In Chapter 6 we return to the functional level of the sentence, expanding the object of analysis from the simple to the complex sentence, and dealing with the issues of co-ordination and subordination at sentence level. Chapters 7, 8 and 9 address themselves to non-finite clauses, and Chapters 10 and 11 look at complex phrases. In Chapter 12, finally, we focus on specific kinds of clause and sentence construction.

0.3 What is syntax?

Syntax describes how words 'hang together': that is, the rules and principles that underlie their **combination** in sentences and phrases. First of all, as a field, syntax should be seen together with its 'neighbours' in language studies: **morphology** and **semantics**. And also, to add two more to those, with **phonetics** and **phonology**, which examine the sounds of speech. These are the different areas of study in the scientific examination of language and languages. But the terms also mean the characteristics of language itself, both generally and specifically. For instance, we can talk about the phonetics of English (in other words, the kinds of **speech sounds** used), or the semantics of a particular phrase or sentence (i.e. its **meaning**), or the morphology of this or that individual word: that is, its **grammatical form**.

These, then, are the different 'departments' of language and language study, and syntax is one of them.

Syntax has an especially close relationship to morphology. Both these fields concern rules about forms and structures. Together, they make up the larger area that we normally call **grammar**. Grammar therefore has two major components: the grammar of individual words (morphology) and the grammar of joining them into larger units like sentences (syntax). For illustration let us apply the two fields to a sentence example:

(1)   Amy enjoys watching sad films.

Picking out examples of 'grammar' here we can say, for instance, that the verb *enjoy* has the third person singular ending, the verb *watch* is in the gerund, and the noun *films* is in the plural. What we have now described is the morphology of those words, i.e. the particular grammatical form in which they appear in this sentence. Morphology, then, is what we might call **word grammar**. But the sentence does not consist of just isolated words, of course. In every sentence there is a grammatical relationship **between** the different words. This second level of grammar ('beyond the word') is what we call syntax. When we say, for example, that *Amy* is the subject of the sentence, *watching sad films* is the **direct object** of *enjoys* and *sad films* is the direct object of *watching*, then we are referring to the grammatical level of syntax. Other **syntactic** points we might observe could concern **word order**: this type of sentence conveys a statement (in contrast, for instance, to a question) and therefore has to have **declarative** word order, with the subject *Amy* in front of its verb *enjoys*. Another point is that here the adjective *sad* has to precede the noun that it describes. And so on.

What must also be taken into account is the connection between syntax and morphology: the grammatical form of a word often depends on its relationship to other words. The reason for the third person singular *-s*-ending on the verb *enjoy*, for example, is that it has to agree grammatically with its subject *Amy*, a noun that also has the morpho-semantic characteristic of third person singular. Or take the gerund form of *watching*. This is triggered by the verb *enjoy* in front of it. With some other verb, e.g. *want*, we would need an infinitive, i.e. a different morphological form of *watch*:

(2)   Amy wants to watch sad films.

The syntax of a sentence, then, can affect the morphology of the individual words. On the other hand, the morphology of the words often tells us something about their actual or possible syntactic relationships to other words in the same sentence. When we look at *enjoys*, say, we know that it has to have a third person singular noun as subject before it. A clause with a gerund verb, like *watching sad films*, is a typical direct object. Other possible positions would be as subject (*Watching sad films is Amy's favourite hobby*), or following a preposition (*Amy is always for watching sad films*). The morphology of a word can therefore indicate its syntactic role and position in a given or possible sentence.

So, although they deal with different areas of grammar, syntax and morphology are really two sides of the same coin and have a two-way relationship:

(3)   Grammar

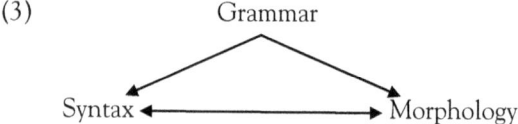

Syntax ⟷ Morphology

0.4 The role of meaning

Our diagram in (3) covers the form side of things, i.e. the shapes of words and the relations between them when they are linked in sentences. This is normally all that we think of when we think of grammar. But actually this leaves a further very important component out. Grammar also reflects meaning. Consider example (1) again. The morphology of *enjoys* that connects it syntactically to *Amy* is not just part of an internal code programme. The syntactic connection represents a meaning: it refers to a link between a person and an action. Specifically it tells us that the person carries out an action and has a particular emotional attitude towards this. Similarly, the tense and aspect morphology of *enjoys* (present tense, simple form) conveys the idea of a present habit or regularity. Syntax and morphology are therefore partly responsible for the semantics of a sentence, i.e. its meaning content. So we should add this to our grammar diagram as follows:

(4)
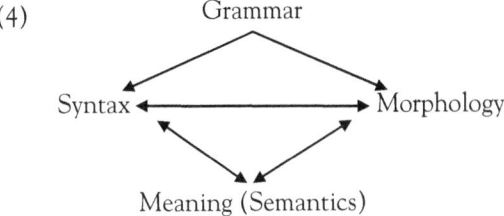

Note that here too we have a two-way relationship. The grammar conveys the meaning, but the intended meaning also determines the grammar.

Though this book is specifically about syntax, we will often refer to its close relation to morphology and semantics.

0.5 The connection to language teaching and training

Our own long experience in the realm of ELT and EFL teacher training shows that many advanced students, and even teachers of English, have only a rather hazy idea of some of the central concepts in applied syntax. Limited cognitive awareness of key characteristics of English sentence structure also means limited ability to grasp and deal with pedagogical issues involved in learning, teaching and using the language. This book aims to fill the gaps. It attempts to provide a comprehensive frame of reference and a fund of systematic descriptive knowledge, supporting both student and teacher in the development of an informed and reflective professional practice.

1 Basic elements of grammatical structure

1.0 Structure

The term **structure** is used in this book to cover the following:

- any kind of **morphological feature**: plural/singular of nouns, verb categories like tense, aspect or person, verb forms like gerund/infinitive, etc., adjective features like comparative/superlative, and so on. (This is just a small selection of examples.)
- any kind of **syntactic construction**: the *of*-genitive, *do*-support, negation, declarative, the interrogative, the imperative, the passive, relative clauses, cleft sentences, extraposition, etc.
- grammatical categories of words known as **word-classes** or **parts of speech**: nouns, verbs, adjectives, prepositions, etc.

All this concerns grammatical characteristics of words and groups of words that are permanent and individual, and do not depend on particular sentences. What contrasts with structure is the idea of **function** (subject, object, etc.), which, as we will see later, is a sentence-dependent concept. For the moment we will stay with structure. Function is discussed in the next chapter. The aspect of structure that we want to look at more closely now is the word-class, which needs some detailed explanation.

1.1 What are word-classes or 'parts of speech'?

Word-classes are a good example of how morphology, syntax and semantics interact with each other. The basis in this case is morphology. Words of the same class have the same grammatical forms. **Verbs**, for instance, change according to the type of subject they have (= **person**: *I am, you are, he is*), and the time they refer to (= **tense: present tense**, *I am*; **past tense**, *I was*). **Nouns** have **number**, i.e. singular and plural forms (*woman* → *women*), **Adjectives** and **adverbs** have the category of **comparison**: *slow* → *slower* → *slowest*; *slowly* → *more slowly* → *most slowly*. And so on. Many members of particular word-classes also show typical endings, e.g. *-ive*, *-ible/-able* for adjectives (*massive, respectable*), *-ion* and *-ity* for nouns (*station, integrity*), *-ise* and *-ate* for verbs (*realise, compensate*), *-ly* for adverbs (*slowly, quickly*), etc. This means that members of one word-class can be converted into members of another (a morphological process called **derivation**): *sensitive* (adjective) → *sensitivity* (noun), *nation* (noun) → *nationalise* (verb), etc.

However, although the external features of word-classes are morphological, it is syntax that shows their real purpose. A word-class comprises members that do the same job syntactically. Members of the same class occur in the same places in a sentence and have similar relationships to members of other word-classes. For instance, we typically start a declarative sentence with a noun or pronoun and follow it with a verb. Sometimes, depending on the verb, this is enough:

(1) noun   +   verb
     Jenny   drinks.

To say more, we might follow this with another noun and extend this further with an adverb:

(2) noun   +   verb   +   noun   +   adverb
     Jenny   drinks   tea   regularly.

But the options are restricted. The second noun cannot swap positions with the verb (**Jenny tea drinks regularly*)[1] and an adjective could not replace the adverb (**Jenny drinks tea regular*). On the other hand, there is nothing to be said against putting adjectives before the nouns:

(3) adjective   +   noun   +   verb   +   adjective   +   noun   +   adverb
     Young   Jenny   drinks   green   tea   regularly.

This is not just about position. Some word-classes are more closely associated than others. Adjectives, we can see here, relate typically to nouns, whereas adverbs relate to verbs and verb sequences. Further examples of close neighbours are articles and nouns, and prepositions and nouns. Conjunctions, on the other hand, combine the larger parts of sentences that we call phrases and clauses (see 1.4 below for a detailed discussion of these terms).

So we can see that word-classes tell us a great deal about what goes where in a sentence.

Finally, semantics also plays a large role in the character of word-classes. Traditionally, in fact, it is meaning, rather than syntax or morphology, that is used to define word-classes, especially in the teaching of children. This is not surprising, as meaning is more easily understood by young learners than grammar. In this approach, nouns, e.g. are said to refer to things and people, verbs are labelled 'doing words', signifying actions, and adjectives are thought of as 'describing nouns'. Linguists have often criticised descriptions of this kind as vague and unreliable. And it is true that they can easily be contradicted. For instance, abstract nouns (such as *love* and *hate*) do not really mean 'things'. Words like *action* and *movement* refer, obviously, to 'actions', yet they are not verbs. On the other hand, verbs are not just 'doing words': they can mean states (*Vanessa strongly resembles her sister*) or experiences (*Alan caught a cold*).

Nevertheless, there is a lot of truth in semantic characterisation. It is not enough for a full definition, but gives us a good indication of typical cases or **prototypes**. Not all nouns refer to 'things' or people, certainly. But the reverse is usually true, i.e. that almost all words referring to things or people do belong to the class of nouns. Similarly, the typical meaning of a verb is that it refers to an event or state, even though a few nouns do the same thing. Furthermore, verbs always link other elements in the sentence together as **participants** in the event or state. This is not only a grammatical relationship, but a semantic one. For instance, in

(4) John kissed Mary

the verb tells us that John and Mary became involved with each other, and moreover in a certain general way: John caused what happened and he caused it to happen to Mary. This is what we call in semantics an **agent–patient** relationship. It is not exclusive to verbs, nor is it always present when verbs are used, but it **is** prototypically part of verb meaning in sentences that have the pattern Noun + Verb + Noun. This shows generally that when we use grammar, we also **think meaning**. In the more detailed discussion of the individual word-classes further below, we will therefore examine matters from both grammatical and semantic perspectives. The next section, meanwhile, introduces the important concept of **phrase**, an analytical category closely allied to word-class.

1.2 The phrase

The sentences in the examples (1)–(4) look as if they are composed simply of strings of individual words in sequence. This is not the whole story, however. We said above that certain word-classes associate particularly closely with each other, e.g. articles and adjectives with nouns. Certain words, that is, form groups. If we want to show word relationships in sentences more accurately, we have to take account of this. A more exact portrayal of (3) above, for instance, could look like this:

(5) (adjective + noun) + verb + (adjective + noun) + adverb
    (Young   Jenny)   drinks (green   tea)   regularly.

Young and *Jenny* on the one hand, and *green* and *tea* on the other, belong together. The verb *drinks* and the adverb *regularly* are just single words. But we could expand these too (grammatically speaking, that is) into groups, e.g. *has drunk* and *quite regularly*:

(6) (Young Jenny) (has drunk) (green tea) (quite regularly).

Such groupings as now shown in the brackets in (6) are vital building-blocks of the sentence, and are known as phrases. Each one acts as a unit. If a phrase is moved to another part of the sentence (for stylistic reasons, say, or because the sentence construction changes syntactically), it must be the whole phrase that moves, and not just a part of it, as, e.g. with the passive:

(7) (Green tea) (has been drunk) (quite regularly) (by (young Jenny)).

Though there are certain exceptions to this rule, phrases in principle remain together and act as a group. This applies particularly to sentence functions (discussed in detail in Chapter 2), which relate to phrases as a whole: for instance, the subject of (6) is *Young Jenny* and the direct object *green tea*, which becomes the subject in the passive version in (7). It is phrases, therefore, rather than individual words, that comprise the first level of sentence organisation.

Notice that each phrase has a main word (respectively *Jenny*, *drunk*, *tea* and *regularly*). This is called the **head** of the phrase. The word-class of the head gives its name to the phrase. As *Jenny* and *tea* are nouns, *young Jenny* and *green tea* are **noun phrases**. The phrase *quite regularly* has the adverb *regularly* as its head, and is therefore an **adverb phrase**. The verbs in a sentence form the **verb phrase**, here *has drunk* (with *drunk* as the head). Similarly, there are **adjective phrases** (e.g. *very big*, with the adjective *big* as the head), and **prepositional phrases** (e.g. *in the house*, with the preposition *in* as the head). Phrases can also include others, as shown in (7) by the prepositional phrase *by young Jenny*, which contains the noun phrase *young Jenny*.

The concept of being 'included' or 'contained' within a particular unit of sentence organisation is expressed by the linguistic term **constituent**, which refers to component elements of larger units. Words are therefore constituents of phrases and phrases can be constituents of sentences or of other phrases.

A final word must be said on single words: *drinks* and *regularly* in (5) above were 'expanded' into units of more than one word. We did this in order to explain the term phrase and demonstrate its central features. In actual fact, however, linguistics treats single words already as phrases. It does so precisely because they are capable of extension into a multi-word unit with themselves as potential heads. Looked at from the opposite point of view, most multi-word phrases can be reduced syntactically to their heads alone and the phrase structure of the sentence will remain intact. *Drinks* and *regularly*, then, represent phrases (a verb phrase and an adverb phrase respectively), i.e. phrases with only one constituent. And by the same token the single-word constituents of (1), (2) and (4) can now be described, more accurately in a syntactic sense, as phrases:

(8)   noun phrase   +   verb phrase
      Jenny   drinks.

(9)   noun phrase   +   verb phrase   +   noun phrase   +   adverb phrase
      Jenny   drinks   tea   regularly.

(10) noun phrase   +   verb phrase   +   noun phrase
      John   kissed   Mary.

10 Basic elements of grammatical structure

1.3 What word-classes are there, and what are their characteristic features?

If you look a word up in a dictionary, you will find that its word-class (part of speech) is given before the meaning. For instance:

house, noun:	A building for human habitation
make, verb:	to construct, build, or create, from separate parts

This underlines a point made above: that word-class is a **permanent feature** of a particular word, i.e. part of its individual character.

We generally distinguish between the following main word-classes: nouns, pronouns, verbs, adverbs, adjectives, prepositions, conjunctions, determiners.

We will now point to basic features that identify each word-class, using the three different perspectives of semantics, morphology and syntax. The functional aspect of syntax will not be discussed here, however, as functions are not introduced until the next chapter. Under the 'syntax' heading we will confine ourselves for the moment to other kinds of relationship between words.

1.3.1 Nouns

- Semantics:
  Nouns denote **entities**, i.e. living things (*person, woman, plant, animal*), objects (*table, road, car*), other physical phenomena (*weight, distance, electricity, rain, wind*), and abstractions like concepts and ideas (*wish, religion, memory, economics, friendship*). Names such as *Peter, London, Christianity, Communism* are called **proper nouns** and are spelt with capital letters. Nouns have further semantic features that not only identify them as nouns but also influence their morphology and syntax. Many can be counted, but others cannot. Those referring to persons can imply male or female identity (i.e. sex or gender).
- Morphology:
  An important feature of nouns is what we call number: that is, they can be **singular** or **plural**. The singular is the 'normal' or unmarked form (*cat*) and the plural is marked, usually just by adding the ending -*s* (*cats*). There are various irregular plural forms, e.g. internal change of vowel (*man*→ *men, goose*→ *geese*), same form as singular (*sheep*→ *sheep*), etc.
  Another important feature related to this is **countability**. Most nouns are what we call **count** nouns, i.e. they appear in the singular and plural with numbers (*one girl, ten girls*). But there are also many **non-count** nouns. These cannot appear with numbers. Some are only singular (*tea, wheat, information*), others are only plural (*surroundings, clothes*).
  And finally, a third central feature of nouns is their **person status**. This is a wholly semantic factor, but it has a kind of 'sleeping' morphological character that appears grammatically in the relationship to other word-classes like pronouns and verbs. Consider the sentence:

(11) Our neighbour is celebrating in her garden, but although we like her, she has not invited us.

> Note that the noun *neighbour* 'controls' the choice of any following pronoun that refers back to it. As the garden belongs to the (apparently female) neighbour we have to say **her** *garden* and not *our *garden*, followed by *we like* **her** (and not, for instance, *We like them), and **she** *has not. . .* (rather than **You have not. . .*). This is the morphology of a category that we call person. It forces pronouns to correspond in certain ways to their 'parent' nouns (i.e. their **antecedents**), which can only be referred back to by *he, she, it* or *they*. As these are known grammatically as **third person** pronouns, nouns are also regarded as having third person status. (The division of **person status** into three sub-categories numbered first, second and third is explained fully under Pronouns below). Example (11) also shows us that pronoun choice (in the singular at least) is further restricted by whether the noun refers to a thing or a person and in the case of a person whether the person is male or female. This is known as **gender**, and is differentiated according to **masculine** (*he*), for male persons, **feminine** (*she*), for female persons, and **neuter** (*it*) for things.

- Syntax:
  Nouns
    o can be preceded by **determiners**, such as **articles** (see below), and also by adjectives:
      The big cat.
      These accompanying words form a unit with the noun that we call a noun phrase.
  Nouns
    o occur (alone or in a phrase) **before** and **after verbs**:
      The dog followed **the boy**.
    o occur (alone or in a phrase) **after prepositions**:
      On the table; in anger; under a large tree.

1.3.2 Pronouns

Pronouns are specialised semantic and morphological variants of nouns. They are not really a separate word-class, but form a sub-division of nouns. Basically, they are used to **stand for** nouns, i.e. represent them, in certain grammatical and communicative contexts.

- Semantics:
  Pronouns step in as substitutes for **full nouns** that speakers cannot use, or do not wish to use, in particular circumstances. The most general reason is to avoid repeating a noun (and more usually a whole noun phrase) which has already been mentioned:

(12) The milkman usually comes around 11 o'clock, but today **he´s** very late. Maybe **his** cart has broken down. **That** was the reason why he was late on one day last week. The cart is an old **one that** he's been driving for years.

Back-reference to previous elements of texts and dialogues is known generally as **anaphora**. The back-referring item is called the **anaphor**. Pronouns are one of the most common examples of anaphor. In (12) the pronouns printed in bold type all show this anaphoric relationship. Note, however, that what they refer back to is different in each case. That is, each pronoun here represents a particular sub-category with its own distinct kind of use:

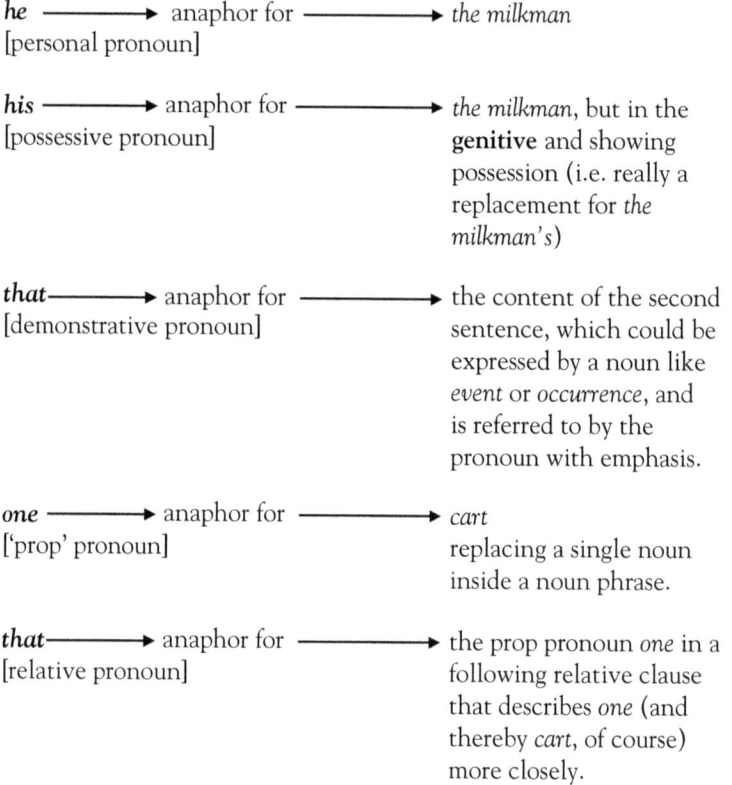

he ⟶ anaphor for ⟶ *the milkman*
[personal pronoun]

his ⟶ anaphor for ⟶ *the milkman*, but in the **genitive** and showing possession (i.e. really a replacement for *the milkman's*)
[possessive pronoun]

that ⟶ anaphor for ⟶ the content of the second sentence, which could be expressed by a noun like *event* or *occurrence*, and is referred to by the pronoun with emphasis.
[demonstrative pronoun]

one ⟶ anaphor for ⟶ *cart*
['prop' pronoun] replacing a single noun inside a noun phrase.

that ⟶ anaphor for ⟶ the prop pronoun *one* in a following relative clause that describes *one* (and thereby *cart*, of course) more closely.
[relative pronoun]

Further pronoun types are: **reflexive pronouns** (*myself, yourself, himself*, etc.), **interrogative pronouns** (*who?, what?, which?*, etc.), and **indefinite pronouns** (*somebody, anybody, no-one*, etc.). **Numerals** (*one, two, three*...) and **quantifiers** (*much, many, some, any*, etc.) can also do duty as pronouns, even though that is not their basic job and not their primary word-class. This does not exhaust the list, but what we have mentioned so far is enough to illustrate the general meaning of the word-class, and at the same time the individual semantic variety among its members. At its most extreme this can be seen with the indefinite pronouns, which unlike the other types are not anaphoric. They do, nevertheless, have a kind of representation function semantically.

- Morphology:
  Corresponding to the semantic variety, the different pronoun types all have their own individual and specific morphological features. Most prominent are the **personal pronouns**. These dominate the pronoun scene, so to speak. They are the most common type, and when we think of pronouns we tend automatically to think of personal pronouns as a prototype. They are also closely related to two other groups: the **possessive pronouns** and the reflexive pronouns.

  o Personal pronouns are sub-divided into persons, as mentioned above, and distinguished also in terms of number:

Person	Singular	Plural
First	I	we
Second	you	you
Third	he, she, it	they

A point to note is that gender is marked only in the third person singular. A further point is that, unlike full nouns, the personal pronouns are marked for **case**. That is, their syntactic status in a sentence (position and function) is marked **morphologically**. There are two case forms, subject (= those in the box above), and object, as follows:

Person (object forms)	Singular	Plural
First	me	us
Second	you	you
Third	him, her, it	them

The category of person originates in the social situation of speech, i.e. has to do with what we call **pragmatic meaning**. It belongs to the more general pragmatic category of **deixis** (= speaker-related meaning). In personal deixis speakers do three things: they refer to themselves as speakers (**first person**: *I/we*); they refer to the people they are addressing (**second person**: *you*); and they refer to third parties, i.e. people and things not involved in the *I–you* exchange (**third person**: *he/she/it/them*). This explains why nouns have the morphological idea of person attached to them, since full nouns are always used in the sense of third parties to a conversation. Third person pronouns are basically the only ones that are **directly anaphoric**. First and second persons can be regarded as representatives of proper nouns, i.e. the names of the speaker and the addressee: but they do not really 'refer back' to them, except perhaps in a rather abstract way.

○ Possessive pronouns follow the pattern of the personal pronouns:

Person	Singular	Plural
First	my	our
Second	your	your
Third	his, her, its	their

Possessive pronouns are not pronouns syntactically, however (see below under Syntax). If we want to use them as 'real' pronouns, i.e. standing alone, they have to be in their **'pronoun possessive'** forms, as in:

(13) This book is **mine**, not **yours**.

This is the complete table of pronoun possessives:

Person	Singular	Plural
First	mine	ours
Second	yours	yours
Third	his, hers	theirs

○ Reflexive pronouns follow partly the possessive pronouns and partly the object forms of personal pronouns, adding the ending *-self/-selves* to them. Semantically, reflexive constructions mean literally that the subject does something 'to itself', as in

(14) **She** has hurt **herself**.

Reflexive pronouns therefore have to signal **person agreement** with the subject pronoun:

Person	Singular	Plural
First	myself	ourselves
Second	yourself	yourselves
Third	himself, herself, itself	themselves

Demonstrative pronouns are marked for number, i.e. they have separate forms for singular (*this/that*) and plural (*these/those*). The same applies to the **prop pronoun**: *one* (singular), *ones* (plural).

The **relative pronouns** *who*, *which* and *that* are differentiated in use according to semantic criteria, which we will not discuss further here (see Ch. 10.1, on relative clauses). *Who* has an object form (*whom*) and a genitive (*whose*). Note that *who* and *which* can also be interrogative pronouns.

A further *Doppelgänger* is *that*, which, as we have just seen, also features as a demonstrative pronoun (see below under Syntax).

- Syntax:
  Anaphoric reference with most pronouns generally involves the whole noun phrase, and not just part of it:

(15) **The big brown** dog had hurt **itself** badly. **It** could not stand on **its** back legs.

An exception here is the prop pronoun, whose job is to replace just the noun part of a noun phrase:
  I wanted to buy red **shoes** for my daughter, but she preferred white **ones**.
Other major syntactic points are the following:
  o Possessive pronouns, as was said above, are **not** pronouns syntactically, but determiners (see further below). That is, they have the function of article words in larger noun phrases. We will therefore refer to them from now on as **possessive determiners**. Only what we called above the pronoun possessives have real pronoun status syntactically. The same is true of demonstrative pronouns. Only when they appear **without** a following noun, as in (12) above, are they pronouns in a syntactic sense. But with a noun following (**this** problem, **that** cat) they are **demonstrative determiners**.
  o Anaphora is a semantic relationship (i.e. it is a form of reference). But it also has a variety of morphological consequences, as we saw above, e.g. personal pronouns, reflexive pronouns, possessive determiners, pronoun possessives have to **agree** morphologically with their antecedents. This is therefore a syntactic relationship too, as the grammar of one word in a sentence affects the grammar of another. Another example is the case of personal pronouns. Case is a morphological feature, but is dependent on sentence function (see next chapter), which is a syntactic relation. This is just a further pointer to what we said at the beginning of this chapter: semantics, morphology and syntax **interact** in a sentence to produce its total meaning.
  o Relative pronouns introduce relative clauses.
  o Interrogative pronouns introduce questions and interrogative clauses (see Chapter 3, 3.1).

1.3.3 Verbs

- Semantics:
  Verbs, as we have already said, typically denote **actions** and **states**, i.e. things that 'happen', 'last' and 'go on in time':

(16) a. The dog **followed** the boy.
b. Karen **is** a teacher.

The close relation to time is shown by the fact that we can ask questions referring to the verb using expressions like *When?* and *How long?*:
For how long/When did the dog follow the boy?
How long has Karen been a teacher?
Another close connection to time is that verbs always show us, through tense, how an occurrence or state relates to the moment of speech, e.g. before it (**past**), simultaneous with it (**present**), both at once (**present perfect**), and so on. Tense is part of morphology, as we will see immediately. Nevertheless, it points to something semantic, i.e. a time reference that is a basic component of verb meaning.

In a more general way we can say that verbs have a semantically **connecting** effect: they link the other 'participants' named (typically the subject noun and any elements following the verb) with each other. In doing so they produce a message, or what is sometimes referred to as a **proposition**. In (16)a. above, for instance, the two noun phrases *the dog* and *the boy* are brought into a meaningful relationship with each other through the verb. The same applies to *Karen* and *a teacher* in (16)b. Some verbs, it is true, can create a proposition without anything following:

(17) a. David snores.
b. Karen sang.

But they still form a link, i.e. bind the noun to themselves to form a sense unit or message.
It is the semantic conception of a proposition that lies behind the **sentence** as a **grammatical unit** (see below under Syntax).

- Morphology:
In English the verb is the word-class with the most complex system of forms. We can see this already in a relatively simple statement like

(18) Jenny drinks coffee.

Firstly, the verb has an ending (*-s*) that is connected grammatically with the noun *Jenny*, which refers to the 'doer' (or **agent**) of the action. The agent, in sentences like this one, generally has the function of subject. Functions belong in the next chapter, as we have said, but the term subject is important here already, as it is this (or, more exactly, the noun in that function) that determines the ending of the verb. It does this according to the person status of the noun, here third person singular. In other words a third person singular noun requires this characteristic to be shown also in the verb ending. Syntactically, this is another example of agreement, this time **subject–verb agreement**, also known as **concord**. Verbs, then, are also marked for person, or, more exactly, they are marked according to the person status of their subject noun (since person is properly speaking a characteristic of nouns, not verbs).

Tables like the following, showing all the person forms of a particular verb (here *be*) are familiar to every language learner:

Person	Singular	Plural
First	I am	we are
Second	you are	you are
Third	he/she/it is	they are

This is what we call a **conjugation**. To **conjugate** a verb means to put it in all its person forms like this. But we can also speak of an individual verb form (such as *he is*) as a **conjugated** verb form, i.e. one that agrees with its subject noun. A verb like this is also known traditionally as a **finite** verb. By contrast, a **non-finite** verb has no subject agreement and is unchangeable: very often, in fact, it has no subject at all. Non-finite verbs are the various **participle** and **infinitive** forms, and the **gerund**. This is an important distinction, because finite verb forms have other characteristics too. In (18), e.g. the third person singular *-s*-ending does not just signify person, but also tense (present) and **aspect** (**simple**). An example such as *You were driving* is marked for second person (singular or plural, as the case may be), past tense, and **progressive aspect**. In English, that is, finite verbs always show – apart from subject–verb agreement – also tense and aspect. By contrast, non-finite verbs usually do not. Take, for instance the infinitive in

(19) Jenny decided **to drink** coffee.

To drink here relates to the past; yet it has no past tense marking of its own, any more than it is marked for person. It simply takes over these meanings (i.e. that *Jenny* is the subject and the action of *drink* is past-related) from the preceding finite verb. It is true that non-finite verbs have certain tense and aspect forms of their own, but they are used only in a limited way.

Further prominent morphological characteristics of verbs are the following:

o   Composite verb forms:
    Finite verbs like *drinks* in (18) consist of just a single verb. Most, however, are composed of two or more separate verbs in partnership, such as *have drunk, were drinking, have been drinking, will drink, can drink*, and so on. These are **composite** verb forms. Most of them are made up of one auxiliary verb + lexical (or main) verb, though some have two or even three auxiliaries:

Auxiliary verb(s) ↓	+	Main verb ↓
have	+	drunk
were	+	drinking
can	+	drink
have been	+	drinking
should have been	+	drunk

Auxiliary verbs are 'helping' verbs. They form a supporting partnership with main verbs in various ways. For instance, they help in creating tense (*have* + past participle = perfect), aspect (*be* + present participle = progressive), the **passive** (*be* + past participle = passive form), and so on. These are purely morphological operations, and the auxiliaries concerned (*be* and *have*) are therefore called **grammatical auxiliaries**. These contrast with **modal auxiliaries**, like *can*, *must*, *should*, etc., which have individual meanings (as well as helping with grammar). Auxiliaries are also essential for certain syntactic operations, such as forming questions and negatives (see below). A further grammatical auxiliary for this purpose is *do*. Note that the lexical verb here is always a participle or infinitive. It is the auxiliary that gives the partnership its finite features (i.e. concord, tense and aspect). Nevertheless, the partnership as a whole, as a unit, is regarded as finite. All the verbs involved work together, as one phrase. For this reason we call these units verb phrases. A **composite verb form** is always **one** verb phrase, and the cases listed here are all **finite verb phrases**.

o   Regular and irregular verb forms:
    This is a distinction that affects morphology mainly in the formation of the past tense and **past participle**. With **regular** verbs both are derived simply by adding *-ed* to the infinitive (or just *-d* if the verb already ends in *-e*), for instance:

Infinitive	Past tense	Past participle
walk	walked	walked

Irregular verbs, by contrast, form past tense and past participle in a variety of quite distinct ways:

Infinitive	Past tense	Past participle
swim	swam	swum
bring	brought	brought
come	came	come
put	put	put
give	gave	given

A general feature here is that instead of an *-ed*-ending internal changes to the word are made, usually affecting the vowels, but in some cases also consonants. Certain past participles are additionally inflected with *-en*. In a few cases all three forms are the same. These patterns usually repeat themselves wholly or partly with other irregular verbs, so that certain close neighbour groupings occur (e.g. *sing-sang-sung*, *shut-shut-shut*, *take-took-taken*, etc.). Several, however, are highly irregular, and show person divergence also: *have*, *do* and *go* have irregular forms in the third person of the present tense, *be* even in the second person, and between singular and plural in the past tense.

- Syntax:
  As was said above, it is the semantic idea of the proposition that is the basis for the grammar of a sentence. Or, regarded from the opposite perspective, it is the sentence as a grammatical unit that gives form and structure to propositions. Propositions are conceptualisations of relationships between entities. When they are expressed through language this is done via a sentence. As verbs hold propositions together semantically, so they hold sentences together grammatically. This translates into the grammatical rule that every sentence needs a verb. And it needs at least one noun for the verb to connect to. How much more it needs depends on the individual verb and what is required or allowed to follow that particular verb. This is known in modern linguistics as the verb's **complementation**, and in (9) and (10), for instance, consists of the noun phrases *tea* and *Mary* respectively. The shape of a sentence is therefore determined prominently by the verb. In order to establish the network of relationships in a sentence we need to refer not just to the word-classes and the phrases they form, but in particular to the **roles** those phrases play in their connection and relation to one another. This is the domain of sentence function, as we will see in the next chapter.

  Basic features of syntactic behaviour that characterise verbs are the following:

  o   Position in declarative sentences (statements):
      Verb phrases always follow the subject noun or pronoun (for a definition of the function of subject, see Ch. 2), and in general follow it directly: *They were dancing.*
      An exception is with certain types of adverb that can occur between subject and verb: *They often dance.*
  o   Negation:
      Verbs are negated by adding *not* after an auxiliary verb: *They were not dancing.* If there is no auxiliary verb in the affirmative sentence (as with the simple aspect of the present or past tense), *do* has to be added as a 'dummy' auxiliary (known as *do-support*): *They did not dance.*
  o   Position in interrogative sentences (questions):
      Like negation, questions require an auxiliary verb. Again, if there is no auxiliary, *do*-support is necessary. Then subject and auxiliary simply change places: *Were they dancing? Did they dance?* This turn-around of subject and verb is called **inversion**. Note again, though, that only the auxiliary is involved, not the full verb. This remains in the same position as in the declarative sentence.
  o   Abbreviated forms:
      These are also known as **weak forms**, and affect certain auxiliaries and negation. In less formal language certain auxiliaries are shortened (abbreviated), and in writing attached to the subject noun or pronoun by apostrophe:

      I am ⟶ *I'm*; *you are* ⟶ *you're*; *he is* ⟶ *he's*;
      the car has gone ⟶ *the car's gone*; *we will* ⟶ *we'll*; and so on.

The negative particle *not* is also reduced to *n't* and attached to the auxiliary:

aren't, doesn't, hadn't, won't, can't, mustn't, etc.

1.3.4 Adjectives

- Semantics:

  Adjectives denote **qualities** or **characteristics** of **entities**, i.e. they are 'describing words' relating to nouns. When they are derived from proper nouns, i.e. names, they are known as **proper adjectives** and are spelt with capital letters. Proper adjectives typically refer to characteristics such as national and regional identity (*French, British, Texan*), religion (*Christian, Protestant, Buddhist*), historical, cultural and political groupings (*Victorian, Impressionist, Marxist, Keynesian*), etc.

  As with other word-classes, certain semantic features of adjectives have an effect on their morphology and syntax. A typical feature is their **gradability**, i.e. whether they can be considered in terms of **degree** or extent: *a little tired, rather bored, highly sensitive*. Associated with this is **comparability**: you might be *happier* now than in the past, when you were *more wealthy* but *less relaxed*. On the other hand you cannot be *slightly married or *somewhat dead, and nor can you be less or more of either than anyone else. This is because the state referred to is thought of as absolute.

- Morphology:

  As with other word-classes there are no specific forms that all adjectives must have. Many cannot be distinguished from verbs or nouns. But there are certain typical endings (suffixes) that are used to derive adjectives from other kinds of words, such as *-ful* (*wonderful*), *-ious* or *-ous* (*envious, mountainous*), *-ic* (*tragic*), *-al* (*tropical*), *-ish* (*selfish*), *-ible* and *-able* (*sensible, considerable*), *-ive* (*primitive*), *-ent* and *-ant* (*different, significant*), *-y* (*sleepy*), and so on. On the other hand there are many members of other word-classes that are simply used as adjectives with no change made to them. For example,

  - participles: *a passing car, falling rain, the broken ladder*;
  - gerunds: *singing lessons, diving apparatus, a cleaning woman*;
  - nouns: *the car driver, a grass verge, a door handle*;
  - numerals/quantifiers: *the two men, his many hobbies*.

  A further feature, with comparable adjectives, is that of comparison:

Base form	Comparative	Superlative
big	bigger	biggest
small	smaller	smallest
violent	more violent	most violent
selfish	more selfish	most selfish

- Syntax:
  Adjectives typically occupy two positions:

  o as parts of noun phrases, placed between a determiner, such as an article (see below), and a noun:
     The **big** cat.
     This is known as an attributive position. It is usually **premodifying** (before the noun), but in some cases can be **postmodifying** (after the noun): *a woman alone, the people responsible, nobody special.*
  o after a small number of verbs like *be*, *seem* or *feel*, that denote a characteristic of the subject:
     Simon was lazy.
     He feels ill.
     That sounds good.
     This is known as a **predicative** position. A further kind of predicative position is after nouns following verbs of cause:
     Father painted the ceiling **yellow**.
     The bad food made Julia **ill**.

  Adjectives also form their own ***phrases***. If they are **gradable**, e.g. they can have adverbs like *very* or *slightly* before them (*very lazy, slightly ill*). Adverbs like this are called **adverbs of degree** (see below).
  Another typical kind of adjective phrase has a preposition and a noun following:
  full of water, pale with fright, keen on films.

  And of course also with comparative and superlative constructions:
  lazier than Simon, better than me, simplest of all the problems.

1.3.5 Adverbs

- Semantics:
  Adverbs add various kinds of information to phrases and sentences. One of their most typical jobs is to describe **how** an action takes place. In this respect they are like adjectives, i.e. they are 'describing words'. An important difference, however, is that they do not refer to nouns, but to verbs. Compare the following:

(20) a. Babs is a **quick** thinker.   [quick = adjective]
     b. Babs thinks **quickly**.   [quickly = adverb]

Thinker is a noun and needs an adjective to describe it. *Thinks* is a verb and can only be described by an adverb. Note the difference in form. Making the adjective into an adverb requires the addition of an *-ly*-ending (more on this point under Morphology below). The business of adverbs is broader than just describing how something happens, however. They can also tell us **when** (*tomorrow, yesterday*), **where** (*here, there*), **how often** (*sometimes, always, once, twice*), and **to what extent** (*highly, deeply, much*). These core meanings are generally referred to as **manner** (how), **place** (where), **time** (when, how often) and **degree** (to what extent). The question words used to ask about them (*how?, when?, where?, how much?*, etc.) are known together as **interrogative adverbs**.

In all of these cases the adverb relates to the verb. Technically, we call this **modifying** the verb. Adverbs can also modify other parts of a sentence. As we saw in 1.3.4, adverbs of degree (*very, slightly, completely*, etc.) modify gradable adjectives. Adverbs of **focus** direct our attention to particular phrases (*only, also*), emphasise them in some way (*particularly*) or restrict point of view (*socially, politically*, etc.). They may also apply to a whole sentence: **Psychologically**, *he's a broken man*; *I **only** wanted to say 'hello'*; *Federico repaired the washing-machine **too**.*

Connective adverbs like *however, therefore, furthermore*, etc., are important semantic links between one sentence and another: **So** *what did you do next?*; **Anyway**, *we had a great time*; **Incidentally**, *how is Federico?*

Comment adverbs (**modal** adverbs) show the speaker's attitude to his or her utterance, or indicate in some other way how it is intended to be understood: **Well**, *he **obviously** doesn't love her*; **Unfortunately**, *we lost all our money*.

- Morphology:
As already mentioned, adverbs can be derived from adjectives by the addition of the suffix *-ly*:

rapid ⟶ *rapidly; conscious* ⟶ *consciously; powerful* ⟶ *powerfully*.

Most adverbs are like this. Nevertheless, there is a lot of 'anarchy'. A large number of them have no special adverb marking, chiefly because they are not related to adjectives at all. Among these are many common adverbs, such as *perhaps, now, often, also, soon*, etc. Others that do have an adjective partner have the same form and add no suffix, e.g. *fast, hard, deep, far, near, late, high, low*. Some of these also have *-ly* versions, but they are either not related in meaning to the adjective, or reflect just a specialised adjectival meaning: *hardly, nearly, lately, deeply, highly*. And there are a number of further exceptions.

Like adjectives, adverbs can be gradable (*very quickly, rather dangerously*), and then usually participate in comparison:

Base form	Comparative	Superlative
hard	harder	hardest
fast	faster	fastest
violently	more violently	most violently
selfishly	more selfishly	most selfishly

- Syntax:
  The main syntactic issue with adverbs is their position in the sentence, which can vary, depending on factors such as emphasis and style, and also the meaning of the adverb. General principles are the following:
  - Adverbs modifying individual items (single words or phrases) usually come immediately before them, e.g. **very** *nice*, **right** *after lunch*, **about** *a boy*, **even** *you*.
  - Apart from this, the most general position, especially with adverbs of manner, time and place, is **final**, i.e. at the end of the sentence or clause, following any phrases that are part of the verb's necessary complementation:
    She spoke to the horse **softly**.
    I saw Mike **yesterday**.

  General exceptions to this are as follows:
  - Certain adverb types, especially those of frequency (*often*, *sometimes*, *always*, etc.) are attracted to a **medial** position, i.e. between subject and verb, or after the first auxiliary:
    I have **never** been to Scotland.
    McCaverty **occasionally** drank at Bewlin's Bar.
    This also applies to common adverbs of focus that restrict, add or emphasise:
    Jane had **only/already/also** been working at the hospital for six months.
    I **especially** enjoyed the picnic on the beach.
  - Most adverbs that give speaker comments, focus on viewpoint or connect with previous sentences favour **initial** position, i.e. the beginning of the sentence:
    Basically, *the company is no longer profitable*. **Moreover**, *it has been like this for at least the last six months*. **Frankly**, *I don't see that it can survive much longer*.

1.3.6 Articles and 'article words' (Determiners)

These are words that precede nouns and help to identify them. Apart from the articles themselves (**definite** – *the*, **indefinite** = *a/an* or 'zero'), this category includes a variety of other words, i.e.:

- quantifiers: ⟶ There weren't **many** people at the concert.
- numerals: ⟶ **Two** men came into the room.
- possessive pronouns: ⟶ I like **your** new jacket.
- demonstrative pronouns: ⟶ Where did you get **this** watch, Mr Breene?
- the interrogative pronouns *which* and *whose*: ⟶ **Which/Whose** bicycle did you take this afternoon, Paul?
- the relative pronoun *whose*: ⟶ Mary is the woman **whose** husband works for Cruikshank Chemicals.

A modern term in linguistics that is used to cover all these is determiner. But there is an objection to this: as we will see later in Chapter 4 (4.1.1.1), the expression determiner really refers to a phrase function and not a word-class. However, we will nevertheless use the term here (exceptionally) to cover **both** function and word-class. It is important to have an expression that brings all these sub-groups together in one overall word-class, for as we will see immediately, they have a common basic meaning as 'identifiers'. It is also necessary to replace the traditional term 'pronoun' in the last four categories above by a more appropriate one. Although the 'pronoun' label has a certain semantic justification, syntactically these are 'article words' and not 'pronouns', as was already indicated under 1.3.2 above in the case of possessives and demonstratives. We will refer here, then, to **possessive determiners, demonstrative determiners, interrogative determiners** and, in the case of *whose*, to the **relative determiner**.

- Semantics:
  Two forms of identification are involved with determiners: definite and indefinite. These terms are derived from the traditional names for the two kinds of article, *the* and *a/an*. But as terms they are a little misleading. There is a tendency to think, e.g. that the 'woman' in the phrase *a woman* is automatically a less specific one than the 'woman' referred to by *the woman*. But this is not necessarily so. If I tell you, *There is a woman outside*, I mean a specific one, not just 'any woman'. If, on the other hand, I make a statement like *The modern woman is very different from the Victorian woman*, I mean 'any woman' from each respective period, although I have used the definite article. So what is the difference?

  o The indefinite article identifies an entity by **category**. This is the central meaning of *a/an*. For instance, if I say *This is a table*, I mean 'an object belonging to the category "table"'. If I say *That's not a cat; it's a rabbit*, I mean 'the category of the animal referred to is not "cat", but "rabbit"'. This is the way we identify and refer to an object, animal or person that we mention for the first time.

  However, we cannot use an indefinite article twice for the same entity. That is, when something or someone has been introduced 'by category', subsequent reference to the same thing or person has to be definite:

(21) I was waiting for **a bus** one day in Beresford Square when **an old woman** approached me and asked for money. **The woman** looked shabby and ill. Then **the bus** came and unfortunately I had to get on it quickly without giving her anything.

Bus and *old woman* are introduced by the indefinite article. But after that, reference back to them requires the definite article (or some other form of definite reference like a pronoun). The definite article here is therefore a kind of anaphor pointing back to an entity already known to the hearer. It may also point forwards, as a **cataphor**, to an identifying part following:

(22) a. **The** man **in the corner** is smoking.
b. **The** couple **we met on holiday** have written to us.

The identifying information, on the other hand, may be entirely understood through context, and not stated at all:

(23) a. I put **the** dirty plates in **the** dishwasher.
(= the plates we have just used for the meal; the dishwasher in our kitchen.)
b. I like **the** new jacket.
(= which you are now wearing, i.e. that one that you have on.)

We can therefore say generally that

- the definite article identifies an entity through association with a known or stated context. This may be the utterance itself (forward or backward reference), or a social context in which speaker and listener already share knowledge of the identity of what is being referred to.

Examples of definite or indefinite reference by other determiners are as follows:

  o Definite: demonstrative, possessive, interrogative determiners and the relative determiner; the quantifiers *both* and *every*.
  o Indefinite: no article at all (known as the **zero article**), numerals, the quantifiers *much, many, all, every, some, any*.

- Morphology:
The articles differ in form only according to pronunciation rules (i.e. phonology): *a* before consonants, *an* before vowels; [ðə] before consonants, [ði:] before vowels. Demonstrative determiners have singular (*this/that*) and plural (*these/those*) forms.
Possessive determiners, as seen above under Pronouns, have the same pronoun characteristics (person, number, gender) as the personal pronouns.

- Syntax:
Determiners are parts of noun phrases. Some, such as the demonstratives, numerals and most quantifiers, can be used also as independent pronouns (see under Pronouns above), but then lose their determiner status.
Numerals, quantifiers and the indefinite article are affected by the number and count status of the nouns they refer to, chiefly in the form of restrictions. The following are just a few illustrative examples (more details in Chapter 4, 4.1):

  o The indefinite article is restricted to count singular nouns, the zero article to plurals and non-count singular nouns.
  o Numerals can only precede count nouns; *one* is restricted to singular and all other numerals to plural nouns.
  o The quantifiers *much, little* and *less* can combine only with non-count singulars, while *many* and *few* are restricted to count plurals.
  o The quantifiers *some* and *any* precede non-count singulars and count plurals, *all* and *both* only count plurals, *each* and *every* only count singulars.

1.3.7 Prepositions

Prepositions are words like *at, in, of, from, to,* etc. They precede noun phrases (e.g. *to the cinema*) and express a relationship between them and other parts of the sentence. Or rather, as the 'other parts' come first, between those parts (e.g. *Stella went . . .*) and the noun phrase following: *Stella went to the cinema*.

- Semantics:
  In their concrete meanings, most prepositions express a connection of **space** or **time**, e.g. *to/at/from the cinema* (space), or *at 8 pm, on Wednesday, in the evening* (time).
  Abstract meanings include the following:

  o 'regarding' or 'concerning': *a story about a lion, a book on bee-keeping, a quarrel over a damaged car,* etc.
  o 'belonging' and origin: *the works of Dickens, a woman from Jamaica, a problem with a client, his reasons for refusing, a painting by Turner,* etc.
  o abstract location/place: *at high speed, in a bad mood, under pressure, above suspicion, beyond belief,* etc.

  Abstract meanings like these underlie many **collocations** with nouns and adjectives: *attitude towards, love for, interest in, hatred of, dependence on, good/bad at, aware of, angry/happy/disgusted with, keen on, nice to, fond of,* etc.
  Verbs in particular combine with prepositions to produce special meanings: *wait for, rely on, tire of, decide on, deal with, look for, enquire into.* These are known as **prepositional verbs**. The preposition in these cases mostly loses its original meaning and is simply 'absorbed' into the meaning of the verb. For example, *decide on* means *choose, look for* is 'try to find', and *deal with* means to process in a certain way or subject to a certain procedure. Sometimes the verb takes on a special meaning too: *come across* (*find*), *look after* (*guard, take care of*), *take to* (*start to like/do*), *wonder at* (*be surprised by*), *make for* (*move in the direction of*), etc.
  All collocations of this kind, whether involving verbs, nouns or adjectives, can be called **composite lexical items**. That is, they form one unit of vocabulary, a semantic phrase that is **idiomatic** (= not literal in meaning). Often verbs are involved together with nouns or adjectives, as well as prepositions: *take into consideration, take care of, pay attention to, keep an eye on, set one's sights on, lose one's head over, get rid of.*

- Morphology:
  Prepositions undergo no morphological changes at all. Because of this and the fact that they are short, they are traditionally called **particles**. However, they do have a morphological effect on following pronouns, requiring an object form: *for me, towards him/her, above us, from them.*
  Some prepositions form composite units with other items preceding them (**complex prepositions**): *in spite of, because of, up to, out of,* etc. Syntactically, these all count as 'one preposition', just as if they were composed of only one word.

- Syntax:
  In simple sentences prepositions are always followed by nouns. In most cases the preposition forms a syntactic unit with the noun phrase that follows it: *at the station, by car, from south-east Asia, with a large black dog*. These are known as prepositional phrases.
  An exception to this is the prepositional verb. Here, as the name implies, the preposition forms a syntactic unit with the verb: *look after, wait for, decide on, deal with*. We still need a noun phrase after the preposition, e.g. *look after **the children**, wait for **me**, decide on **a particular plan**, deal with **the day's mail***, etc. But the noun phrase is regarded as separate from the preposition and, as we will see later, is treated as an object of the prepositional verb (called a **prepositional object**).
  Finally, many prepositions can also become adverbs. This happens as soon as the noun phrase is left out, e.g.:

(24) a. We waved to them on the other side of the street and they came **across** (= across the street).
  b. My young son had started to climb up a dangerous ladder in the garden. I told him to come **down** immediately (= come down the ladder).

Across and *down* in these examples are no longer prepositions but **adverb particles**. These also form a syntactic unit with their verbs, which are then called **phrasal verbs**. It is important to distinguish carefully between phrasal verbs, prepositional verbs and prepositional phrases (see Chapter 4, 4.2).

1.3.8 Conjunctions

These are words like *because, when, although, since, if*, etc., as in the following examples:

(25) a. Stanley quit his job **because** it bored him.
  b. **Although** the day was cloudy and grey, it did not rain.
  c. The man has not left the house **since** he arrived home last Friday.
  d. **When** you get to the next set of traffic lights, you will see the station on the left in front of you.

- Semantics:
  Conjunctions express a connection between two potential sentences. For instance in (25)a. the two sentences would be: *Stanley quit his job. It bored him.* In (25)b. they would be: *The day was cloudy and grey. It did not rain.*
  In each case the conjunctions bring the two sentences together and relate the clauses in meaning: *because* gives a reason, and *although* a contrast or contradiction. In (25)c. and (25)d. the conjunctions *since* and *when* express time relationships between the two respective sentence parts. Other connections of meaning are:

- Condition: *If you had been at the party you would have had a good time.*
- Place: *There is a big park now where the old slum used to be.*
- Purpose: *We stood on tiptoe so that we could see the game properly.*
- Addition: *Clara will do the shopping and cook the meal.*
- Content: *I don't think that we should react too quickly.*

- Morphology:
Like prepositions, conjunctions do not change morphologically and traditionally also belong to the particles. Conjunctions that consist of more than one word, like *so that* in the example above, are called **complex conjunctions**. Other examples are: *as soon as, as if, even if, even though, no matter how*. Certain constructions consist of two separate conjunctions working together as a pair: *You must **either** change your job **or** take a long vacation.* These are known as **correlative conjunctions**.

- Syntax:
When two base sentences are joined together grammatically by a conjunction, they become **clauses** of the same sentence. We can therefore say that the syntactic task of a conjunction is to **link clauses** in a sentence **grammatically** (as well as **semantically**, as we saw above). In this book we will call the clause with the conjunction before it the **conjunction clause**, and the other one the **free clause**. One of our main topics later will be the explanation of the various syntactic relations between the free clause and the conjunction clause. We do not need to talk about these yet, though.

1.4 Phrase, clause and sentence

Finally, we will look briefly at three basic units in sentence analysis and see how they are related to each other. The term phrase has already been introduced, but as a reminder we give a summary of the concept immediately below. What a sentence is has been regarded so far as intuitively understood, but at this point we will consider the meaning of the term more exactly. The third type of unit, the clause, has hardly been mentioned at all and now needs to be introduced properly. First of all, a word of general explanation concerning all three concepts. The sentence, the clause and the phrase are **units of syntactic structure**. To these, for the sake of completeness, we must add two more: **words** and **morphemes**. These five units of syntactic structure represent five levels of analysis related to each other in a hierarchy. From 'top to bottom' and from left to right, this can be shown as follows:

sentence → clause → phrase → word → morpheme.

Starting at the top of the hierarchy[2] and going downwards level by level, we can therefore say that sentences consist of clauses, clauses of phrases, phrases of words and words of morphemes. Or, if we look at it 'bottom up', we can say that an utterance is made up of morphemes (= the smallest unit of syntactic structure), which form words, which are grouped into phrases, which in turn combine into clauses, from which a sentence is immediately composed. The introduction of the clause-level between the phrase and the sentence may appear to conflict with the impression possibly given earlier that the phrase is the immediate constituent of the sentence. With sentences of the kind shown so far this is actually the case, at least in effect, since here the terms *clause* and *sentence* refer to the same unit. The sentence, in other words, is equal to the clause. With other types of sentence, as we will see further below, this is not so.

1.4.1 The sentence

The sentence, as we have just seen, is at the top of our syntactic hierarchy: it is **the largest unit of syntactic structure** and is **independent**, i.e. it stands alone grammatically. In this respect it contrasts with the other four types of unit, none of which can stand alone. At first sight, however, there appear to be certain objections to the idea that only sentences are independent. Take, for instance, the following conversation:

(26) a. 'Where are you going?'
 b. 'To the shops.'

(26)b. is clearly a complete utterance, typically of an ordinary conversation and therefore giving an intelligible answer to the question in (26)a. Yet it is not a sentence but just a prepositional phrase. In real speech complete messages are often conveyed like this by isolated phrases and even just individual words. This appears to contradict the principle that only sentences can stand alone. However, such a phrase does actually represent a sentence communicatively, and can be expanded into one: *I am going to the shops*. Utterances like the answer in (26)b. are sometimes called **sentence fragments**. They are properly regarded as **ellipses**, i.e. context-bound 'shortened versions' of full sentences.

A further problem for our definition is that even formally complete sentences may contain elements that refer to other sentences, and are therefore only fully interpretable if those other sentences are known. This is the case with both the following examples:

(27) a. 'What did Celia do then?'
 b. 'She called the police.'

In (27)a. the adverb *then* is obviously a back-reference to an event or point of time previously mentioned. The sentence is therefore not strictly independent: to understand it fully we need to have knowledge of what was said beforehand. A counter-argument to this is that back-reference here is a semantic problem, not a grammatical one; and what we mean in the definition by 'independence' is **grammatical independence**. However, if we look at (27)b. (meant as a reply to (27)a.), we are still not off the hook: the personal pronoun *she* points back to

Celia in (27)a. This is a pronoun connection, and is therefore not only semantic but also grammatical. And the connection here crosses a sentence boundary. Other very common examples of this phenomenon occur with tense and aspect. The need for the past tense with *did* and *called* in both sentences in (27) would be dictated by a time reference already established in the immediate context, i.e. in preceding sentences. So again we have an example of grammatical influence on the sentence from outside it, and this appears to contradict the claim of independence. Trying another counter, we could protest that the grammatical elements just mentioned are morphological rather than syntactic. This is largely true. Nevertheless, they have a syntactic influence in that they impose constraints on the forms of other words co-occurring with them, even across sentence boundaries.

The solution to these objections actually lies in a more narrow interpretation of the term syntactic in the definition. If we see syntactic in the more restrictive sense of **functional**, then the sentence is actually an independent unit, not influenced by anything outside itself. And it is this in both an internal and an external respect. Firstly, a sentence is self-contained in that it does not play a functional role (subject, object, etc.) in relation to any larger unit. Secondly, its internal **functional characteristics** are determined entirely internally. This will become clear from our introductory discussion of sentence functions and functional patterns in Chapter 2.

1.4.2 The clause

Consider the following:

(28) a. Jane made the tea.
      b. Benny cooked breakfast.
      c. Jane made tea and Benny cooked the breakfast.

Here we have three sentences. The last one, (28)c., has been formed by combining (28)a. and (28)b., using the word *and* to join them. In (28)c. the formerly separate sentences in a. and b. have now become clauses of the same sentence. We could of course take (28)c. as our starting-point and reverse the process. In this case we would divide sentence (28)c. up by making each clause into a **separate sentence**. Sentences become clauses when they are **joined** to form larger sentences (they cannot then still be called 'sentences', because if they were, this would violate our definition of a sentence as being the 'largest unit of syntactic structure').

The clauses of a sentence need not be identical in structure with separate sentences. Let us assume now that tea-maker *Jane* is ill and *Benny* does both jobs:

(29) a. Benny made the tea and cooked breakfast.
      b. Benny made the tea.
      c. Benny cooked breakfast.

Notice now that when *Benny* is the subject of both clauses, he is only mentioned once. In other words, if the subject is the same in each clause, it is ellipted in the second one. If we make the clauses into separate sentences, as in b. and c., of course the ellipted subject in a. must be reintroduced in c. (otherwise we would not have a complete sentence). What we are saying here, then, is that when sentences become clauses, they often have to be integrated into the syntax of the larger sentence. As we will see later, this adaptation can be quite drastic, making some clause types look very different from how they would have to look if they were independent sentences. Nevertheless, every clause can be called **a sentence-like unit**, and this is so for a simple reason: every clause has **its own separate verb phrase** (functioning, as we will see in Chapter 2, as **predicator**).

We have used the term sentence to illustrate what a clause is. But actually we can define the clause quite independently of the sentence:

- A clause is a unit of phrases held together by one of them in the role of predicator.
- The predicator must always be a verb phrase.

This will allow us to reverse the logic above and define sentence in terms of clause:

- A clause or group of connected clauses that can stand alone syntactically is known as a sentence.
- A sentence consisting of just one clause is known as a **simple sentence**.
- A sentence consisting of more than one clause is known as a **multiple sentence**.

In Chapter 4 we will go into detail on multiple sentences, distinguishing two kinds: **compound sentences** and **complex sentences**. But for the moment we will let this aspect of the matter rest there.

1.4.3 *The phrase*

The phrase is the most basic unit in sentence analysis. The major phrases of a sentence or clause are its immediate constituents, i.e. those phrases not contained inside any other phrases. These major phrases are the first elements that must be identified before we can establish sentence functions, as we will see in Chapter 2. In a simple sentence, all sentence functions are filled by phrases. Phrases, to return to basic definitions, are structural word units based on word-classes. This is illustrated again, by way of summary, in (30). (30)b. is the phrase analysis of (30)a.:

(30) a. My daughter reads crime novels.
b. noun phrase (*my daughter*) + verb phrase (*reads*) + noun phrase (*crime novels*).

As already mentioned above (1.2), a phrase may consist of just one word, or of more than one. If there are more than one, the unit will depend for its grammatical existence on one major member representing the particular word-class. This is known as the head of the phrase. The head of a noun phrase must be a noun, that of a verb phrase a main verb, that of an adjective phrase an adjective, and so on. In (30) the heads of the two noun phrases are *daughter* and *novels*, respectively. As the verb phrase consists of just one member (*reads*), this, obviously, is the head. The second noun phrase actually consists of two nouns, *crime* and *novels*, but only *novels* is the head, as this is the element we cannot leave out, i.e. the member on which the unit *crime novels* depends. Grammatically speaking, phrases are of flexible length and can be expanded or reduced, but the head always has to be present. Conversely, it is the head around which expansion takes place, i.e. around which the further elements of the phrase are grouped. Taking the example in (29)c., we could expand the phrases in it as follows:

(31) (My brother Benny) (had cooked) (our breakfast).

Notice also that if a phrase is shifted in the sentence, e.g. due to the passive operation, it must move **as a whole**:

(32) (Our breakfast) (had been cooked) (by (my brother Benny)).

We cannot split phrases up and place their parts in other sentence positions. (33) is ungrammatical and, for that reason of course, nonsense:

(33) *Our had been breakfast my Benny cooked by brother.

In Chapter 4 we discuss the structure of phrases in more detail.

Exercises

Exercise 1

Bracket the phrases in the following that are constituents at sentence-level (see 1.2).

1. Old Bob walks five miles a day.
2. The three small children crossed the busy road very quickly.
3. Mrs Simpson's daughter has gone into town by bus.
4. Large vehicles should be parked behind the house on the grass.
5. We are meeting at 6 o'clock inside the main entrance to the concert hall.
6. All kinds of wild animals gather on the edge of the lake in the early morning.
7. Kalinda always did her maths homework on the table in the dining room.
8. Many visitors like the Impressionist paintings in Gallery B most.

Exercise 2

Give the word-class of each of the underlined words in the following. In the case of pronouns, verbs and determiners name also the particular sub-type, e.g. determiner: definite article, possessive determiner, modal auxiliary verb, reflexive pronoun, etc.

1 <u>We</u> walked <u>to</u> the beach <u>this</u> morning.
2 <u>Charis</u> waited for Brendan <u>outside</u> <u>a</u> hairdresser´s in McBride Street.
3 They <u>should</u> arrive at the <u>theatre</u> <u>early</u>.
4 A band <u>of</u> <u>four</u> young women were <u>playing</u> <u>loud</u> rock and blues on a small stage.
5 Julie has <u>played</u> very <u>well</u> in <u>her</u> <u>last</u> three basketball games.
6 <u>After</u> <u>she</u> got <u>home</u>, Sounis asked her mother <u>which</u> dress she should wear to the party.
7 I <u>didn´t</u> know <u>that</u> you were not <u>well</u>.
8 Farouk didn´t <u>have</u> <u>much</u> luck in the race, <u>but</u> at least he enjoyed <u>himself</u>.
9 Kim Chok went to the concert <u>with</u> Gary <u>yesterday</u>, <u>although</u> she had sworn she would <u>never</u> <u>see</u> him <u>again</u>.
10 The children <u>had</u> not visited <u>their</u> grandparents <u>since</u> the <u>previous</u> Christmas.

Exercise 3

Show how semantics, morphology and syntax all contribute to the meaning of these sentences:

1 My father reads a newspaper only on Sundays.
2 Colin´s wife gave him an expensive painting for their wedding anniversary.
3 Have you made your bed and tidied up your room, Eric?
4 Samira is from Kenya, but her parents are Indian.

And how is each of these language fields responsible for the differences in meaning between the a. and b. sentences in the following?:

5 a. She offered me a seat, but I didn´t want it.
   b. She offered me a drink, but I didn´t want one.
6 a. I wasn´t going to drink wine or beer.
   b. I wasn´t going to drink wine and beer.

Notes

1 An asterisk (*) signifies an incorrect item of language.
2 Structures above the level of the sentence are referred to as *text* and *discourse*.

2 The simple sentence and its grammatical functions

2.0 Structure and function

Let us go back first of all to structure. As we saw in the last chapter, an important basic item of grammatical structure is the phrase. The phrase, just to refresh our memories, is a grammatical unit based on a word-class. For example, in the sentence

(1) My daughter reads crime novels.

we have three phrases: *my daughter* and *crime novels* are both noun phrases and *reads* is a verb phrase. The structure of the sentence, that is, is as follows:

(2)   noun phrase (*my daughter*) + verb phrase (*reads*) + noun phrase (*crime novels*).

However, this does not tell us much about how the phrases are related to each other in terms of meaning and grammar. One noun phrase comes before the verb and the second follows it. But what does that say about their relationship to each other and to the verb? This is where the idea of **grammatical function** comes in. The first noun phrase, *my daughter*, functions as the subject of the sentence and the second, *crime novels*, as the object (more specifically, as the direct object). The verb phrase functions as the predicator: that is to say, it joins the two noun phrases to form the sentence, and determines their parts in the meaning of the message:

	subject	predicator	direct object
(3)	My daughter	reads	crime novels.

For a basic description of the sentence, then, we need both levels of analysis, i.e. structure **and** function. And for our sentence in (1), this can be expressed as follows:

(4)   The first noun phrase (*my daughter*) functions as subject;
       the verb phrase (*reads*) functions as predicator;
       the second noun phrase (*crime novels*) functions as direct object.

As concepts, it is important to keep structure and function distinct from each other. But we use both when describing the basic syntax of the sentence. In a sense, they are 'partners' in the description. As we will see a little later, however, function is the 'senior partner'. It is the functions in a sentence that reflect its general shape and pattern.

In summary, then, we can say that the term function means the role that a phrase has in a particular sentence. This role:

- represents the relationship of that phrase to other phrases in the sentence;
- represents the relationship of that phrase to the sentence as a whole;
- is therefore a sentence-dependent concept (as opposed to structure, which is not);
- has both a grammatical and a semantic character.

There are seven different sentence functions, which we will now look at in detail (2.1.1–2.1.7). Our object of analysis in this chapter is confined to the simple sentence (i.e. containing only one predicator) in its declarative form (i.e. expressing a statement), with its verb in the **affirmative** (i.e. not negative) and in the **active voice** (i.e. not passive).

2.1 Sentence functions explained

Sentence functions are **syntactic categories**. However, as with word-classes (see Chapter 1), we can define them according to both grammar and meaning.

2.1.1 Predicator (P)

- Syntax/morphology:
  The predicator:
  - is always a verb phrase;
  - **follows** the subject;
  - contains a verb (always the first, if there is more than one) which **signals the subject grammatically** in terms of person and number (called agreement or concord, see also Chapter 1). In a simple sentence, in other words, the verb phrase must be finite:

		P	
(5)	The children	**have been eating**	strawberries.
	Mike	**is**	a student.
	Maxine	**did not like**	Robert.

Every sentence needs a predicator. A string of phrases with no predicator is not a grammatical sentence. It is the predicator which 'makes' phrases into sentences by joining them in a certain grammatical way: e.g. by placing one phrase in the role of subject and another in the role of object. Such functions are only possible if they are related to a predicator.

- Semantics:
  Also in terms of meaning it is the predicator which pulls the other members of the sentence into a coherent message. Without a predicator there would be no message. The predicator is the core of the statement.

2.1.2 Subject (S)

- Syntax/morphology:
  The subject
  o   is always a noun phrase,
  o   **precedes** the predicator,
  o   must be present in every simple sentence,
  o   imposes *concord* (morphological agreement, see Chapter 2, 2.1.1) on the verb in the predicator role:

	S		
(6)	**The children**	have been eating	strawberries.
	Mike	is	a student.
	Maxine	did not like	Robert.

Furthermore the subject role requires a particular morphological form for personal pronouns. This is often called the **subject case** (or, more traditionally, the **nominative case**). If we make pronouns out of the subjects in (6), this gives us:

	S		
(7)	**They**	have been eating	strawberries.
	He	is	a student.
	She	did not like	Robert.

These pronouns change forms in other functions, i.e. take on a different **case** (see also below).

- Semantics:
  When the verb refers to an action, the subject is always the person or thing performing the action, in other words the 'actor' or 'doer' (the agent, to use a technical term, cf. SAGE, pp. 20, 422, 423ff.). If the verb refers to a state or feeling, the subject is usually the person or thing that experiences it. In (6), e.g., *the children* perform an action (*eat*), whereas *Mike* and *Maxine* experience particular states: a state of being, in the case of *Mike*, and an emotion in the case of *Maxine*. (Note, again, that in this chapter we are referring only to active sentences.)

2.1.3 Direct object (Od)

- Syntax/morphology:
  The direct object
    o is always a noun phrase;
    o **follows** the predicator;
    o but only when the predicator function is filled by certain kinds of verbs.

			Od
(8)	The children	have been eating	**strawberries.**
	Maxine	did not like	**Robert.**

Verbs followed by a direct object are called **transitive**. As can be seen in (8), only two of our examples have transitive verbs: *eat* and *like*. The noun phrase after *is* in the other example sentence (*a student*) is not a direct object. Reasons for this are given immediately below.

The object function also means a change in morphology for pronouns, which then have to be in the **object case**. So if *strawberries* and *Robert* are made into pronouns, we get *them* and *him* (rather than *they* and *he*, which are the subject case versions, as shown in (7)):

			Od
(9)	The children	have been eating	**them.**
	Maxine	did not like	**him.**

- Semantics:
  The direct object is always the person or thing that 'suffers' from, or is the target of, an action or feeling (known technically as the patient, cf. SAGE, loc. cit.). This already shows us why *a student* in *Mike is a student* cannot be a direct object. On the level of meaning, the verb *be* does not create a target relation between the two noun phrases. It gives no sense of the first one 'aiming' any kind of affecting experience at the second. Verbs that do not have direct objects following them, like *be*, are called **intransitive**.

2.1.4 Indirect object (Oi)

- Syntax/morphology:
  The indirect object
    o is always a noun phrase;
    o **follows** the predicator;
    o can only occur **together** with a direct object;
    o must immediately **precede** the direct object;
    o only occurs, again, when particular verbs fill the predicator function.

			Oi	Od
(10)	The children	gave	**their mother**	some strawberries.
	Maxine	sent	**Robert**	a letter.
	Joe	bought	**his sons**	new cars.

Verbs followed by an **indirect object + direct object** are also transitive, of course: in fact they are 'doubly transitive', as they have two objects. For this reason we call them ditransitive, as opposed to the first type with just a direct object (as shown in 2.1.3), which is often referred to as **monotransitive**, to distinguish it from this second type.

Personal pronouns as indirect objects also need the object case, of course:

			Oi	Od
(11)	The children	gave	her	some strawberries.
	Maxine	sent	him	a letter.
	Joe	bought	them	new cars.

We can nearly always express an indirect object alternatively by using a prepositional phrase, usually with the prepositions *to* or *for*:

			Od	A
(12)	The children	gave	some strawberries	**to their mother.**
	Maxine	sent	a letter	**to Robert.**
	Joe	bought	new cars	**for his sons.**

Here there are two things to note. Firstly, there is **no** indirect object in this case. That is, the verb is now monotransitive and the noun phrase that was the indirect object in (10) now becomes part of a prepositional phrase, which functions as an **adverbial (A)**: more explanation of the adverbial function follows below. Secondly, the prepositional phrase **follows** the direct object, in contrast to the ditransitive version, where the indirect object **precedes** the direct object. A final point and a word of warning on correct usage: not all prepositional phrases like those in (12) can be expressed as indirect objects. One must know which verbs can be ditransitive and which cannot. Several verbs with similar meanings to those of ditransitive verbs can in fact only be monotransitive, e.g. *tell* is ditransitive, but *say* and *explain* are both only monotransitive; *show* is ditransitive, but *demonstrate* is only monotransitive.

So although all indirect objects can be paraphrased by the prepositional phrase version, the reverse is **not** true. It just depends on the individual verb. The point is mentioned again immediately below, under Semantics.

- Semantics:
  The indirect object is the **receiver** (or recipient) of the direct object. This is clear from (10): the *mother* gets the *strawberries*, *Robert* receives *a letter* and *Joe's sons* get *new cars*. The prepositional phrase variants underline this receiver meaning especially clearly.

However, we must emphasise the last point mentioned under Syntax/morphology. Not all prepositional phrases with receiver meanings can be converted into noun phrases as indirect objects. It depends on the particular verb. As already mentioned, the verb *show*, for example, can be ditransitive, but not the verb *explain*. So in (13)a. both variants are permissible, but not in (13)b.

(13) a. Fred showed the maths problem to Claire.
　　　　Fred showed Claire the maths problem.
　　　b. Fred explained the maths problem to Claire.
　　　　*Fred explained Claire the maths problem.

2.1.5 Subject complement (Cs)

- Syntax/morphology:
  The subject complement
  - can be a noun phrase or an adjective phrase;
  - **follows** an intransitive verb in the predicator function;
  - occurs only after the verbs *be, seem, become, feel,* and any of similar meaning, such as *appear, get* (= *become*), *sound, look* (= *appear*), etc.

	S		Cs
(14)	Mike	is	**a student.**
	Mother	seems	**worried.**
	Joe	got	**angry.**

The subject complement occupies the same position in the sentence as a direct object. This sometimes leads to confusion. As we said earlier, there are semantic reasons why the noun phrase in the first example cannot be a direct object. But we can now add a syntactic factor. The subject complement slot can also be filled by an adjective (such as *worried* or *angry*, above). The object function, however, cannot. Only noun phrases can be direct objects. Subject complements occur when intransitive verbs need something following them to complete the sentence (i.e. obligatory complementation). Many intransitive verbs, it is true, need nothing at all, as in (15):

(15) Dogs bark.
　　 Patrick was working.
　　 I have been running.

But with intransitive verbs like those in (14) this is not so. Sentences consisting just of *Mike is* or *Joe got* are ungrammatical. And they do not of course make sense. The sense has to be completed by an adjective or noun, as shown immediately below, under Semantics.

- Semantics:
  The subject complement describes a characteristic of the subject. If left out, of course, the most important part of the message would be missing.

2.1.6 Object complement (Co)

- Syntax/morphology:
  The object complement
    - can be a noun phrase or an adjective phrase;
    - occurs after certain kinds of transitive verb in the predicator function;
    - **follows** the direct object.

			Od	Co
(16)	Bad food	made	the guests	**sick**.
	The pupils	elected	Robin	**class-monitor**.
	Jenny	considers	Alan	**stupid**.

Object complements, like subject complements, are compulsory after certain verbs. Leaving them out would result in ungrammatical sentences and an incomplete message. They have a similar relation to the object as a subject complement has to the subject, especially in a semantic sense. Transitive verbs that have object complements are called **complex transitive**, to distinguish them further from the other two transitive types.

- Semantics:
  Just as a subject complement refers to a characteristic of the subject, so the object complement describes a characteristic of the direct object. The relation to the verb, however, is slightly different in the case of the object complement. Generally speaking, the verb **confers** (or imposes) the characteristic on the direct object. This might be a concrete case of cause and effect, as in the first two sentences in (16); or a more abstract sense of imposition by thought or feeling, as in the last example. Complex-transitive verbs are a relatively small group. Among them are verbs of judgement and thought, like *think, find, consider, imagine, prove, judge, confirm, rank*, etc.; and verbs expressing declarations, such as *call, name, declare* and *pronounce*:

			Od	Co
(17)	The parents	called	the baby	**Wanda**.
	The chairman	declared	the meeting	**open**.
	A doctor	pronounced	the patient	**dead**.

2.1.7 Adverbial (A)

- Syntax/morphology:
  An adverbial

The simple sentence: grammatical functions 41

- can be a noun phrase, prepositional phrase or an adverb phrase (occasionally also even adjective phrases);
- can be obligatory after certain verbs, but is usually an **optional** addition to the sentence;
- usually **follows** the objects and other complements of the predicator (though there are two other frequent positions discussed below).

(18)   A
     They completed the job   **last week**.
     People were waiting   **at the bus stop**.
     Morton crossed the road   **quickly**.

The adverbial function is an extension of the adverb itself as a word-class. The position in the sentence is therefore the same. The **final** position, as in (18), is probably the most common. Other positions are medial and initial (see also discussion of adverbs in 1.3.5). The medial position, i.e. between subject and predicator, or inside the predicator (if there are auxiliaries), is preferred with single adverbs that express frequency, focus and emphasis (for more comment on adverbial meaning, see under Semantics below):

      A
(19) I **often** eat fish.
             A
     We should **always** be optimistic.
            A
     Stella had **only** washed three of the shirts.

The initial position (at the beginning of the sentence) is common with adverbials that comment on the sentence, or connect it to a preceding statement. It is also used with other types to emphasise them:

      A
(20) **In the town square** a large crowd had gathered.
     Frankly, I don't think that the plan will succeed.
     In that case, we ought to call the police.

Note that although the terms adverb and adverbial are connected, they must be carefully distinguished as concepts. An adverb is a word-class. An adverbial is a sentence function, like subject and predicator. So, for instance, we say that the word *frankly* in the second sentence is an adverb filling the function of an adverbial in that sentence. Adverbs, as we will see later, do not always function as adverbials. And adverbials are certainly not always adverbs, as our examples show. In (18), e.g., *last week* is a noun phrase and *at the bus stop* a prepositional phrase. In (20) *in the town square* and *in that case* are also prepositional phrases. Sentence functions and word-classes are not the same thing, even though they occur together when we are talking about sentences.

Another point concerns the question of when adverbials are optional and when they are obligatory. Syntactically speaking, most adverbials are optional, i.e. they are not required grammatically. Some, however, are needed to complete the sense and grammar of the sentence, particularly with verbs that express movement from one place to another:

                                             A

(21) This train goes   **to London Bridge**.
      My grandfather came   **from Scotland**.
      Mrs Bleckford put the letter   **on the table**.

Another major case of compulsory adverbials arises when **ditransitive** verbs are converted into **monotransitive** verbs:

            Oi   Od   Od   A
(22) We gave **our son** some money ⟹ We gave some money **to our son**.

In contrast to other functions, there can be more than one adverbial in a sentence:

                A   A   A
(23) This train **only** goes   **to London Bridge**   **on Sundays**.
      Maureen   **just** put the letter **on the table**   **slowly**.

In the case of final position, the compulsory adverbial comes first, and any others follow. Other factors affecting the order of adverbials are mentioned briefly in the Semantics section immediately below.

- Semantics:
It is customary to classify adverbials according to the same meanings as those of adverbs. Typical concrete meanings are time, place and manner, answering the questions *When?*, *Where?* and *How?* (see also SAGE, p. 23). This is the order of the adverbials in the three example sentences in (18). Other common categories include adverbials of **frequency** such as *always* and *often*, adverbials of **circumstance** (*in that case*), focus adverbials like *only*, *especially* and *particularly*, and adverbials of comment and **connection**, such as *anyway*, *however*, and *so*. Further meanings will be mentioned later in the course of the book.

As we have seen at certain points in this and the last chapter, the meanings of adverbs and adverbials has some influence on their position in the sentence. Two or more adverbials in final position are usually found in the order manner, place, time:

                             A   A   A
(24) He washed his hands **quickly** **in the kitchen sink** **before the meal**.

There are no strict grammatical rules on this, though, and the order may vary according to style and speaker emphasis. A full guide to usage is given in SAGE, pp. 196–208.

2.2 Verb complementation

The structural elements and functions of a sentence following the verb are known as the **verb complementation**. As we saw in 2.1, the individual verbs filling the predicator function present a variety of complementation requirements and possibilities which have a large influence on determining the shape of a sentence. Here we want to give a short overview of them.

2.2.1 Transitivity

Transitive verbs are subdivided into the following types:

- Monotransitive verbs take a direct object (**Od**):

            Od
    (25) Fred was eating a **hamburger**.

- Ditransitive verbs take an indirect object (**Oi**) + a direct object (**Od**):

        Oi   Od
    (26) Dick bought **his girlfriend a present**.

- Complex transitive verbs take a direct object (**Od**) + an object complement (**Co**):

        Od   Co
    (27) We found **the wine too sweet**.

An important point to note is that when we apply a particular transitivity feature to a verb (monotransitive, ditransitive, intransitive, etc.), we are talking about the use of the verb concerned in a **given sentence**. There may, in addition, be other complementation possibilities. This is information that we will find in a dictionary. A dictionary would tell us, for instance, that *eat* is not only transitive, as in (25), but can also be used intransitively, as in (28) below; or that with *buy*, apart from the monotransitive version of the ditransitive meaning, i.e. with compulsory adverbial (*Dick bought a present for his girlfriend*), there is also a 'straight' monotransitive possibility without the adverbial, i.e. *Dick bought a present*. (With *give*, for instance, this is not the case). On the other hand, *find*, in the meaning of (27), has no alternative complementation types, and can only be used in a complex transitive way. From the practical point of view, knowing how to use a verb means, among other factors, knowing its **complementation potential**.

Intransitive verbs are those without objects. Some have other types of complementation, while others do not:

- **without** complementation:

(28) Fred was eating.

- **with** complementation:

(29)
                    Cs
Karen   is   **Dick's wife**.
Jill   felt **happy**.
                               A
The children had been **in the garden**.

Again, we can see here that the same verb may have various possibilities of complementation. *Eat*, as already said, can be transitive or intransitive. (29) shows that *be* can take a subject complement or an adverbial. This is not the case with *feel*, which occurs only in the form seen here, i.e. solely with a subject complement. Furthermore, *be* and *feel* are examples of intransitive verbs which, unlike *eat* in (28), always need complementation.

2.3 Functions in the sentence

Having focused on the various functional parts of the sentence, we now want to consider the sentence as a whole. How are typical sentence patterns expressed in terms of function and how should we approach the task of analysing a given sentence? Let us look at the general patterns of sentence architecture first.

2.3.1 Basic sentence patterns

The foundation plan of a sentence depends very much on the complementation of the verb in it. And as we have seen, complementations vary. In accordance with these, there are seven basic functional sentence patterns:

(30)
a. S   P
    The letter has arrived.   [S + P]

b. S   P   Cs
    Janine became a teacher.   [S + P + Cs]

c. S   P   A
    This train goes to Leicester.   [S + P + A]

d. S   P   Od
    The painters are decorating the kitchen. [S + P + Od]

e. S   P Oi   Od
    Our son sent us a postcard.   [S + P + Oi + Od]

```
          S     P       Od            A
   f. Craig   put   his hands   in his pocket.    [S + P + Od + A]
          S         P        Od      Co
   g. His success has made   us   very happy.    [S + P + Od + Co]
```

These patterns represent the **minimum** type that is permissible with each verb. But one should bear in mind what was said in the previous section. A verb may have several complementation possibilities. For example, the minimum pattern with *sing* is the absolute minimum shown in (30)a. But further optional patterns are those in (30)c., d., e. and f., as illustrated in (31)a.–e.:

```
            S    P
(31) a. Rita is singing.                              [S + P]
            S   P      A
     b. Rita sings in the shower.                     [S + P + A]
            S   P        Od
     c. Rita sings Elizabethan love songs.            [S + P + Od]
            S   P       Oi               Od
     d. Rita sang her children Elizabethan love songs. [S + P + Oi + Od]
            S   P          Od                A
     e. Rita sang Elizabethan love songs every evening. [S + P + Od + A]
```

And of course we could add an adverbial to (31)d. as well (*Rita sang her children Elizabethan love songs every evening*).

2.3.2 First steps in analysing the simple sentence functionally

Finally we will look at procedures of analysis. How do we approach the task of functional sentence analysis in its application to whole sentences? And what part does structural description play? We will use the following examples to answer these questions:

(32) a. They sent some money to the woman in Brighton.
     b. The hot soup was getting cold in the draught from the open window.
     c. A light plane suddenly appeared between the mountains.
     d. Bad service in restaurants nearly always made Brian very angry.
     e. After the hectic years in London we bought ourselves a small cottage in the country.

It is the answer to the second question that concerns us first. We need first of all to identify the major phrases in a sentence, those, that is, that are constituents at sentence level. In (33) we have used brackets to do this. Each phrase is numbered for reference and described briefly in the comments further below:

(33) a. ¹(They) ²(sent) ³(some money) ⁴(to the woman in Brighton).
b. ¹(The hot soup) ²(was getting) ³(cold) ⁴(in the draught from the open window).
c. ¹(A light plane) ²(suddenly) ³(appeared) ⁴(between the mountains).
d. ¹(Bad service in restaurants) ²(nearly always) ³(made) ⁴(Brian) ⁵(very angry).
e. ¹(After the hectic years in London) ²(we) ³(bought) ⁴(ourselves) ⁵(a small cottage in the country).

Note again that it is not our task yet to identify all the phrases in each sentence, but just those that are the major constituents. It is only these that are relevant for the sentence functions. Type of phrase, position and meaning are the further points of orientation. For (33)a. this gives us:

(34) ¹(*They*) = noun phrase functioning as subject (**S**)
²(*sent*) = verb phrase functioning as predicator (**P**)
³(*some money*) = noun phrase functioning as direct object (**Od**)
⁴(*to the woman in Brighton*) = prepositional phrase functioning as adverbial (**A**).

Graphically we can then represent the functions in the usual way:

```
           S     P      Od                A
(35)     They  sent  some money   to the woman in Brighton.
```

A detailed breakdown of phrases is not necessary for a functional analysis of the sentence, and that is our first concern here. Note, however, that this does involve identifying sentence-constituent boundaries accurately. Phrase⁴, for instance, actually consists of two prepositional phrases: *to the woman* and *in Brighton*. It is important to see here that the second, *in Brighton*, is not a separate sentence constituent, but is contained within the scope of the first. More exactly, it is a constituent of the noun phrase *the woman in Brighton*, which in turn is a constituent of the larger prepositional phrase *to the woman in Brighton*. That *in Brighton* is not a sentence constituent is seen first of all in the semantic relations: it identifies and describes the noun *woman* more closely. Secondly, and because of this, it cannot be detached syntactically from the noun. If, e.g., we make the noun phrase *the woman* . . . into an indirect object, the prepositional phrase *in Brighton* has to move with it:

```
           S     P          Oi                    Od
(36)     They  sent   the woman in Brighton   some money.
```

We have to pay attention generally in this respect to prepositional phrases and ask ourselves where they belong, i.e. whether they are parts of other

The simple sentence: grammatical functions 47

phrases or independent constituents of the sentence and therefore functional parts of it. We have further examples here in (33)b.[4], (33)d.[1], (33) e.[1], (33) e.[1] and (33) e.[5], all of which involve prepositional phrases contained within major constituents.

(33)b.–e. are analysed further in (37)–(40):

(37) [1] (*The hot soup*) = noun phrase functioning as subject (**S**)
 [2] (*was getting*) = verb phrase functioning as predicator (**P**)
 [3] (*cold*) = adjective phrase functioning as subject complement (**Cs**)
 [4] (*in the draught from the open window*) = prepositional phrase functioning as adverbial (**A**).

Functional overview:

    S   P   Cs   A
The hot soup   was getting   cold   in the draught from the window.

(38) [1] (*A light plane*) = noun phrase functioning as subject (**S**)
 [2] (*suddenly*) = adverb phrase functioning as adverbial (**A**)
 [3] (*appeared*) = verb phrase functioning as predicator (**P**)
 [4] (*between the mountains*) = prepositional phrase functioning as adverbial (**A**).

Functional overview:

   S   A   P   A
A light plane   suddenly   appeared   between the mountains.

(39) [1] (*Bad service in restaurants*) = noun phrase functioning as subject (**S**)
 [2] (*nearly always*) = adverb phrase functioning as adverbial (**A**)
 [3] (*made*) = verb phrase functioning as predicator (**P**)
 [4] (*Brian*) = noun phrase functioning as direct object (**Od**)
 [5] (*very angry*) = adjective phrase functioning as object complement (**Co**)

Functional overview:

                S   A   P   Od   Co
Bad service in restaurants   nearly always   made   Brian   very angry.

(40) [1] (*After the hectic years in London*) = prepositional phrase functioning as adverbial (**A**)
 [2] (*we*) = noun phrase functioning as subject (**S**)
 [3] (*bought*) = verb phrase functioning as predicator (**P**)
 [4] (*ourselves*) = noun phrase functioning as indirect object (**Oi**)
 [5] (*a small cottage in the country*) = noun phrase functioning as direct object (**Od**)

Functional overview:

```
                       A                S   P    Oi              Od
After the hectic years in London we bought ourselves a small cottage in the country.
```

Exercises

Exercise 1

Decide whether the underlined parts in the following sentences are the direct object (**Od**), the indirect object (**Oi**), the subject complement (**Cs**), or the object complement (**Co**).

1 My brother has told <u>me</u> <u>that story</u> already.
2 The weather is getting <u>colder</u>.
3 The committee has made <u>Marley</u> <u>their honorary president</u>.
4 Dahlia got <u>her brother</u> <u>a job</u> at the same company.
5 Ossie became <u>a music teacher</u> in West London.
6 Let me ask <u>you</u> <u>a question</u>.
7 The sun had turned <u>Carrie´s brown hair</u> <u>almost blond</u>.
8 Our mad games with the dog had got <u>him</u> <u>very excited</u>.

Exercise 2

Underline the adverbials (**A**) in the following and identify the kinds of phrases involved.

1 I am going there for the first time next week.
2 You will probably find Maria´s husband in the garage.
3 They often go to the Scilly Isles for their holidays.
4 I´ve been to that restaurant three times with Joe already.
5 The car then drove across the bridge very fast.

Exercise 3

Show all the sentence functions in the following, using the appropriate letter symbols (**S, P, Od, Oi, Cs, Co, A**):

1 Grandmother sent the children some fine toys for Christmas.
2 These days, I am often in Tel Aviv on business.
3 Chocolate always makes my daughter happy.
4 You seemed a bit tired this afternoon at the meeting.
5 We will find Uncle George a quiet seat by the river.
6 During the Channel crossing Roy´s face slowly went green.
7 Unfortunately, Dave´s secretary had sent the letter to the wrong firm.

8   Some students find our exercises rather difficult.
9   I gave the suspicious-looking package to the police at the airport.
10 The directors might consider Bailey unsuitable for the job.
11 I am going to make everyone a cup of tea.
12 The potatoes had turned mouldy in the damp air of the cellar.
13 The damp air in the cellar had turned the potatoes mouldy.
14 Without doubt they will show us their whole collection of holiday photographs.
15 Esther did not explain the plan to us clearly enough.

3 Structural variations of the simple sentence and functional consequences

3.0 Basic sentence operations

In the chapters so far we have been talking only about sentences produced as **statements** (declarative sentences), with verbs that are affirmative and in the **active voice**. How is the syntax, and in particular the functional basis of it, affected by a change in one of these basic features, or 'settings'? Changing one of these settings is what we call here a 'basic sentence operation'. The declarative, affirmative and active sentence is the starting point. From here, in the course of this chapter, we go through the series of operations necessary for the formation of **questions**, the passive, **negation** and the **imperative**. Our first port of call is question formation.

3.1. Questions (the interrogative)

The fundamental operation here is **subject–predicator inversion**. The subject and predicator, that is, are turned around (i.e. inverted), so that the question begins with the predicator:

```
         S    P    Cs                              P    S         Cs
(1)  Mr Creasey is a maths teacher.  ⟹   Is Mr Creasey a maths teacher?
```

This type of question is what we call a *yes-no-question*. Its purpose is to ask whether the equivalent declarative sentence, i.e. the statement, is true. And the required answer, logically, is either confirmation (*yes*) or denial (*no*). A second and communicatively quite different type of question is the **wh-question**. This focuses on an information gap filled by a particular constituent of the equivalent declarative sentence:

```
         S     P     Cs                            Cs   P   S
(2)  Mr Creasey is our maths teacher. ⟹    Who is Mr Creasey?
```

In this case the **wh-word** (the interrogative pronoun) refers to information provided by the noun phrase *our maths teacher*. As this functions as **Cs** in the declarative sentence, so also does the *wh*-word in the question. Notice here that the declarative sentence from which the question is formed is actually the answer to the question. Basically, though less obviously, this is so also with *yes-no*-questions. The answer *yes*, for instance, affirms the truth of the declarative sentence underlying a particular question and is often emphasised by the addition of the equivalent declarative sentence to the answer:

(3) a. 'Is Mr Creasey a maths teacher?' 'Yes, Mr Creasey is a maths teacher.'
     b. 'Who is Mr Creasey?' 'Mr Creasey is our maths teacher.'

So we see that, from the communicative point of view, statements might be regarded as back formations from questions, and could be held on some abstract level to presuppose them.

3.1.1 Yes-no-questions

Simple inversion, as seen in (1) is only part of the story. This sentence, in fact, is an absolute exception. The reason for this is that as a general rule only auxiliary verbs are allowed to participate in subject–predicator inversion:

	S	P	Od		P	S	P	Od
(4)	Denise	is reading	the newspaper.	⟹	Is	Denise	reading	the newspaper?

In other words, we cannot say *Is reading Denise the newspaper? The main verb *reading* has to stay in third position (its declarative position, in fact); only the auxiliary *is* participates in the inversion with the subject. So we have a **split predicator**, and we mark both parts of it as **P**.

If the declarative sentence does not contain an auxiliary, we have to introduce an artificial one in the form of *do*, before inversion can take place (known as *do*-support):

	S	P	Od		P	S	P	Od
(5)	Mr Creasey	teaches	maths.	⟹	Does	Mr Creasey	teach	maths?

Questions are subject, then, to what we will call the **auxiliary-inversion rule**. However, as example (3) shows us, this rule does not apply, exceptionally, to the verb *be*. This is allowed to behave like an auxiliary, even when it is not one, as here.

The questions discussed so far are what we call *yes-no*-questions (meaning that they can be answered with *yes* or *no*). A second major category is that of the *wh*-questions, discussed in the next section.

3.1.2 Wh-questions (the wh-interrogative)

As already seen in the introduction above, the *wh*-word (more exactly labelled an interrogative pronoun, interrogative adverb or interrogative determiner, as

52 The simple sentence: structural variations

the case may be) focuses on a particular item of information in the equivalent declarative sentence. This information is represented by a phrase in a certain sentence function. The *wh*-word takes over this same sentence function:

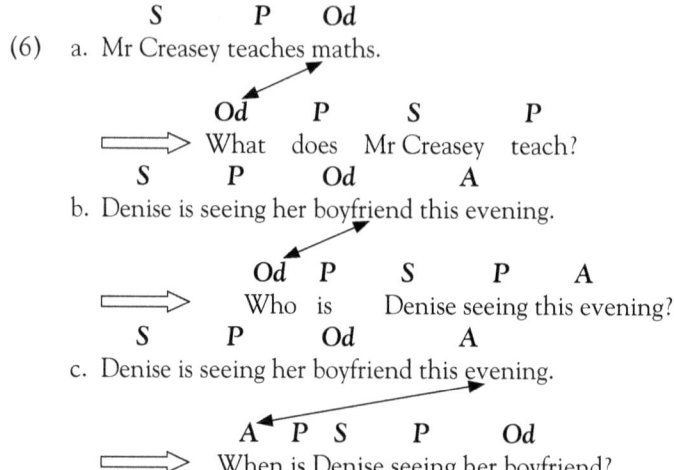

(6) a.
    S   P   Od
    Mr Creasey teaches maths.

    Od P   S   P
⟹ What does Mr Creasey teach?

b.
    S   P   Od   A
    Denise is seeing her boyfriend this evening.

    Od P   S   P   A
⟹ Who is Denise seeing this evening?

c.
    S   P   Od   A
    Denise is seeing her boyfriend this evening.

    A P S   P   Od
⟹ When is Denise seeing her boyfriend?

A point to note by the way is that the interrogative pronoun *who* has an object-case form *whom*. This is not used much today, except in very formal style. (6)b. could therefore be expressed as ***Whom** is Denise seeing this evening?* In ordinary language, especially in speech, this version would not be very likely. There is one case, however, where the *whom*-form is compulsory. We deal with this a little later below.

Notice that in *wh*-questions subject–predicator inversion (with *do*-support, if necessary, as in (6)a.) is the same as in *yes-no*-questions. There is one exception, however: when the *wh*-word refers to the subject of the sentence, **no inversion** takes place, i.e. the declarative word order is kept, and there is no *do*-support:

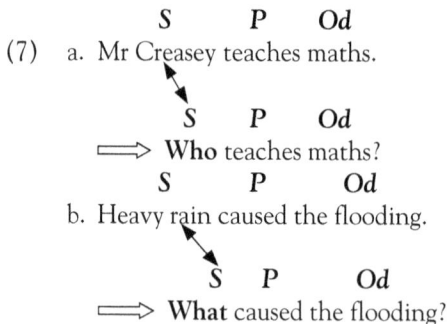

(7) a.
    S   P   Od
    Mr Creasey teaches maths.

    S   P   Od
⟹ Who teaches maths?

b.
    S   P   Od
    Heavy rain caused the flooding.

    S P   Od
⟹ What caused the flooding?

3.1.3 Wh-questions and indirect objects

Another special case, though of a different kind, arises with indirect objects. A *wh*-word **cannot** refer to an indirect object. For example, if we want to know who the recipient was in (8)a., we cannot do it by asking (8)b.:

```
           S    P    Oi   Od
(8)   a. Sharon gave Tracy the book.
      b. *Who did Sharon give the book?
```

The reason is that an indirect object must be followed immediately by a direct object (see 2.1.4). But that rule is broken here because the interrogative pronoun (= *who*) is placed at the beginning of the sentence. So now an indirect object is no longer possible. It must be converted into its alternative prepositional phrase version first. The *who* then refers to the noun following the preposition (i.e. the former indirect object). In other words, the interrogative pronoun and the preposition form a new **interrogative prepositional phrase**. Here the object-case of *who* (*whom*) is compulsory:

```
         S    P    Od        A
(9)   Sharon gave the book to Tracy.
```

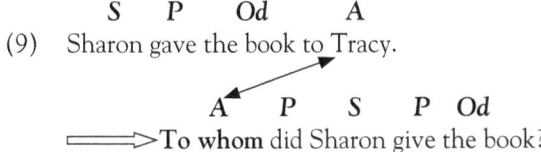

Like an ordinary prepositional phrase, the interrogative prepositional phrase functions as an adverbial. Because of the *whom* this still sounds rather formal. But as long as the interrogative pronoun **follows** the preposition the object-case is necessary. The much-preferred alternative, in neutral and more informal language, is to place the preposition at the end of the sentence. Then the subject form of the interrogative pronoun (*who*) can be used:

```
       A  P    S    P    Od   A
(10)  Who did Sharon give the book to?
```

This is the normal form of an interrogative prepositional phrase. The preposition has been **postposed**. This therefore splits the prepositional phrase, meaning that the adverbial function is also split, so that we have to label each half separately.

Postposing prepositions like this is common in one or two other structures as well, as we will see later in the book.

3.1.4 Wh-questions and subject complements

Wh-words in the function of subject complement also require subject–predicator inversion, with *do*-support where necessary:

```
           S   P      Cs
(11)  a. Bobby is getting fat.
```

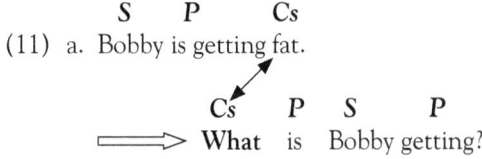

54 *The simple sentence: structural variations*

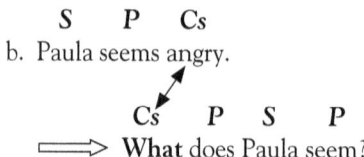

With *be*, as we emphasised above, inversion does **not** need *do*-support:

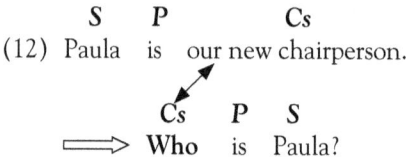

Because there is no *do*-support here, we may think at first glance that *who* is the subject and *Paula* the subject complement. But that would be wrong. The functions in the question <u>must</u> match the functions in the declarative sentence. So if we think of the declarative sentence as the answer to the question, then it is clear that the subject complement *our new chairperson* provides the missing information that the questioner asks about by using *who*. *Who* must therefore be the subject complement of the question. Or, to use another argument, as *Paula* is obviously the subject of the answer (initial position!), *Paula* must also be the subject of the question, leaving only the subject complement slot for *who*. (The different positions of *Paula* in question and answer show also, incidentally, that inversion occurs in the question.)

Let us compare this with a completely different answer to the same question. A teacher asks a group of pupils *Who is Paula?* and one of them replies *I am Paula*. In this case the missing information is the subject:

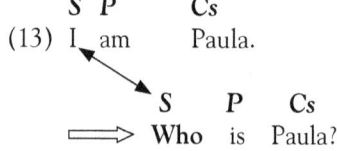

Notice this time that *Paula* is in the same position in both. That is, no inversion takes place in this question because *who* refers here to the subject.

3.2 Voice: active to passive

The term **voice** in this context means 'way or manner of speaking' (*SAGE*, p. 280). It refers to the distinction between what we call active and passive verb forms. All the sentence examples used so far have been active: their verbs, as we say, are in the active voice. (14) shows the contrast between the active and passive voices in the same verb:

(14) a. My son **painted** that picture.   [active]
      b. That picture **was painted** by my son.   [passive]

Voice is usually considered to be something that affects, first and foremost, the morphology of the verb. Focusing on this point for a moment first of all, we should note that the passive voice of a verb is formed by combining its past participle with the auxiliary *be*, as in (14)b. The following is also important to remember:

- passive verbs refer to actions, and must therefore be in the **progressive form** when necessary:

(15) The house **was being renovated** when the fire broke out.
      Departing hotel guests **are** now **being transferred** to the airport.

- only *be* + past participle counts as a passive. Other verbs that can be followed by past participles, such as *get* and *become*, are **not** passive formations. In this case the past participle occurs as an adjective in the function of subject complement. Verbs like *get* and *become* are main verbs, not auxiliaries:

	S	P	Cs
(16)	Sandra	got	married.
	Harry	became	involved.

- depending on meaning, this may also apply even to *be* + past participle:

	S	P	Cs
(17)	The food	was	cooked.

In this analysis *cooked* is an adjective referring to a state, like *married* in (16). The meaning is that *the food* was in a 'cooked state', i.e. it was not uncooked or raw. But in isolation the sentence is ambiguous. It may alternatively refer to an action, i.e. to something that happened. In this case *was cooked* must be regarded as passive, and the functional analysis would be:

	S	P-pass
(18)	The food	was cooked.

3.2.1 Monotransitive passivisation

The last two points in the preceding section show how closely morphology is connected with syntax and semantics. So this puts us in a good position to do what we now want to do, and discuss the syntactic issues involved with the passive. First of all, it can already be seen from our comments and examples here that the passive is not just a verb phenomenon, but affects the syntax of the whole sentence. We therefore speak not just of passive verbs, but also of **passive**

56 *The simple sentence: structural variations*

sentences and 'passive constructions'. Considerable changes come about when an active sentence is **passivised**:

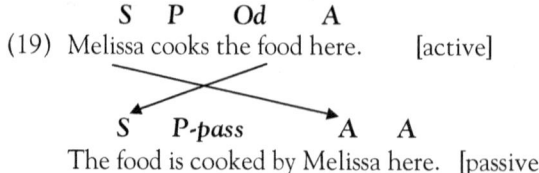

(19) Melissa cooks the food here.   [active]

The food is cooked by Melissa here. [passive]

Apart from the change in the verb form,

- the **active direct object** becomes the **passive subject**;
- the **active subject** becomes – in the passive sentence – part of a prepositional phrase with *by*, functioning as an adverbial;
- and the whole operation is accompanied, of course, by the necessary changes in word order.

All this shows us the main syntactic and semantic purposes behind the concept of voice. The passive operation (**passivisation**) allows us, for one thing, to change the word order of the active sentence. In doing this we shift the emphasis. By bringing the patient to the beginning of the sentence as the passive subject, we change the focus from the agent to the patient. The active sentence in (19), e.g., is about 'what Melissa does', whereas the passive sentence is concerned more with 'what happens to the food'. When we want to stress the patient's experience in this way, we use the passive. The agent in fact may be completely unimportant or unknown, and therefore remain unmentioned:

(20) a. Several players were injured in the game on Wednesday.
     b. Our flat is being re-decorated at the moment.
     c. My car had been badly damaged.

3.2.2 Ditransitive passivisation

Active sentences with ditransitive verbs (i.e. with the complementation indirect object + direct object) can be put into the passive in two possible ways. The first is the same as with monotransitives: the active direct object becomes the passive subject:

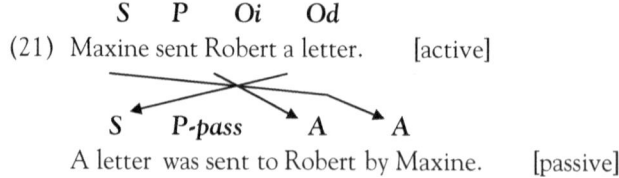

(21) Maxine sent Robert a letter.   [active]

A letter was sent to Robert by Maxine. [passive]

Notice that in this case the indirect object has to be dropped, and expressed by the prepositional phrase variant. This conversion is necessary because of the basic rule that an indirect object can only occur together with a direct object following it (see under 2.1.4 and 2.3.2). In the passive sentence the direct object disappears (having become the subject). So we have to get rid of the indirect object too.

The second form of **ditransitive passivisation** (and probably the most common) converts the active indirect object into the passive subject, and keeps the direct object:

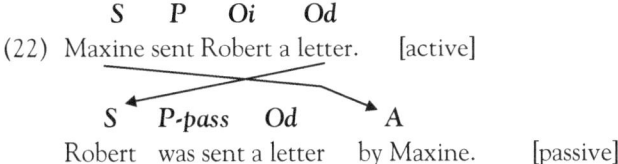

```
          S       P     Oi      Od
(22)  Maxine  sent  Robert  a letter.         [active]

          S     P-pass    Od              A
      Robert  was sent  a letter     by Maxine.    [passive]
```

3.2.3 Complex transitive passivisation

Complex transitive verbs, as a reminder, are those with an object complement following the direct object (Od + Co). In the passive, the object complement becomes the subject complement. The other changes are the same as with monotransitive passivisation:

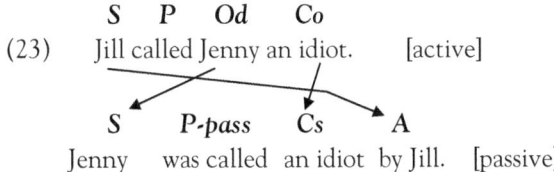

```
           S     P     Od      Co
(23)    Jill  called  Jenny  an idiot.         [active]

           S    P-pass      Cs           A
        Jenny  was called  an idiot  by Jill.    [passive]
```

3.3 Negation

So far all our sentence examples have been affirmative (sometimes referred to as **positive**). That is, they have not been negated. When we negate an affirmative sentence, we turn it semantically into its opposite: we say that something is not the case. This is done by adding *not*, the **negative particle** (technically an adverb), to the verb phrase, as is explained in detail in the following sections.

3.3.1 Negation with declaratives

In the case of the verb *be* the negative particle is simply added to the verb phrase:

(24) Mrs Conway is a fashion designer.   [affirmative/positive]
⟹ Mrs Conway is **not** a fashion designer. [negative]

However, *be* is an absolute exception. In all other cases, as with questions (see 3.1.1 above), an auxiliary verb is necessary: the negative particle *not* then follows the auxiliary (or the first auxiliary if there is more than one):

              S   P   A   A
(25) a. Mike is coming to the dance tonight.
                 S   P   A   A
     ⟹ Mike is **not** coming to the dance tonight.
             S   P   Od   A
     b. She should have been doing her homework at that time.
                 S   P   Od   A
     ⟹ She should **not** have been doing her homework at that time.

As the examples show, the negative particle just counts as part of the verb phrase, i.e. functionally it is part of the predicator.

If there is no auxiliary in the affirmative sentence, *do*-support is necessary, as with questions:

              S   P   A   A
(26) a. Mike came to the dance yesterday.
                  S   P   A   A
     ⟹ Mike **did not** come to the dance yesterday.
             S   P   Od
     b. Mrs Conway designs clothes.
                   S   P   Od
     ⟹ Mrs Conway does **not** design clothes.

In speech, unless stressed, the negative particle becomes a weak form, added as an ending to the auxiliary (an **enclitic**, as it is technically called), and informally written as **n't**:

(27) a. Mike isn´t coming to the dance tonight.
     b. She shouldn´t have been doing her homework at that time.
     c. Mrs Conway doesn´t design clothes.

The weak-form version reinforces the idea that *not* is a part of the predicator.

3.3.2 Negation with questions

Negated questions follow the same general syntactic principles as negated statements. But there are one or two extra things to point out. The first concerns the position of *not*. With the enclitic (i.e. weak form) this is exactly the same as in statements, see (28)a. As a full form, however, *not* follows the subject, as shown in (28)b.:

(28) a. **Didn´t** Sam play darts on Tuesday night?
 b. **Did** Sam **not** play darts on Tuesday night?

Secondly, negated questions and affirmative questions have differing semantic relationships to their respective declarative sentences:

(29) a. **Did** Sam play darts on Tuesday night?
 b. **Didn´t** Sam play darts on Tuesday night?

(29)a. is an open *yes-no*-question. (29)b., however, is not. It expresses a conclusion on the speaker´s part that a formerly held belief (that *Sam played darts*) now may not be true, and seeks confirmation of this.

3.3.3 Varied negation focus

Despite the general attachment of *not* to the predicator, there are one or two exceptions to be mentioned. Sometimes it is not the verb phrase, but other phrases that are negated. The negative particle is then part of those other phrases (technically as an adverb, as mentioned above):

        S   P-pass   A
(30) a. Not a soul could be seen in the street.
      S   P   Od   A
 b. He rejected the criticism, but not angrily.
        S   P A
 c. Not everyone can run fast.
       S   P Cs   Cs
 d. The summer was wet, and not warm.

In (30)a. and c. it is the subject noun phrase that is negated, and *not* is regarded as part of it, i.e. is integrated into the subject function. In (30)b. and d. the negated phrases are added using conjunctions (*though*, *but*). In b. this is an adverb phrase functioning as an adverbial, and in d. an adjective phrase functioning as a subject complement. (As we will see later, these additions to the sentences are really clauses). There are two points to note here. Firstly, **phrase-focused negation** occurs most commonly with subject noun phrases, as in (30)a. and c. It is unusual in the verb complementation, unless there are additions to already existing previous verb complementation, as in (30)b. and d. Otherwise it is nearly always the verb that is grammatically negated, even if the negation refers to parts of its complementation. This can sometimes lead to ambiguity. Out of context, for instance, (31)a. may mean any one of b., c., d., or e.:

(31) a. Sam didn't play darts on Tuesday night in the pub.
   b. Sam didn't play.
   c. Sam didn't play darts, but billiards.
   d. Sam played darts in the pub, but not on Tuesday night.
   e. Sam played darts on Tuesday night, but not in the pub.
   (examples from SAGE, p. 289)

(31)b.–e., then, are four different interpretations of what the negated verb in a. might mean. This shows that the **semantic negation focus** in (31)a. is ambiguous. In b., as we might expect, it is on the verb (*play*); but in c. the intended negation refers to the direct object (*darts*), in d. to the first adverbial (*on Tuesday night*), and in e. to the second adverbial (*in the pub*). The moral of the story is that in all of these cases negation has to be attached syntactically to the verb, even though the semantic negation focus might be on various elements of the complementation. To return to the general point being made, then, negation from a syntactic point of view is generally a matter for the verb phrase, i.e. it is part of the predicator.

3.4 Commands (the imperative)

Along with statements and questions, commands are traditionally regarded as being one of the three basic **moods** of speech, i.e. syntactic and morphological forms showing speaker-attitude to the utterance. The imperative has been left until last in our considerations here, as there is relatively little to say about its effect on syntax. Nevertheless, there are one or two things to point out. First of all, we must distinguish morphologically between two command types: those in the second person (singular and plural), and those in the **first person plural**.

3.4.1 The second person imperative

As there is no difference morphologically between singular *you* and plural *you*, the imperative form is the same for both, and additionally corresponds to that of the base infinitive (i.e. without *to*). With the exception of *be*, this is also the present tense second person form of the ordinary finite verb. For the imperative, then, all we have to do is leave out the subject pronoun (*you*):

      P   Od
(32) a. Have another drink.
   b. Turn left.
   c. Be quiet and eat your crisps!
   d. Keep calm and carry on!

The missing subject, in fact, is the most prominent feature of syntax with imperatives. Apart from this, functional labelling (as indicated in the first example) and word order are the same as in any declarative sentence. In informal language the subject is sometimes even included, usually together with a name, when the speaker wishes to emphasise who is being spoken to:

>   S   P   A   S   P   A
> (33) a. Eric, you stand by the door. Jason, you go to the window.
>   b. You be quiet and eat your crisps, Maurice!

Apart from the use of the name (known as **vocative emphasis**), there is no syntactic distinction in this case between imperative and declarative sentences. A different kind of emphasis (focusing on the verb) is created with *do*-support:

>   P   Od
> (34) a. Do have another drink.
>   b. Do be quiet and eat your crisps, Maurice!

As in other uses of *do*-support, *do* here is an auxiliary followed by a main verb, and therefore belongs to the same verb phrase (= the same predicator). A point to notice here is the use of *do* even with *be*.

Though not very frequent, progressive forms also appear in the imperative when a framework meaning is indicated:

(35) Please be waiting outside the cinema at 8 o´clock.

Negative commands need *do*-support, even in the progressive:

(36) a. **Don´t** move!
     b. **Don´t** be rude!
     c. **Don´t be** still packing your bags at 9 am.

3.4.2 The first person plural imperative

This is formed with the expression ***let us***, and usually appears informally in its weak form ***let´s***:

(37) a. **Let us (let´s)** have a drink.
     b. **Let us (let´s)** go to the circus on Saturday!
     c. **Don´t let´s/Let´s not** go out this evening. **Let´s** stay at home.

As shown in (37)c., there is a choice of two possible negatives. The second is perhaps a little more elegant stylistically.

A word should be said on the syntax of *let us*. As we will see later in the book, *let* can be an independent main verb meaning *allow/permit*. The imperative form *let us* has clearly developed from this, but in doing so has taken on a different meaning. (38)a. therefore has two possible interpretations, either (38)b. or (38)c.:

(38) a. **Let us** go to the circus on Saturday.
   b. Allow us to go and don't forbid it.
   c. What about you and me going to the circus on Saturday?

The different meanings are also based on differences in syntax. In the b.-meaning, (38)a. has the main verb *let* as its predicator and *us* as its direct object. (It is not necessary to comment on the rest of the syntax in the sentence at this point.) In the c.-meaning there is no direct object, **let us go** is simply one verb phrase (and therefore one predicator). That is, it is one unit: a verb phrase in the imperative form. Notice in this case that *us* is invariant, i.e. we could not replace it by any other object. In the b.-meaning, of course, this is not so: here we could equally say *Let **me** go. . ., Let **John** go. . .*, and so on. The invariance of *us* in the imperative form shows that its identity as a separate pronoun is restricted simply to the morphological task of signalling the first person plural character of the imperative. But it has lost its status as a separate object and has simply become a person-marker for the verb. This point is underlined by the fact that in the imperative version we can reduce it to a weak form, *let's*, a total exception (as pronouns are otherwise never weakened), and impossible in the case of the b.-meaning. The moral of the story, then, is that first person plural imperatives, despite their different (derived) form, have the same syntactic status as second person imperatives: as one verb phrase they function also as one predicator:

$$\begin{array}{cc} P & Od \end{array}$$
(39) Let us have/Let's have a drink.

Exercises

Exercise 1

Form yes-no questions from the sentences with **no** underlining. Otherwise, form *wh*-questions relating to the **underlined** parts of the sentences. Mark **all syntactic functions** in each question.

1 Tracy went to Birmingham by train with her sister.
2 Tracy went <u>to Birmingham</u> by train with her sister.
3 Sonny and Jake are repairing <u>Jill's bicycle</u>.
4 I am going to give <u>my neighbours</u> this letter. [*Use* **you** *in the question.*]
5 Tracy went to Birmingham by train with <u>her sister</u>.
6 She has given up her job because of illness.
7 Sam came to London for an interview yesterday.
8 She has given up her job <u>because of illness</u>.
9 <u>Sam</u> came to London for an interview yesterday.
10 Carrie teaches <u>refugees</u> English.
11 Sam came to London for an interview <u>yesterday</u>.
12 Sam came to London for <u>an interview</u> yesterday.

13 Frank and Joan have been writing a book about their journey through South America.
14 Frank and Joan have been writing a book <u>about their journey through South America</u>.
15 You must help <u>people</u> more often. [*Use **I** in the question.*]

Exercise 2

Put the following sentences into the passive and then analyse them functionally. If alternative passive versions are possible, please give them also and mark both versions functionally.

1 The people of this country have elected O'Brien the new president.
2 Eleanor is going to give the stranger in the pub three packages.
3 A teacher was explaining the movements of the planets to some pupils in class 4b.
4 Kevin's son showed me the new family car.
5 Neighbours were looking after the children while the couple were at the theatre.
6 Roberts waits on the guests and his wife does the cooking.
7 An unknown person has sent the mayor threatening letters.
8 Many customers consider the service at this garage to be inferior.
9 Tom's colleagues had bought him an expensive wedding present.
10 When we arrived there several other prospective buyers were already looking at the house.

Exercise 3

Using weak forms of *not*, negate the following sentences and then analyse them functionally.

1 Mrs Conway repairs cars on Sundays.
2 She should have been walking home at that time.
3 Have you brought the wine with you?
4 We're going to Iceland for our holidays. [*Use a full form of **not** here.*]
5 Did Hari meet Yasmin at the dance on Friday?
6 Have another beer.
7 Just be very nice to them.
8 Let us go to the fair in Tewkesbury.
9 *What two different meanings can no. 8 have?*
10 *In what various ways might the negation in the following sentence be understood?*:

Chas did not go fishing with Brian at Yalding on Sunday.

4 Phrases and their structure (I)

4.0 Phrases

As we saw in the last chapter, the phrase is the most basic unit in sentence analysis. It is a structural unit based on word-class, and is the smallest unit that can fill a sentence function. In this chapter we take a close look at what phrases consist of, i.e. what we will call here in a general sense their **composition**. Like sentences, phrases can be analysed internally in terms of both structures and functions. In other words, the composition of a phrase consists of **phrase functions** and the structures that fill them. That is, like sentences, phrases can be analysed on the one hand structurally, and on the other hand functionally:

(1) Composition of phrase

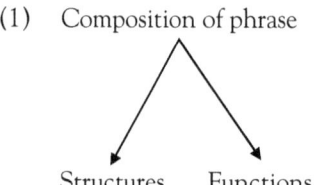

Structures   Functions

What this means concretely we will see in the following. In this first chapter on the phrase, we will be looking at noun phrases, prepositional phrases, adjective phrases, and adverb phrases.

4.1 The noun phrase

Let us look first of all at some typical structural patterns in the noun phrase:

(2) a. *noun alone*
        trees
     b. *article* + *noun*
        the   trees

c. *article* + *adjective phrase* + *noun*
   the   big   trees
d. *article* + *adjective phrase* + *noun* + *prepositional phrase*
   the   big   trees   in our garden

The minimum that we need in order to form a noun phrase is a single noun, as in (2)a. The rest is just a selection, of course. The prepositional phrase could follow the noun on its own (*trees in our garden*), for example, or the adjective could be used without the article (*big trees*). We´re simply looking here at the main possibilities for combining structural elements within a noun phrase. As can be seen in (2)c. and (2)d., other types of phrase unit can also be included, here an adjective phrase and a prepositional phrase. One phrase inside another one is a general phenomenon in syntax. The prepositional phrase itself here (*in our garden*), for instance, also contains a further noun phrase (*our garden*). In fact, as we will see a little later, this is the case with all prepositional phrases. Unlike a noun, a preposition cannot form its own phrase alone.

Now let us consider the phrase functions. The central function on which every other function depends is the head of the phrase, which must be a noun (*trees*). Without this, of course, there would be no phrase. The other elements are optional. These consist of two large functional groups: the one that comes before the head (the **premodification**) and the one following (the **postmodification**):

(3)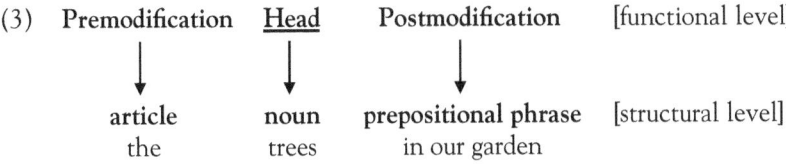

This is only the first step, however. The premodification has an additional lower functional level, which we should also add in our analysis. Articles function as determiners and adjectives as what we call the **modification**:

(4)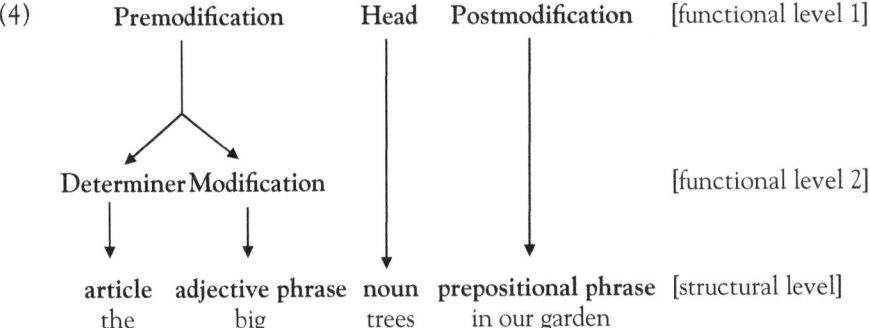

We will later make a further distinction within the premodification on functional level 2. But there are the main elements of premodification to be considered in a little detail first. What is the character of determiners, and why is it necessary to distinguish these from the modification?

4.1.1 Premodification

The functional concept of determiner comprises several different word-classes. These, to re-cap, are:

- the definite and indefinite articles (*the/a*)
- quantifiers (*much, many, all, some*, etc.)
- numerals (*two, three*, etc.)
- possessive determiners (*my, you, their*, etc.)
- demonstrative determiners (*this, that, these, those*)
- the interrogative determiners (*which?; whose?*)
- the relative determiner (*whose*)

To the possessive determiners we will now add the **s-genitive** ('s, s') such as George's, the Smiths' or my uncle's (for more on s-genitives see SAGE, p. 78, LGSWE, pp. 292ff.).

The common semantic relation of determiners to the noun, as we said in 1.3.6, is that of **identification**. They identify the noun following by locating it in certain **fields of reference**. This is either indefinite (type, category or genre) or definite (a known context or a relation to entities mentioned elsewhere in the communication or participating in it). A detailed discussion of individual meanings and usage would go beyond the scope of a book like this one on syntax. For a full guide, see SAGE, pp. 73–140 or LGWSE, pp. 270–2. Nevertheless we come back to one or two syntactically important things about determiners further below. The chief concern at this point is to establish the essential nature of a determiner and distinguish it from the other main sub-category of premodification, i.e. that of the modification. Semantically the modification comprises elements that characterise the noun in a descriptive sense. Whereas the determiner relates to the question *which?* (i.e. which or what entity is being referred to), the modification tells us *what kind of* X is being referred to (i.e. characterises the entity more closely and individually). First and foremost it is adjectives that fill this functional slot. One or two other structural elements in this role are dealt with further below.

4.1.1.1 Determiners and predeterminers

Like most functional slots in both sentences and phrases, the determiner can only appear once in one noun phrase. Determiners cannot be combined. Phrases like the following, in other words, are ungrammatical, if not meaningless:

(5)   *the his car

Phrases and their structure (I) 67

However, some words that are usually determiners can take on the character of adjectives and function as part of the modification. These are numerals and certain quantifiers:

> the *four* cars; Henry's *many* ex-girlfriends:

(6) a.

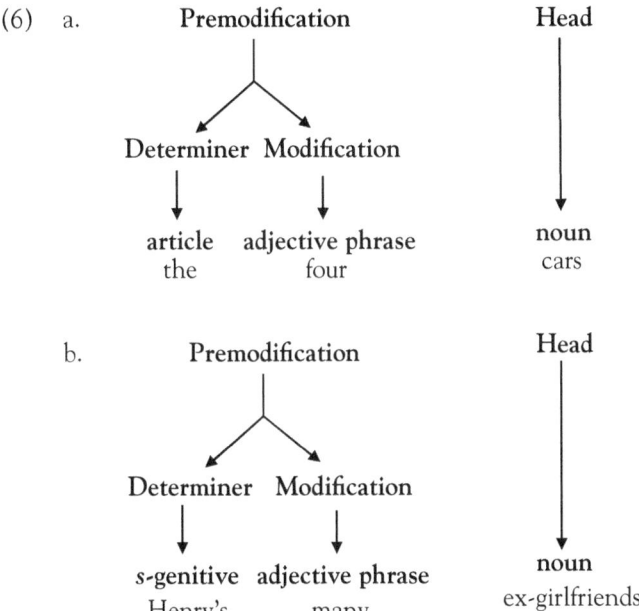

Another point is that certain quantifiers (*all*, *half* and *both*) can precede the determiner:

> *all* the cars; *half* the cake; *both* my friends. In this case they function as what we call predeterminers:

(7)

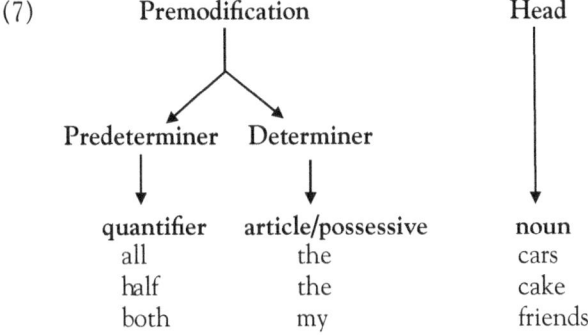

This is what we will call 'direct contiguity': that is, the predeterminer and determiner are direct neighbours, standing shoulder-to-shoulder, so to speak. A stylistically more elegant version places the preposition *of* between them: ***all of** the cars*; ***half of** the cake*; ***both of** my friends*. This then immediately increases the scope of possibilities to numerals and nearly all other quantifiers: *three of these trees, none of the milk, some of Greta's money*. Only *all*, *half* and *both* can have direct contiguity, i.e. appear without *of*. The *of*-construction is therefore the general pattern with quantifiers and numerals as predeterminers:

(8)

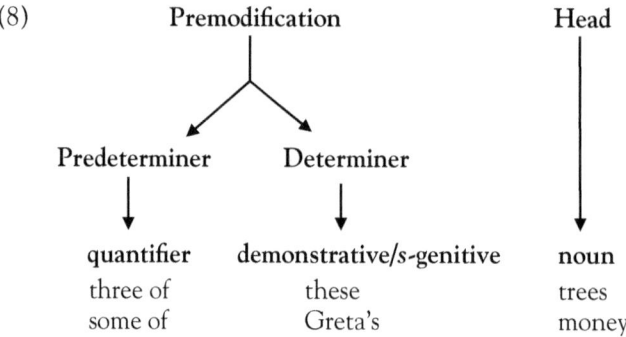

Traditionally, *of*-constructions like these with quantifiers and numerals are called partitive constructions (see also SAGE, p. 109, LGWSE, pp. 258ff.). That is, they refer to a part or portion of a larger group or amount. Fractions and percentages are also common partitive expressions (*three-fifths of the people, 60% of the pupils*). Technically, quantifiers in *of*-constructions are being used as pronouns. However, it is syntactically neater, and more in line with semantics and usage, to treat the whole construction as one composite quantifier, as we have done here. In addition to the word-class of numerals and quantifiers, ordinary nouns referring to an amount or a measure of something can also be regarded as partitive-type expressions:

(9) a pint of milk; two pounds of beef; a drop of blood; a slice of bread; a bar of chocolate

Similarly, nouns denoting containers of various kinds can also be seen as essentially partitive in nature:

(10) a cup of tea; a jug of water; a box of chocolates; a jar of marmalade

Such examples do pose a syntactic question, however. The first noun in each case refers to an individual object and not just to a measure of something. This also goes for *drop*, *slice* and *bar* in (9). Of the two nouns in each phrase, which one is actually the head? In our partitive solution, of course, it is the second noun, i.e. *bread, chocolate, tea, water*, etc. The first, as we have seen, is part of the premodification. But we may also be justified in declaring the first noun as the head. In this case the preposition *of* would form a unit with the second noun and this unit would then function as a postmodification (see under 4.1.2 below). Both types of analysis are possible. The choice of one or the other is basically a semantic issue depending on the particular context of use. If a guest asks for *a bottle of wine* in a restaurant, it is obviously the noun *wine* that is semantically profiled and therefore syntactically the head of the phrase. But to a still-life artist painting a bottle of wine, for instance, the order of priority would probably be reversed, suggesting syntactically the postmodification analysis. (Though of course neither artist nor guest is likely to care much about syntax in these situations!)

This is another pointer to the fact that syntax and semantics are often inextricably bound to one another.

4.1.1.2 *The zero article*

Let us stay with the wine for a moment, though in the interests of syntax (some of the best wine connoisseurs we know are also linguists; after a bottle or two they are fluent in both subjects). If we put *a bottle of wine* into the plural (its most satisfying form), we get *bottles of wine*. The indefinite article, that is, now disappears. What is left, however, is not simply a gap where something that ought to be there is just missing. No article is actually not 'no article' but the **plural equivalent** of the indefinite article. The gap, that is, is itself an article form and represents a grammatical presence. For this reason we call this 'gap' the zero article (see also *LGSWE*, pp. 261–3). It is also necessary for indefinite reference to **mass nouns** like *wine* or *water* (see below). Among other things, this is an important point in connection with partitive constructions. When these are followed by mass nouns and plurals we assume a zero article as a determiner in-between. The partitive expression thus remains in its role of predeterminer:

(11)

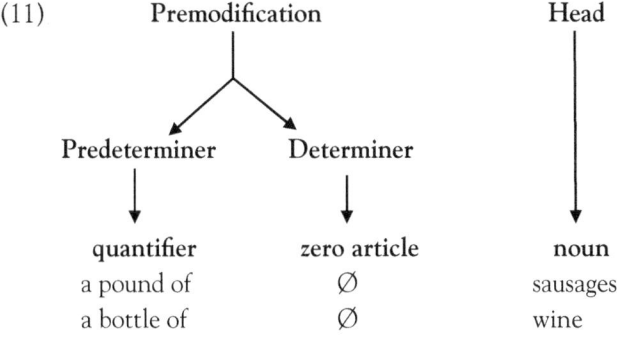

4.1.1.3 The modification

Unlike most other functional slots, the modification can have single or multiple representation, for example, *two **beautiful big white** swans*:

(12)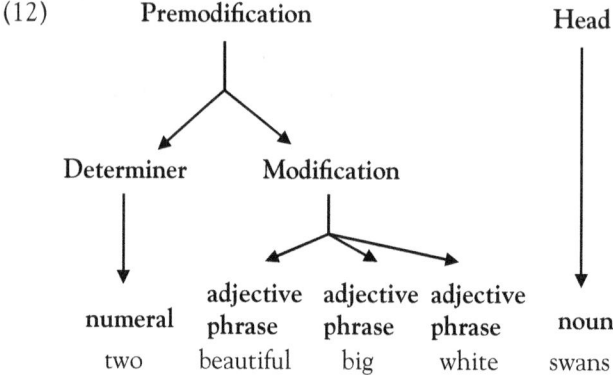

Elements of modification (**modifiers**) can also be nouns:

(13) a. a bus stop, the kitchen window, the garage roof
     b. Victoria Station, Leicester Square, Piccadilly Circus

Two nouns together, as in (13)a., are sometimes traditionally called 'compound nouns', and regarded (in our terminology) as 'double heads'. Some are frequently spelt with a hyphen (*bus-stop, taxi-driver*) to underline the fact that they belong together. In our analysis, however, we will not recognise compound nouns or double heads as such. Where they are hyphenated they will be regarded here as one word, and without a hyphen, as in (13)a., as two words, with the first as a modifier, i.e. serving as a kind of adjective characterising the head noun more exactly. The second type, in (13)b., which are names, will be regarded in the same way, with the common noun (i.e. the 'ordinary' second noun) as the head and the proper noun (i.e. the naming element) as the modifier. A significant point to be made here in passing is that as a general rule proper nouns have no definite article before them (though there are admittedly a number of individual exceptions to this, see SAGE, pp. 95–8).

(14)

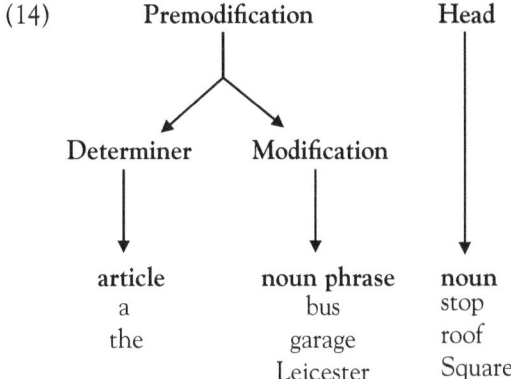

Premodification		Head
Determiner	Modification	
article	noun phrase	noun
a	bus	stop
the	garage	roof
	Leicester	Square

Finally, non-finite verb forms are also used as modifiers in the noun phrase:

(15) a. a walking stick, an ironing board (**gerunds**, often with hyphens)
b. a passing car, a used vehicle (**participles**)

These are discussed in detail in Chapters 8 and 9.

4.1.1.4 Order of modifying elements

There are certain general principles governing the order of modifiers. We cannot, for example, express (16)a. as (16)b.:

(16) a. a small fat white dog
b. *a white fat small dog

The principles are semantic and have to do with certain categories of meaning. Generally speaking, the modifiers referring to the qualities most intrinsic or essential to the identity of the entity come closest to the head. There is therefore a kind of progression in meaning from 'general' to 'particular' in a left-right direction.

Phrases and their structure (I)

Although there is some scope for variation, the following order is usually kept:

General quality/ assessment	More specific quality/ assessment	Size	Age	Shape	Colour	Origin	Material	Purpose/ type	Head
a	fine		old	curved	white-handled	Indian	ivory	hunting	knife
the	pleasant	good-looking	tall	young		olive-skinned	Israeli		maths	teacher
a	smart	powerful		new		blue-and-white	French	fibre glass	speed	boat
that	awful	tuneless	fat	middle-aged			London		rock	singer

4.1.2 Postmodification

Just as the premodification comprises everything that precedes the head, so the postmodification comprises everything that **follows** the head. Elements of postmodification are typically clauses:

(17) a. the man **who is standing on the corner**
  b. my fears **that our son would lose his job**
  c. Lavinia's fateful decision **to marry Paul**

In (17)a. we have a relative clause, in (17)b. a finite appositive clause introduced by the conjunction *that*, and in (17)c. a non-finite appositive clause introduced by the infinitive. These are constructions which we deal with in detail under 'The Complex Noun Phrase' in Chapter 10. Clauses like these involve **subordination**, which we introduce and discuss fully in Chapter 6. At this point we are just explaining the general principle of postmodification. In diagram form the composition of the noun phrases in (17) looks like this:

(18)

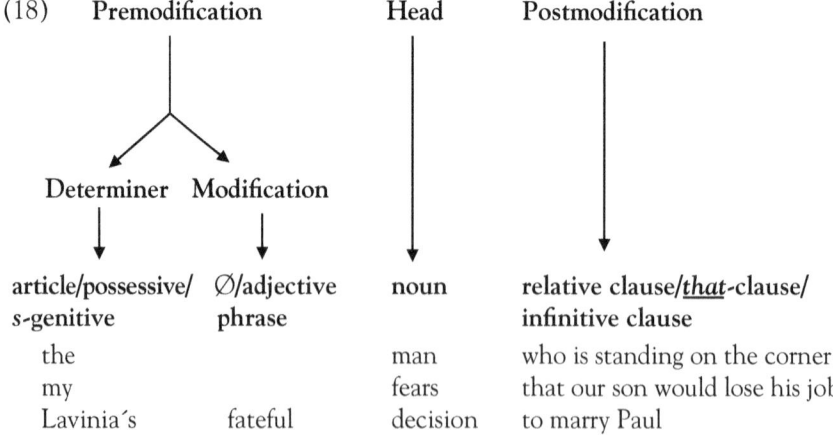

We will not go into the further analysis of the postmodifying clauses now. As we have just said, this comes later. For the moment we will stay with phrases. Easily the most common phrase-type **postmodifier** is the prepositional phrase. In fact the relative clause in (17)a. can be reduced to the prepositional phrase *on the corner* without changing the meaning. This and further prepositional examples are shown in (19):

(19) a. the man **on the corner**
      b. the legs **of the table**
      c. our grave doubts **about the economy**

And in diagram form, for the sake of clarity:

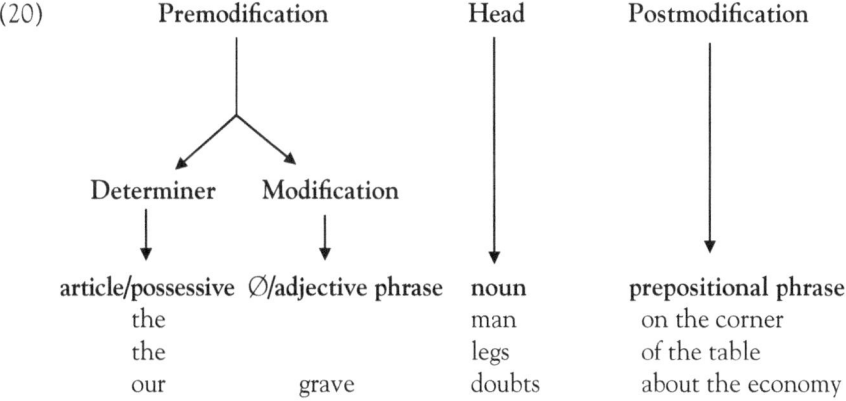

Traditionally, the **head noun** is called the antecedent of the postmodification. This may seem like just another term to refer to the same thing, but in fact it is a useful expression when talking specifically about the head noun in its **relation** to the postmodification and vice versa.

Further structural elements functioning as postmodifiers are adverb phrases (*here, over there, just now, then,* etc.) and noun phrases with an adverbial-type meaning, such as *last year* and *next door*. As we will see further below, certain types of adjective phrase also appear as postmodifiers (see under 4.3).

4.1.2.1 The concept of restriction

Most postmodifications are **restrictive**. This means that they identify or define their antecedent (and for this reason are known alternatively as *defining* postmodifications). For instance, our example above, *the man on the corner*, means 'only that man; he alone out of all other possible men'. In other words, a **restrictive postmodification** narrows the choice down to that particular antecedent, so that the reader or listener knows which one is meant. All our examples so far have been restrictive. By contrast, the postmodifications in the following are **non-restrictive**:

(21) a. Alan's house, **in Mill Lane**, was being re-decorated.
   b. The two antique chairs, **from the reign of Queen Anne**, were no longer in my grandfather's study.

Here the postmodifications are separated by commas from both the antecedent and the rest of the sentence. The commas indicate that if the sentences were spoken there would be a pause at that point, also causing a change of intonation:

(22) Alan's house, **in Mill Lane**, was being re-decorated.

This creates a **parenthesis**, i.e. a 'slotting in' of additional information as a kind of extra thought, which implies that the reader or listener does not need it to identify what the antecedents refer to, as this is already known. In any case, *Alan's house* (if he has only one house) is sufficiently identified by the premodifying s-genitive. As the additional information is not necessary to identify the antecedents, it does not need to be given in a postmodification, but could just as easily be shifted to a different clause or sentence:

(23) a. Alan's house was being re-decorated. It was in Mill Lane.
   b. The two antique chairs were no longer in my grandfather's study. I was worried, as they were from the reign of Queen Anne, and were very valuable.

Let us assume now that *Alan* has two houses and that the *study* contained three further *antique chairs* from a different period (Victorian, for example), which were still there. In this case we need defining information for each antecedent. This must be given in restrictive postmodifications:

(24) a. Alan's house in Mill Lane was being re-decorated (= only that one, not the other two in Forbes Road and Pinkett Way).
   b. The two antique chairs from the reign of Queen Anne were no longer in my grandfather's study (although the three Victorian ones were still there).

Notice now that there are *no* commas, meaning no parenthesis, and in the spoken version no pauses. The whole of each noun phrase is now pronounced with the same intonation, and in one breath:

(25) a. Alan's house in Mill Lane...
   b. The two antique chairs from the reign of Queen Anne...

Non-restrictive postmodification is less common with prepositional phrases, but frequent with noun phrases as postmodifiers, and occurs sometimes also with adjective phrases:

(26) a. The sales manager, **Mrs Tomlin**, was interviewing candidates for a post.
      b. Jane's husband, **a keen fisherman**, is on the quay every Sunday with his rods and nets.
      c. Grandmother, **unsure about her visitor's identity**, called the police.

Traditionally, noun phrase examples like those in (26)a. and b. are called **apposition**. The antecedent and the postmodifier are said to be in apposition, i.e. **side by side**, to one another. We will come back to this term later when we discuss clause examples (see Chapter 10.3). Although for clarity commas are desirable with all forms of non-restrictive postmodification, the comma principle is not a fixed grammatical rule. The commas are sometimes left out, although usually only with cases of apposition:

(27) a. Our maths teacher Ms Landsdowne is away ill at the moment.
      b. Jane's husband Robert is a keen fisherman.
      c. My brother Terry has two motor-bikes.

It is now sense and context that decide whether the postmodifications are restrictive or non-restrictive. They look restrictive (i.e. there are no commas – commas must definitely **not** be used with restrictive postmodifications!). But context and social custom tell us at least with (27)a. and b. that women can have only one husband and school classes (usually) only one maths teacher at one time. The postmodifying names (proper nouns) are therefore most likely to be non-restrictive. (27)c. is a different case. It is not unusual for people to have more than one brother. So does the writer here mean 'only Terry but not my other brother, Simon' (restrictive), or is this a case of a comma left out, i.e. 'my only brother, whose name is Terry' (non-restrictive)? Only contextual knowledge will help us to decide that one – as long, that is, as we only have the written form to go on. The spoken form of the non-restrictive cases would still be distinct (= slight pause and fall in intonation, see example in (22) above).

4.1.2.2 Multiple postmodification

Like the modification, the postmodification can have multiple representation. That is, it may contain more than one postmodifier relating to the same head noun:

(28) a. the woman in the red dress by the fishpond
      b. the neighbour in the corner-house with the four children

For these examples, we assume contexts in which either of the postmodifying prepositional phrases are sufficient alone to identify the head noun. This means that with (28)a., for instance, there is only one woman by the fishpond and that she is the only one (at least in the direction possibly indicated by the speaker) who is wearing a red dress. So the person concerned could be equally identified as *the woman in the red dress* or *the woman by the fishpond*. Similarly, for (28)b., we will take it that there is only one neighbour with four children, and that she (and no other neighbour) lives in the corner-house.

This state of affairs is shown syntactically in the following phrase diagram.

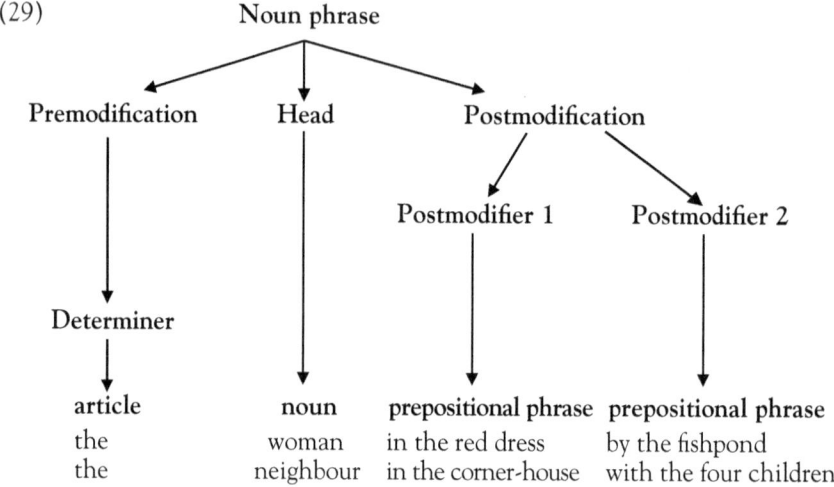

(29)

For these contexts, then, there is a choice of postmodifiers. Either postmodifier in each sentence could do the job as a solo performer. Both together simply provide alternative signals of identification and therefore possibly better insurance against misunderstanding. It is important to stress that the two postmodifiers in each case are restrictive, but independent of one another. We will say here that they function **in parallel**.

Let us now assume slightly different contexts: for (28)a. more than one woman in red (say, in the garden as a whole), and more than one by the fishpond (though of course only one in a red dress by the fishpond). And for (28)b. a corner-house with two flats, each housing a different neighbour, only one of whom has four children. Regarding identification, the situation now is more complicated. The first postmodifier now narrows the choice down ('only the women in red dresses') but not enough to be unambiguous. It is only the second postmodifier that makes the focus exclusive. On the other hand, the second one is also not sufficient to do the job by itself. Both postmodifiers have to act in co-operation, so to speak. In fact, each one has a different task in contributing to the combined effect: **postmodifier 1** describes the head noun alone; **postmodifier 2** describes the head noun + postmodifier 1. So actually the two postmodifiers have distinct antecedents. Only the first postmodifies the head noun. In doing this, it expands the head noun into a unit which we will call the head phrase. It is the head phrase which is the antecedent of postmodifier 2. The second postmodifies the head phrase. What we must now also say in addition is that the two postmodifiers no longer belong to the same postmodification. As we have two different antecedents, we also now have two distinct postmodifications. These function **serially**, i.e. one is applied after the other. In linear form, and using brackets, we could represent this generally as follows:

(30) premodification + head phrase [head + postmodification 1] + postmodification 2

A phrase diagram with all the details looks like this:

(31)
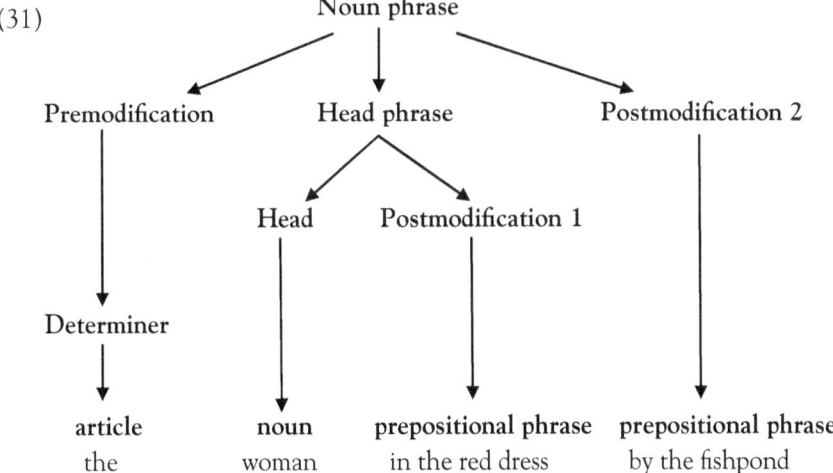

This is a good example showing that syntax and meaning are two sides of the same coin and go hand-in-hand. In this case the individual situation and context have to be interpreted semantically before the syntax of the phrase can be properly defined.

4.1.3 Number and countability

These are morphological and semantic categories, but have a certain effect on syntax. The specific issue here, from a syntactic point of view, is the compatibility of certain types of nouns with numerals, particular quantifiers, and the indefinite article. This is a particular issue in EFL. The following, for instance, are typical learner errors:

(32) a. *much cars (*There weren´t much cars in the street)
　　 b. *an information (*Can you give me an information?)
　　 c. *a surrounding (*He grew up in a poor surrounding)

(32)a. wrongly combines a quantifier restricted to singular use (*much*) with a plural noun. By contrast, the error in (32)b. does not arise from a singular-plural problem. The noun is singular and the indefinite article also, of course, but there is nevertheless an incompatibility. This has to do with a certain morphological property of nouns known as countability. Particularly affected are what are often categorised semantically as mass nouns, of which *information* is an example (further examples are terms referring to elements and substances, such as *air, water, sand, sugar*, etc., or to abstract entities like feelings: *love, anger, disgust*, and so on). These are singular, but cannot be individualised grammatically as defined single units. They are therefore not compatible with the numeral *one*, or with the indefinite article (which has a similar meaning), and, accordingly, have no plural form either. In short, they cannot be counted, and are hence known as uncountable or non-count nouns.

A further large semantic category of non-count nouns are **collective** nouns, representing groups or sets of individual items, such as *furniture, luggage* or *crockery*. These also have no equivalent plural form. On the other hand, many collective nouns are 'plural only': *clothes, goods, contents*, etc. Here we cannot talk about *a clothe or *a good, just as we cannot refer to *furnitures or *luggages in the case of the singular type. We therefore have **non-count plural nouns**, as well as **non-count singulars**. One such is the noun *surroundings*, falsely rendered in (32)c. as a singular. In a sense (if the correcting hand was inclined to be nasty) this might be viewed as a kind of 'double error', since in addition to being plural only, the word is non-count: in (32)c. it appears (erroneously) as a count noun. Non-count plurals, in other words, are just as incompatible with numerals as non-count singulars. This brings us to a further group of non-count plurals known semantically as **pair** nouns (see also SAGE, p. 33). Here, too, of course, numerals and other individualising quantifiers are taboo:

(33) a. *three scissors
     b. *several trousers
     c. *a few shorts

The countability type (count/non-count) and number status (singular/plural) of nouns are therefore factors influencing determiner compatibility, though only because determiners themselves also exhibit these characteristics (otherwise there would be no compatibility problem). The use of *much* in (32)a. is a violation of determiner number status. (32)b. and c. contravene the count status of their respective nouns, as do the errors in (33). In cases of error, countability and number often appear to be separate factors, as they do here. This is because one rather than the other is predominantly involved in the mismatch. In fact, however, the two properties are mostly intertwined, and condition each other. Non-count nouns always have **bound number status** (i.e. they are exclusively 'singular only' or 'plural only'). The great majority of count nouns, on the other hand, have **free number status**, i.e. can occur in both singular and plural. (Nevertheless, there are exceptions. For a full account see SAGE, pp. 29–31.)

On the determiner side, countability and number status are highly variable. Among the numerals, *one* (along with the indefinite article) is restricted to count singular nouns, the rest to count plural. Among the quantifiers, *some*, *any* and *enough* are confined to plurals and non-count singulars, *many* and *a few* to count plurals, *each* and *every* to count singulars. *Both* and *neither* are restricted to pair relations, the first to count plurals and the second to count singulars. Other determiners like the definite article, possessives and s-genitives are unrestricted, while the demonstratives distinguish between singular and plural. These are just a few examples showing the importance of countability and number status for the syntax of the noun phrase.

4.1.4 Sentence functions of noun phrases

In the sentence, noun phrases can fill all functions, apart from that of predicator:

- subject (**S**) ⟶ **Dogs** bark.
- direct object (**Od**) ⟶ Carrie liked **her teacher**.
- indirect object (**Oi**) ⟶ Your friends sent **you** this.
- subject complement (**Cs**) ⟶ Her husband became **an alcoholic**.
- object complement (**Co**) ⟶ The group made Albert **their leader**.
- adverbial (**A**) ⟶ I saw Wendy **last night**.

In phrases, noun phrases can function as:

- modifiers in noun phrases ⟶ the **kitchen** door
- postmodifiers in noun phrases ⟶ my brother **Tim**
- prepositional complements
  in prepositional phrases ⟶ on **the table**

As prepositional phrases have an important part to play in noun phrases, and vice versa, our next port of call will be the prepositional phrase.

4.2 The prepositional phrase

The prepositional phrase is a unit consisting of a preposition + noun phrase:

(34) *preposition* + *noun phrase*
　　　in　　　　　our garden
　　　on　　　　　the dining room table
　　　at　　　　　work

80 Phrases and their structure (I)

As we said in 4.1. above, a preposition cannot form its own phrase alone. It always requires an accompanying noun phrase, which functions as **prepositional complement**:

(35) Prepositional phrase

```
         Head        Prepositional complement
          |                    |
          ↓                    ↓
      preposition          noun phrase
          in              ◢──────◣
                          our garden
```

The triangle under the noun phrase slot indicates that the noun phrase is not further analysed. We have not used this symbol in previous diagrams, but will do so from now on for every phrase that is not broken down into its end components. That, however, is precisely what we will do now for (35). The final, complete analysis looks like this:

(36) Prepositional phrase

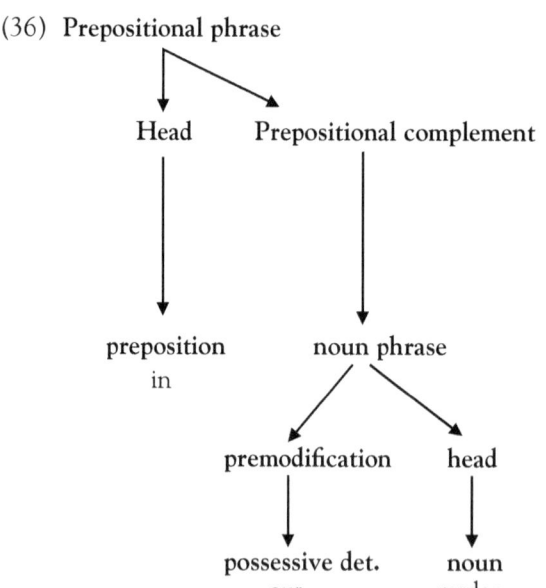

As we can now break down prepositional phrases properly into their final components, we are able to provide the following complete analysis for the noun phrase *the woman in the red dress by the fishpond* from 4.1.2.2. This is based on the serial postmodification version shown in example (31):

(37)

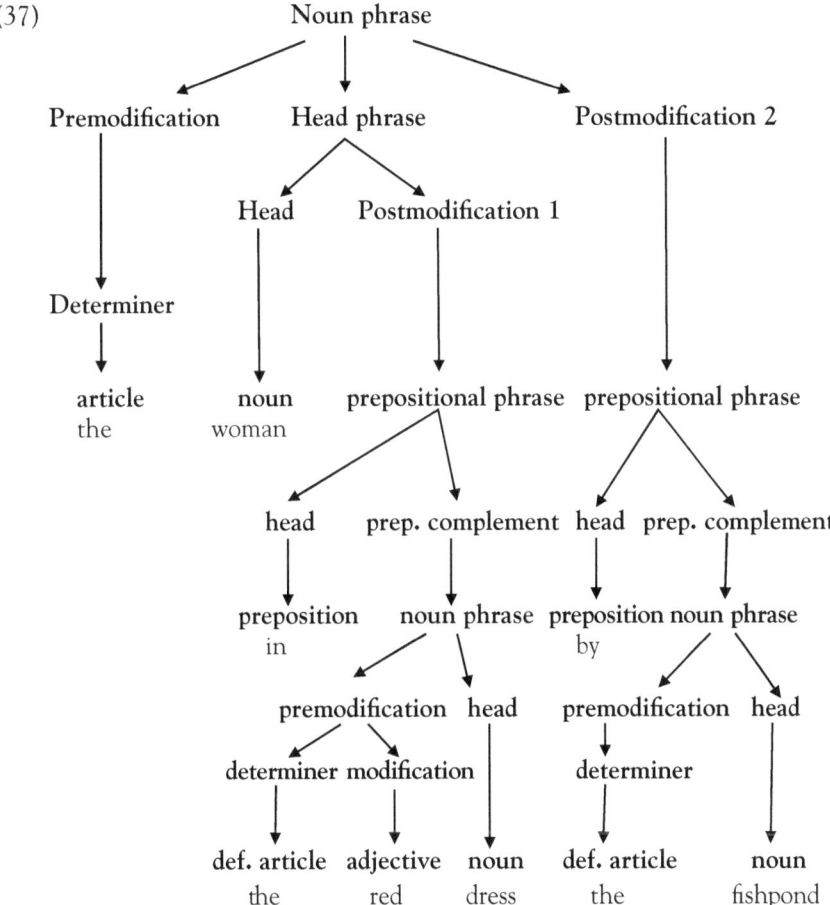

4.2.1 Premodification of prepositional phrases

In the ordinary way, prepositional phrases cannot be premodified. However, a restricted type of premodification does occur with specific types of degree adverbs: **right** *outside the station*, **just** *by the door*, **directly** *after lunch*. We deal with these later in a section on special kinds of adverbs (see under 4.4.1).

4.2.2 Sentence functions of prepositional phrases

In the sentence, a prepositional phrase always functions as an

- adverbial (A) ──────────▶ Billie was waiting **at the station**.

82   Phrases and their structure (I)

There may, of course, be several in one sentence:

(38) **On Saturday** we are flying **to Spain** **for a holiday**.
           A   A   A

In other phrases, prepositional phrases function as:

- postmodifiers in noun phrases ⟶ the man **on the corner**
- adjectival complements ⟶ red **with anger**

The term **adjectival complement** is explained in the next section.

4.3 The adjective phrase

Typical structural patterns in the adjective phrase are the following:

(39) a. *adjective alone*
        good
     b. *adverb + adjective*
        very   good
     c. *adjective + prepositional phrase*
        good   at grammar

Putting b. and c. together, we get *very good at grammar*. This gives us all the possible functional slots of the adjective phrase, which look like this:

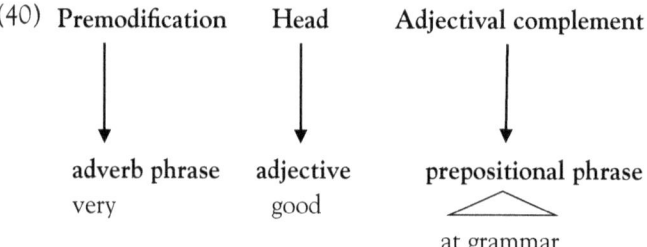

(40) Premodification   Head   Adjectival complement

    adverb phrase   adjective   prepositional phrase
    very   good
                                              at grammar

Note again the use of the triangle symbol indicating that the phrase concerned could be analysed further if desired. The only form of premodification in the adjective phrase consists of adverbs of degree (and this only with gradable adjectives, see 1.3.4). (40) is the basis of our phrase diagram. But it does not yet show clearly how different relations of 'closeness' between the three members of the phrase are arranged. There is a certain hierarchy which we could represent in bracketed form like this:

(41) [[very (good)] at grammar]

That is, the adverb premodifies the adjective and both together, as a unit, are complemented by the prepositional phrase. This means that for the phrase diagram we need our concept of the **head phrase** again to distinguish different levels of 'belonging':

(42)
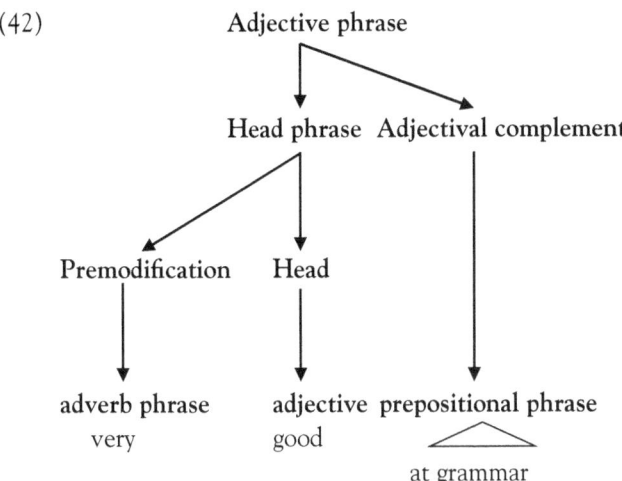

There is one adverb of degree, *enough*, that follows the head as an adjectival complement (*good enough*). As with postmodification in noun phrases, there may be more than one adjectival complement. The connection is then always serial (see 4.1.2.2 above):

(43) a. She was **blue in the face with cold**.
     b. I´m not **good enough at maths**.

This means that the first phrase complements the head and the second complements the head plus the first phrase. This is a mirror image of the arrangement of premodification and head in (41) and (42). In bracketed form:

(44) a. She was [[(blue) in the face] with cold].
     b. I´m not [[(good) enough] at maths].

Here also, as with (42) and the corresponding noun phrase pattern, we need the head phrase slot to account for the unit head + first adjectival complement, as represented in the internal set of square brackets in (44):

84 *Phrases and their structure (I)*

(45)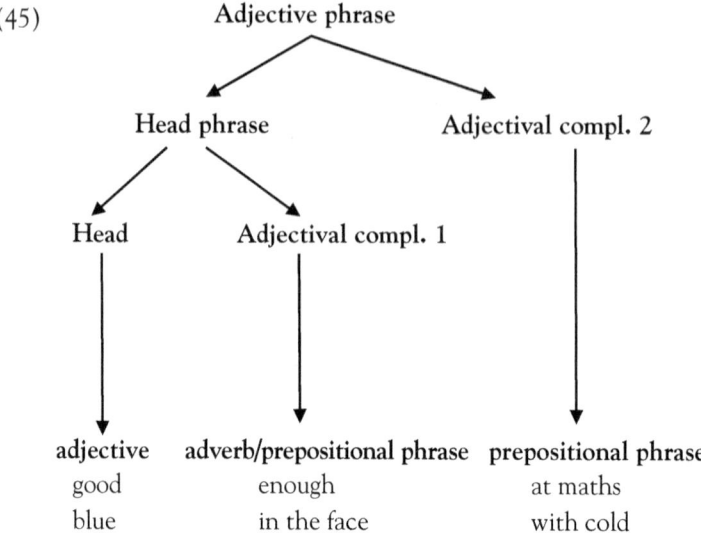

Multiple adjectival complementation occurs more often when one of the complements is a clause (see Chapter 11 for a detailed account on this issue).

4.3.1 Comparison

Semantically, comparison tells us how much of something one entity has in relation to another. It can involve various word-classes, but is probably most typical with adjectives and adverbs (though gradable ones only!). With adjectives, which is what we are focused on here, the 'something' referred to is a characteristic of some kind. **Comparative constructions** express that one 'comparison partner' has more, less, or equal amounts of this characteristic relative to the other partner:

(46) a. Gerry is shorter than Mike.
 b. Mrs Sims is more generous than her husband.
 c. Wanda is as tall as her father.

For full guidance on formation and use of comparatives see *SAGE*, pp. 166–87 (or *LGSWE*, pp. 521–44). We will not go into semantics and morphology at length here, but one or two morphological aspects should be mentioned briefly in connection with the syntax. First, adjectives can have **inflectional** (for example, *shorter*) and/or **periphrastic** (for example, *more generous*) comparative forms, depending on the length of the adjective concerned. Periphrastic comparison involves the use of *more* and *less*, which are adverbs of degree functioning as premodifiers. Secondly, a **comparative phrase** follows the adjective as the adjectival complement. The **comparative particle** *than* is a preposition in the examples in (46). Similarly, the comparative particle *as* is a preposition when it follows the adjective, i.e. when it introduces the adjectival complement. In the premodifying position we will treat it is an adverb since it expresses an 'amount relation'. In keeping with the prepositional character of *than* and *as* (in complement position), comparative phrases are therefore prepositional phrases and fit into the ordinary functional phrase diagram as follows:

(47)

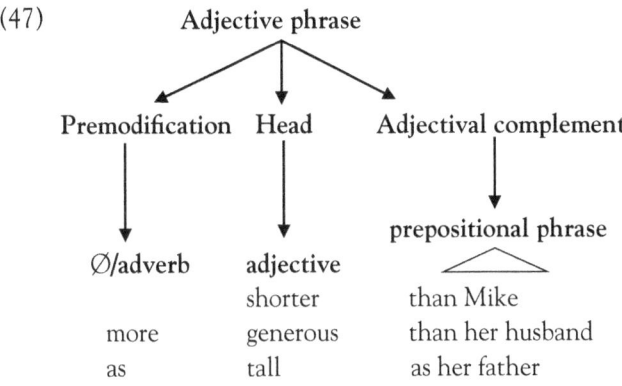

Notice that premodifying comparative adverbs operate together syntactically with the adjectival complement and are therefore on the same level. Here, that is, they do not form a phrase with the head.

Comparative constructions may also involve more than one adjectival complement:

(48) a. Conny is **better than Gary at maths**.
b. Gary is not **as good as Conny at maths**.
c. Mrs Sims is **more generous than her husband with money**.

As was said above, multiple adjectival complements are always serial, see examples (43)–(45). Internal phrase patterns here are therefore the following:

(49) a. [[as (good) as Conny] at maths]
b. [[more (generous) than her husband] with money]

Together with the head, the first adjectival complement thus forms a head phrase, with the premodification included. That is, pattern directly under the adjective phrase slot in (47) remains the same, but 'drops a slot downwards', so to speak, so that the second adjectival complement can be shown as complementing the whole first pattern of premodification + head + adjectival complement 1:

(50)

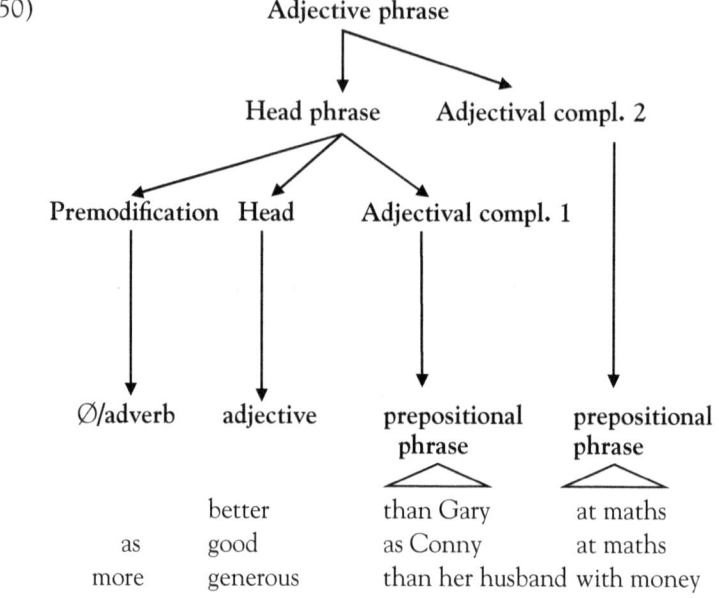

It is also possible for the two prepositional phrases to swap positions, so that we get:

(51) a. Conny is **better at maths than Gary**.
 b. Gary is not **as good at maths as Conny**.
 c. Mrs Sims is **more generous with money than her husband**.

This changes the internal relations a little:

(52) a. [as [(good) at maths] as Conny]
 b. [more [(generous) with money] than her husband]

The head phrase now no longer includes the premodifying comparative adverb. In the phrase diagram the premodification therefore has to feature on the same level as the second adjectival complement:

(53)

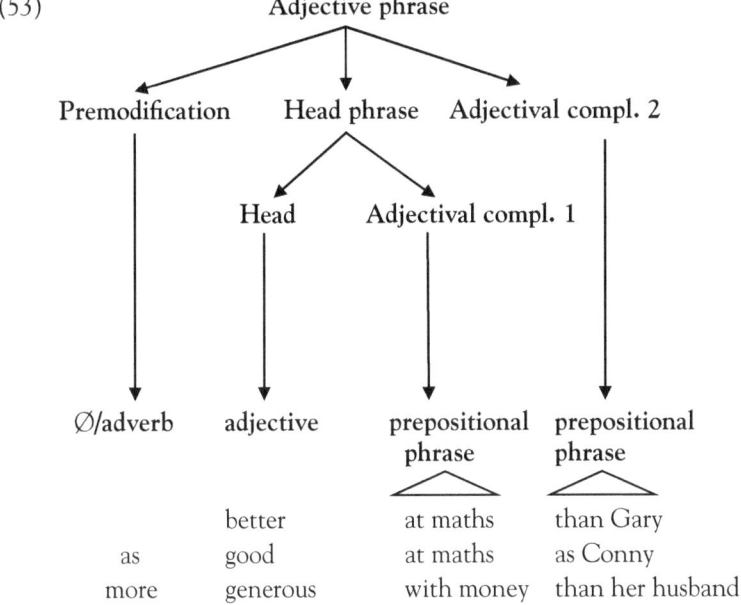

4.3.2 Sentence functions of adjective phrases

In the sentence, adjective phrases function as

- Subject complement (**Cs**) ─────────→ The food was **cold**.

In the phrase, adjective phrases function as:

- Modification in noun phrases ─────────→ the **black** jacket.

4.4 The adverb phrase

Adverbs typically occur alone, especially when they premodify adjectives. But they can also be premodified themselves by other adverbs. If, like many adjectives, the head is a gradable adverb, a particularly frequent premodifier is an **adverb of degree**. This is most common when the adverb phrase is used independently in its sentence-functional role of adverbial:

(54) a. He fell off a chair and hurt himself **rather badly**.
    b. Manchester United are now challenging Liverpool **very strongly**.

But it occurs also in adjective premodification, particularly with adjectives in participle form:

(55) a. Liverpool are now a **very strongly** challenged side.
    b. They do **quite hotly** spiced curries at the Star of India.

The most common structural patterns in the adverb phrase are thus the following:

(56) a. *adverb alone*
        strongly
    b. *adverb + adverb*
        very   strongly

The functional diagram looks like this:

(57)

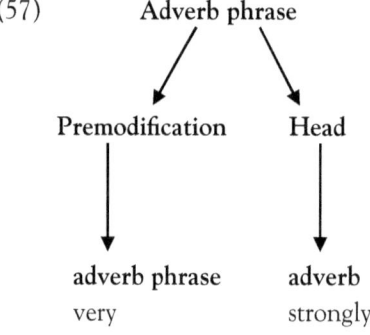

Unlike adjectives, adverbs generally have no further complementation following the head. An exception is with comparative phrases (see below under 4.4.2). Drawing a parallel to the adjective phrase, one might object here that prepositional phrases, for example, follow adverbs in the same way. Compare, for instance, the two sentences in (58):

(58) a. Sally is bad at maths.
    b. Sally has done badly at maths.

There is an important difference, though. In (58)a. the prepositional phrase is closely related to the adjective in sense, and cannot be moved independently to another part of the sentence. In (58)b., on the other hand, the prepositional phrase relates to the sentence as a whole, and functions as an independent adverbial. A functional analysis of the sentence shows the difference:

```
          S    P    Cs
(59) a.  Sally is [bad at maths].
          S    P    A    A
     b.  Sally has done badly at maths.
```

We now want to see how the adverb phrase fits into larger phrase patterns, for example within an adjective phrase inside a noun phrase. Here a diagram of the noun phrase *the quite hotly spiced curries of Sri Lanka*:

(60)
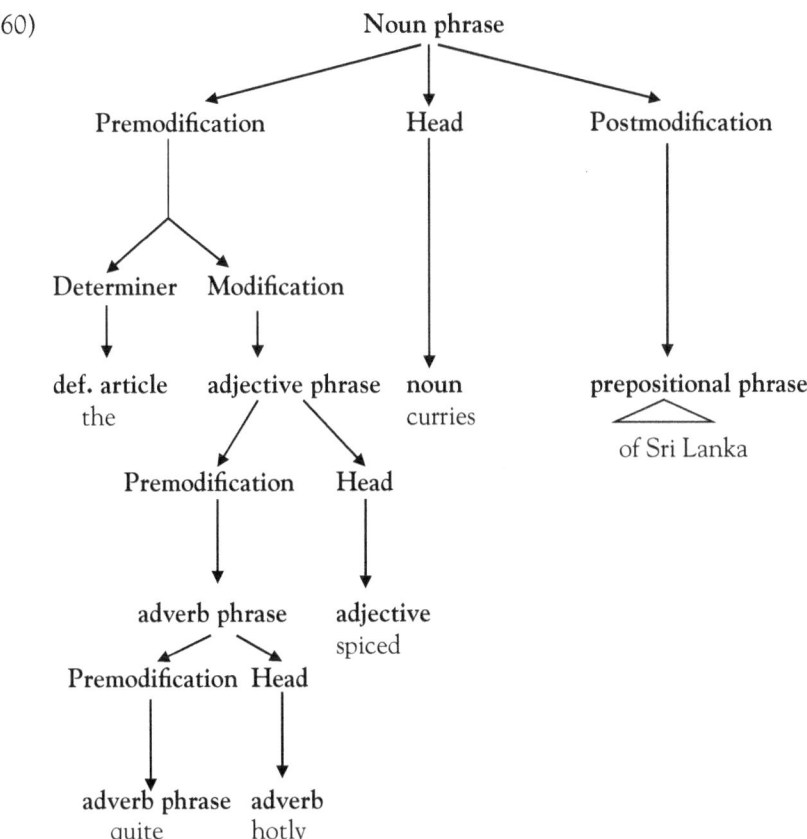

4.4.1 Adverbs in strange places: some special cases

Adverbs of place and time have their own particular kinds of degree adverb, with which they usually form fairly restricted collocations: *right behind, well ahead, close by, far away*; *just then, right now*, etc. Though they may not look like it, these are structurally and functionally quite normal adverb phrases, with the second adverb as the head and the first as the premodification.

90   *Phrases and their structure (I)*

Adverbs of place and direction can themselves act as premodifiers, not as degree adverbs, but as a kind of what we might call 'specifier', giving more semantic exactness to common generalised place adverbs like *here* and *there*. The premodifier in this case is usually an adverb particle (see 1.3.5 and 5.1): *over here, up there, out there, down here*. But there are also combinations with prepositions: *through here, along there, from here, until later, by now, since then*. These must be seen as prepositional phrases, with the adverb as prepositional complement (see also 3.2):

(61) Prepositional phrase

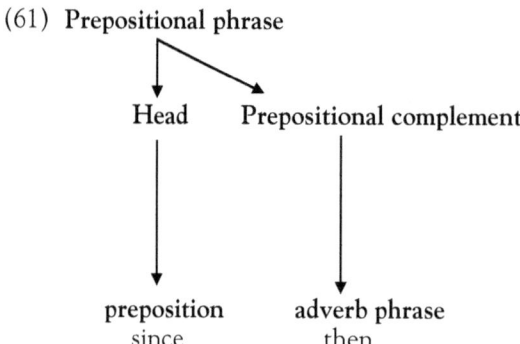

As mentioned briefly in 4.2.1, prepositional phrases can also have adverb particles as a kind of 'specifying' premodification: *up in Scotland, over in France, down in the south*:

(62)

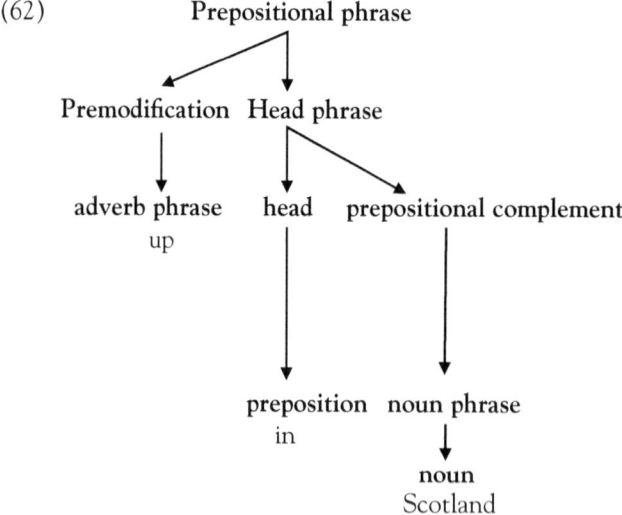

Note that we need the head phrase slot here because the adverb premodifies the whole prepositional phrase, i.e. in the form

(63) [up [(in) Scotland]]

Mentioned at the beginning of this section above were particular kinds of degree adverb premodifying adverbs of place and time. Quite logically, they can also premodify prepositional phrases (since prepositional phrases are also adverbial in function): *just behind the door, right outside the bank, shortly after midnight* (see also 4.2.1). The phrase patterning is that of (62). Certain degree adverbs focus specifically on numerals and quantifiers: *about fifty students, almost all children, practically every pupil*:

(64)

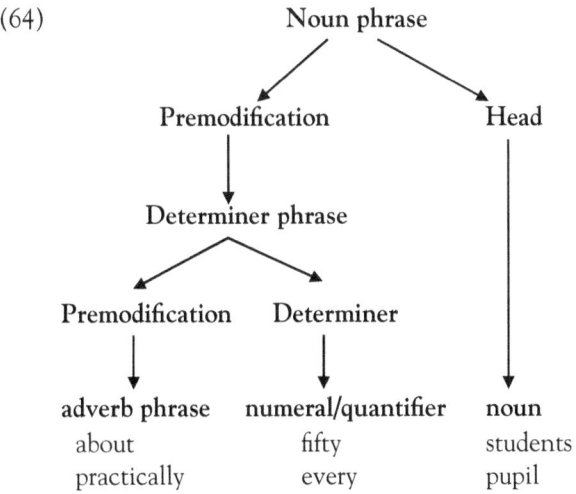

Some common degree adverbs take a 'predeterminer' position: *such a nice boy!; quite a good performance; rather a bad beginning*. The position is optional for *rather* and *quite*, which can also follow the article (*a rather bad beginning*). However, they seem to be generally preferred in the predeterminer position. With *such* there is no choice.

The predeterminer position only applies when the indefinite article is used. All other determiners trigger the regular post-article position (*some rather sour apples; this quite humorous remark; many such doubtful characters*). This in fact represents their meaning more faithfully, for like any degree adverbs, they modify the adjective. The predeterminer position does not change this semantically, i.e. there is no difference in meaning between *quite a good performance* and *a quite good performance*. In other words, even as predeterminers, these adverbs still belong semantically to the modification. Nevertheless, in functional-syntactic terms they should be regarded as filling the predeterminer slot. What underlines this point is that they also occur without adjectives, i.e. when there is no modification. Both cases are illustrated in the following diagram:

(65)

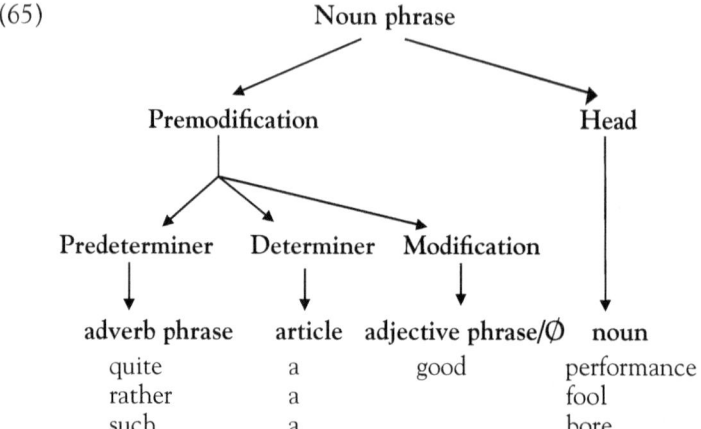

Adverbs of place and time can also appear in noun phrases as postmodifiers:

(66) a. My relatives **here** are all on my father's side.
b. The workplace **nowadays** is more flexible than it used to be.

This applies especially to those that specify directions with nouns referring to dimensions of time and space:

(67) a. four months **ago**; three years **hence**.
b. three feet **wide**; four yards **long**; ten miles **away**.

The diagram pattern is then, quite simply:

(68)

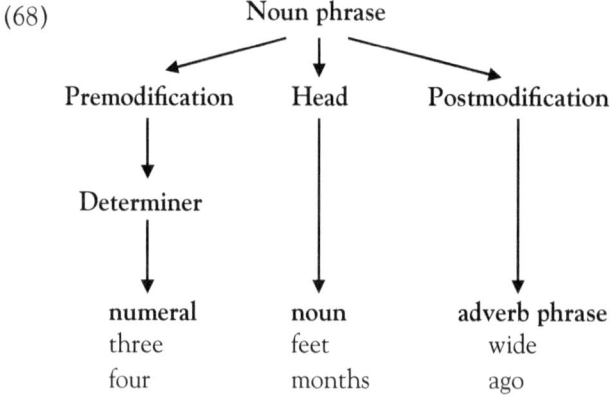

4.4.2 Comparison of adverbs

The comparison of adverbs is similar to that of adjectives:

(69) a. Brad drives faster than Mike.
 b. Mrs Sims drives more patiently than her husband.
 c. Wanda drives as well as her mother.

Here, too, there are inflectional forms (*faster*) and **periphrastic** forms (*more patiently*), depending on the length of the word concerned, with periphrastic comparison involving *more* and *less* as premodifiers. The comparative phrase with *than* or *as* functions as the adverb complement. Again, full details on usage can be found in *SAGE*, pp. 218–20 or in *LGSWE*, pp. 544–50:

(70)

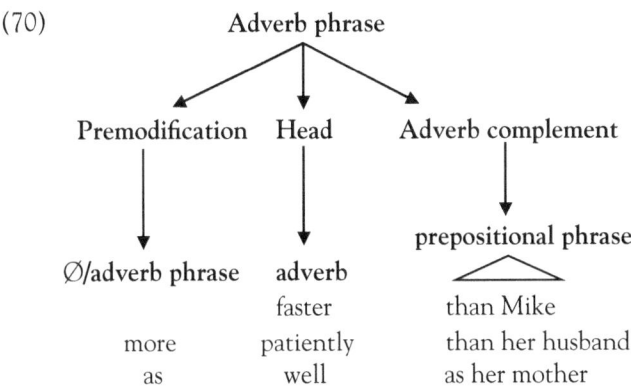

As has already been said, adverb complements occur only with comparative constructions. That is, if we add a prepositional phrase, it is not part of the adverb phrase, but an independent sentence adverbial (see comments on (58) and (59) above):

(71) a. Brad drives faster than Mike in heavy traffic.
 b. Mrs Sims drives more patiently than her husband under stress.

That is, we can quite comfortably put the prepositional phrase also at the beginning of the sentence:

(72) a. In heavy traffic Brad drives faster than Mike.
 b. Under stress, Mrs Sims drives more patiently than her husband.

Rather confusingly, however, the prepositional phrase can also precede the comparative phrase:

(73) a. Brad drives faster in heavy traffic than Mike.
   b. Mrs Sims drives more patiently under stress than her husband.

Even here, however, the meaning does not change. The prepositional phrases *in heavy traffic* and *under stress* could equally have other sentence positions and are therefore still independent functional units of the sentence as a whole. The comparative phrases, though, cannot be shifted. Admittedly, they have been cut off from the rest of their 'home' in the respective adverb phrases, but they still belong there and only make sense in combination with their adjectives. The independent prepositional phrases are 'intruders'. They can be represented like this:

$$\text{S} \quad \text{P} \quad \text{A}_1 \quad \text{A}_2 \quad \text{A}_1$$
(74) Brad drives faster in heavy traffic than Mike.

This indicates that the two parts of A_1 belong together as a single phrase with a single sentence function. What we have here is the phenomenon of phrase **postponement**. It is caused by a kind of 'interrupting' external phrase which acts as a parenthesis. The interrupting element may also be a whole clause. This point is taken up again in Chapter 10.1.10.

Exercises

Exercise 1

Analyse the following phrases using phrase diagrams:

1. a glass of fine Scottish malt whisky.
2. a few young football fans from Manchester.
3. the many students in our big city.
4. four beautiful statues of Greek gods.
5. all the guests at Terry's wedding.
6. more clever than Ryan in difficult business negotiations.
   Give both a parallel and a serial interpretation of the following sentence:
7. the boy with the dark hair next to Sarina.

Exercise 2

Identify the errors in the following and describe them in terms of countability and number status:

1. *She lived in an unfriendly surrounding where she didn´t have much people to talk to.
2. *Can I have an attention please? I have some important informations for you.

3   *None of the two boys had brought any towel with them, so they were both unable to go swimming, although every one of them had two swimming trunks in his bag.

Exercise 3

State the differences in meaning between the a. and b. sentences in the following, and say how those differences arise. Pay attention to possible contexts:

1   a. The hotel guests in eighteenth-century costume were admitted to the ball free of charge.
    b. The hotel guests, in eighteenth-century costume, were admitted to the ball free of charge.
2   a. The choir members, with bouquets in their hands, posed on stage for press photographs.
    b. The choir members with bouquets in their hands posed on stage for press photographs.
3   a. The old pub at the western end of Blakely High Street has been forced to close.
    b. The old pub, at the western end of Blakely High Street, has been forced to close.

Exercise 4

Analyse the following according to sentence functions:

1   Kate works much better alone.
2   Theresa is writing a book on flower gardens in Kent.
3   The school rugby team get better in defence after a few training sessions.
4   Courtney has been doing well in English again.
5   He has been good at English since Grade 1.
6   None of the guests at Terry's wedding were from Scotland.

5 Phrases and their structure (II)

Finally we come to the verb phrase, the most important phrase in the sentence and the one with the most far-reaching effects on sentence structure as a whole.

5.1 The verb phrase

Structural patterns in the verb phrase look like this:

(1) a. *main verb alone*
    work
  b. *auxiliary verb* + *main verb*
    am   working
  c. *auxiliary verb* + *auxiliary verb* + *main verb*
    have   been   working
  d. *auxiliary verb* + *auxiliary verb* + *auxiliary verb* + *main verb*
    should   have   been   working

The **main verb** gives the verb phrase its individual lexical meaning (and for that reason is alternatively called the **lexical verb**). This is the head of the verb phrase. Any other members of the phrase must be auxiliary verbs and these precede the head. In a sense they 'modify' it in very important ways: i.e. by indicating its tense, aspect, person, and also, in an example like (1)d., its modal colouration (for modality see SAGE, pp. 430ff.). However, apart from their semantic content, the basic nature of these categories is morphological: that is, they represent compulsory morphological characteristics of a finite verb phrase (see 1.3.3). The auxiliaries that express them are therefore not 'premodifiers' as such, but carriers of formal grammatical features applying to the **phrase as a whole**. Sometimes these carriers are contained in the main verb alone, as in (1)a. As a finite verb, for instance in the form *I work*, this shows all the necessary tense, aspect and person features by itself: first person, **present tense** and **simple aspect**. With composite verb forms (e.g. perfect or progressives, see 1.3.3) these features are partly 'outsourced' to the preceding auxiliaries:

(2) a. Terry was lying on the couch.
b. He had arrived the day before.

In (2)a. the verb phrase *was lying* is **marked** (as it is usually called) for third person singular, past tense and progressive aspect. The marking for the first two categories, and also for half of the last one, is carried by the auxiliary. That is, *was* is a third person singular, past tense verb form, and also contributes 50%, so to speak, to the aspect marking, which requires a form of the verb *be*. The remaining 50% of the progressive form is added by the **present participle** form of the main verb. In (2)b. the auxiliary *had* indicates the past element in the past perfect, half of the perfect tense marking (which requires a form of the verb *have*) and third person singular; the past participle form of the main verb is responsible for the remaining 50% of the perfect form and for the simple aspect. Our phrase diagrams then have the following forms:

(3) a.

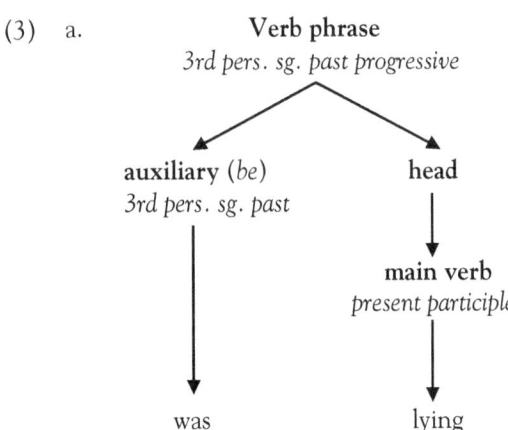

b.

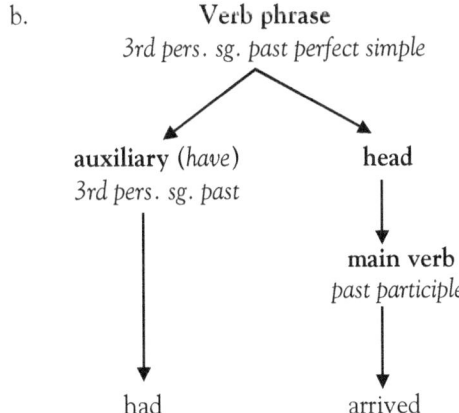

We thus have to see the verb phrase a little differently from the other phrases. There is no modification and verb phrases consist entirely of verbs, without any further components (except, of course, the negative particle *not*). It is important to bear this point in mind. It is true, as we said in Chapter 1 (see 1.3.3), that the verb phrase influences the architecture of any remaining parts of the sentence. For that reason, what follows the verb is often called its complementation. This is a rather loose term, however, and should **not** be taken to mean that its components are actually part of the verb phrase itself (as is usually done, for instance, in generative grammar models). From the functional-structural point of view this would be a contradiction. If following phrases are analysed according to their sentence functions (e.g. direct object, adverbial, etc.), then they must be regarded as belonging to the sentence-level. Equally, the verb phrase can only fulfil its function as a predicator if the rest of the phrases in the sentence are regarded as separate from it and on the same level as each other and the verb phrase. So when we speak of the verb complementation, what we really mean is that its parts actually 'complement' the sentence, in the sense that they 'complete' it. This is mentioned here simply to explain why a verb phrase does not include anything beyond its verbs (for further reference see SAGE, pp. 273–310, or LGSWE, pp. 358–450).

Complementation as such is no longer relevant at this point, and we will leave it for the time being and turn our attention back to the actual phrase components. Note that we include morphological information in the phrase diagram, as this is relevant to the syntax of the phrase. As we said above, a finite verb phrase must be marked for tense, aspect and person. This information is given for the whole phrase beneath the main phrase slot in the diagrams. Beneath the sub-slots we show the individual components of these categories, as they are distributed over the different members of the phrase.

5.1.1 More on auxiliaries

We will now look in more detail at how auxiliaries are represented in phrase diagrams, particularly when there is more than one auxiliary. The first point is to recall the distinction between grammatical and modal auxiliaries (see also 1.3.3). Grammatical auxiliaries help in performing certain grammatical operations. These are *be* and *have* (necessary for the construction of tense and aspect forms), and *do* (for certain question types). Modal auxiliaries are those like *should, will, must*, etc., which add individual meanings of their own to the lexical meaning of the main verb. In the phrase diagrams in (3)a. and (3)b. above we have a single grammatical auxiliary. A single modal auxiliary, as in *Kate should arrive tomorrow*, looks more or less the same, though with slightly different morphological specification:

(4)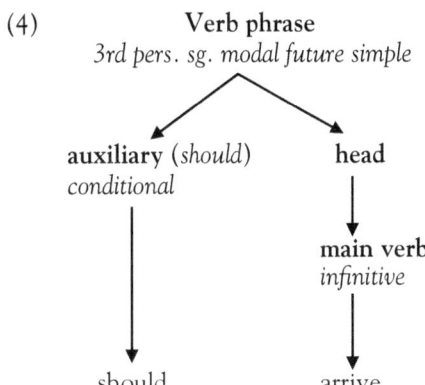

If a further auxiliary is added (as for instance in *Kate should be arriving tomorrow*), it must be a grammatical one, in its infinitive form, and must follow the modal. More than this, however, the second auxiliary is morphologically attached to the main verb, as it helps to form the progressive of the infinitive. In order to capture the hierarchy of elements properly, we therefore need to introduce a head phrase slot, as with the other phrases we looked at in Chapter 4 (see, for instance 4.1.2.2, and the diagrams there in (29) and (31)):

(5)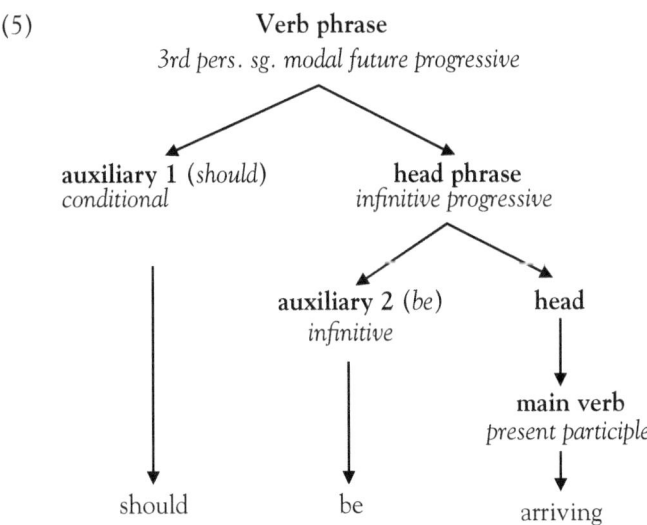

In morphological specifications auxiliaries can be additionally marked as modal or grammatical. However, this is not necessary. The verb phrase specification already notes that the overall meaning is modal, and if a second auxiliary follows, as in (5), it is clear because of its position that it must be grammatical. It is also worth pointing out that only grammatical auxiliaries have infinitives. Indeed to a great extent they behave in formal terms like main verbs. Modal auxiliaries, by contrast, are what is known traditionally as 'defective': they have no non-finite forms, no aspect and hardly any tense distinctions (for full information, see SAGE, pp. 430–1).

What has just been said leads directly into our next point: grammatical auxiliaries, being like main verbs, also have perfect forms.

(6)   a. Trisha had been running.
      b. Kate should have been working.

The grammatical auxiliary *be* appears in the past perfect in (6)a. and in the perfect infinitive form in (6)b. As this involves splitting the auxiliary *be* into two further auxiliaries, we need to introduce the idea of an **auxiliary phrase** within which this can be done (see also the **head phrase** slot in (5) above). For (6)a. the diagram is therefore the following:

(7)   a.

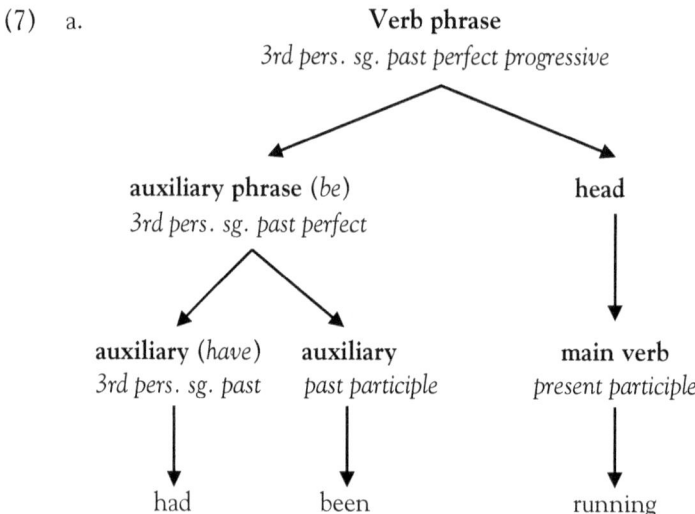

In (6)b. the grammatical auxiliary *be* followed the modal just as it does in (5). But this time its tense form necessitates lower level splitting and therefore the introduction of the upper level auxiliary phrase slot, as in (7)a.:

(7) b.

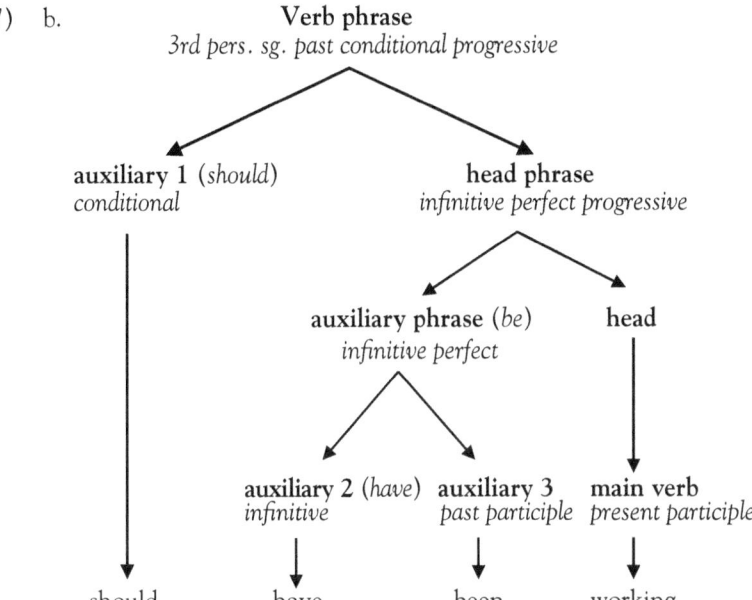

5.1.2 Non-finite verb phrases

We have just seen how participles and infinitives play a role within the finite verb phrase.

But we will now consider how they look when they are verb phrases in their own right. First of all compare the following three sentences.

(8) a. The children should see Tom.
 b. The children ought to see Tom.
 c. The children want to see Tom.

Each of them contains two verbs. The second verb in all three sentences is an infinitive. In (8)a. and (8)b. the infinitive follows an auxiliary verb. As we can see here, the infinitive comes in two variants, one with and one without the preposition *to* before it. The normal form of the infinitive after auxiliaries is the version without *to* (e.g. *must see, can see, would see*, etc.). The auxiliary *ought* is one of the exceptions, but there are others too, for instance *to be to, going to* and *to be supposed to*, all of which also count as auxiliaries. The point to remember in this connection is that auxiliaries are always parts of other verb phrases: that is, they cannot stand alone and therefore do not form separate verb phrases of their own. (8)a. and (8)b. therefore contain only one verb phrase each. (8)c., however, is a different case. Using pronouns, we could express (8)c. as *The children want something* or *The children want this*. The verb *want*, that is, can stand alone. It is therefore not an auxiliary, but a main verb. As a consequence, (8)c., unlike the preceding sentences, contains two separate verb phrases, one finite (*want*), and the other non-finite, i.e. the infinitive form *to see*. There are a large number of main verbs like *want* that can be followed by the infinitive or other non-finite verbs (e.g. *promise, expect, try, learn, remember, seem,* etc.). We call such verbs traditionally **catenatives** (= 'connecting verbs'), in order to distinguish them from auxiliaries. This is important, because two separate verb phrases in the same sentence mean that it consists of two separate clauses. In other words, the infinitive and its direct object in (8)c. form a subordinate clause. This is dealt with in detail in Chapters 7–9, and we will not go into the aspect of subordination further here. The significant point here is that infinitives can form their own verb phrases. This is the case with the other non-finites too. In the following examples the catenatives *stop* and *regret* are followed by gerunds:

(9) a. Sally has stopped smoking.
    b. I regret moving from London.

In phrase diagrams these look exactly the same as finite verbs. Here the infinitive and gerund phrases from (8)c. and (9):

(10)   **Verb phrase**
        non-finite

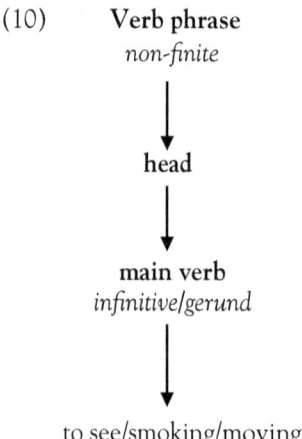

        head

        main verb
        infinitive/gerund

        to see/smoking/moving

And the same applies, essentially, when auxiliaries are involved. Non-finites can appear in perfect and progressive forms:

(11) a. I regret having moved from London.   [gerund perfect]
     b. She claims to have been working all day.   [infinitive perfect progressive]

And the diagrams:

(12) a.

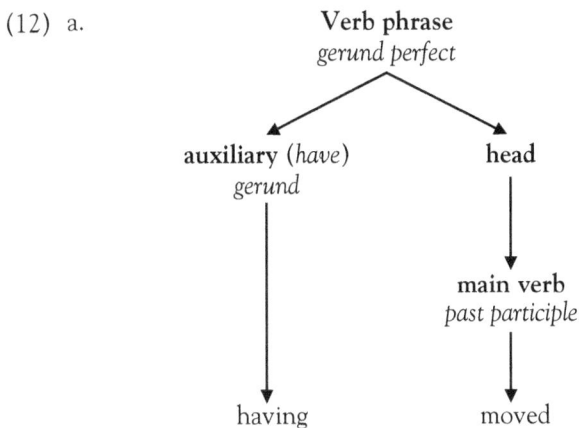

b.

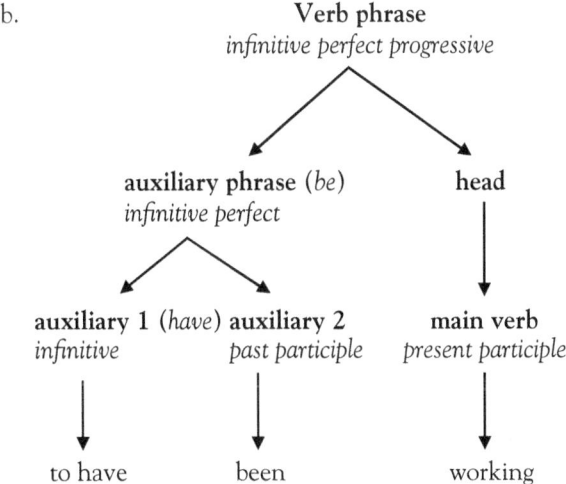

5.2 Effects of negative, interrogative and passive on the verb phrase

As was pointed out in Chapter 3, questions and negation require a composite verb form. This is because both operations need the presence of an auxiliary. Only auxiliaries can participate in inversion, i.e. the position change of subject and verb in questions. Only auxiliaries can be followed by *not*, the **negative particle**, when verbs are negated. If there is no auxiliary in the equivalent affirmative (i.e. positive) and declarative (statement) form of the

5.2.1 Negation

Negation was dealt with thoroughly in 3.3. However, we want to re-consider it here firstly as a reminder and, secondly, from the perspective of a **procedure**. What is the **process** involved in negating verbs? As our starting point we will take the two affirmative sentence examples in (13):

(13) a. Christine **has read** a lot of crime fiction.
　　 b. Christine **reads** a lot of crime fiction.

What mental steps should we observe when proceeding from affirmative to negative? For (13)a. these would be:

(14) a. Christine **has read** a lot of crime fiction.　　[affirmative]
　　　　　⇓
　　　　auxiliary present
　　　　　⇓
　　　　negative particle follows
　　　　　⇓
　　 b. Christine **has not read** a lot of crime fiction.　　[negative]

And for (13)b.:

(15) a. Christine **reads** a lot of crime fiction.　　[affirmative]
　　　　　⇓
　　　　no auxiliary
　　　　　⇓
　　　　do-support needed, then negative particle
　　　　　⇓
　　 b. Christine **does not read** a lot of crime fiction.　　[negative]

As pointed out in 3.3, using the weak form of the negative particle (n´t) tends to emphasise the importance of the auxiliary in negation, as in writing the particle is treated as an affix of the auxiliary:

(16) a. Christine **doesn´t read** a lot of crime fiction.
     b. Christine **hasn´t read** a lot of crime fiction.

In sentence-analytical terms we will therefore treat the negative particle, even in its separate full form *not*, simply as a morphological part of the auxiliary verb.

5.2.2 The interrogative

As said above and shown in 3.1, questions are subject to the same auxiliary condition as negatives. Conversion of a declarative sentence into an interrogative one therefore involves the same procedural issue as that shown in (14) and (15): *do*-support must be given if there is no auxiliary present. After this point has been resolved, inversion of subject and auxiliary follows. Taking the declaratives in (13) as the base, we then get

(17) a. **Has** Christine **read** a lot of crime fiction?
     b. **Does** Christine **read** a lot of crime fiction?

As the subject noun phrase now interrupts the phrase, we have a case of phrase postponement. Functional labelling should therefore read as follows:

$$P_1 \quad S \quad P_1 \qquad Od$$
(18) a. **Has** Christine **read** a lot of crime fiction?
     b. **Does** Christine **read** a lot of crime fiction?

Sub-script numbering shows that the two verbs belong to the same predicator. The phrase diagram looks like any other in which an auxiliary precedes the main verb, since inversion (as a clause construction) cannot be shown inside the verb phrase:

(19) a.
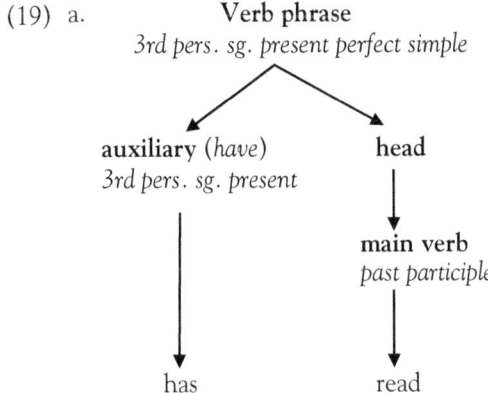

106 *Phrases and their structure (II)*

b.
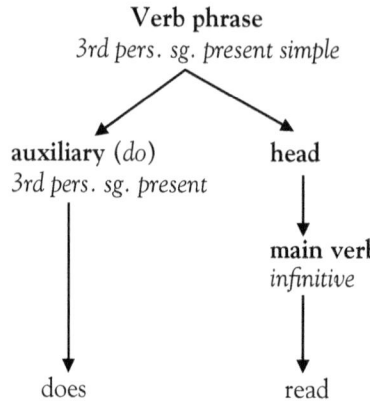

5.2.3 The passive

As was shown in 3.2, verb phrases in the passive consist of auxiliary *be* + past participle, and are functionally marked as **P-pass**:

       S   P-pass   A
(20) a. Crime novels are read by many people.
       S   P-pass
    b. Food was being prepared.

In the corresponding phrase diagrams the verb phrase slot is marked as passive. The rest is just a case of auxiliaries and the past participle form of the main verb:

(21) a.
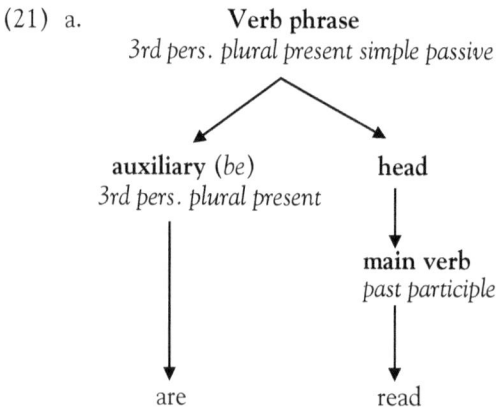

b.

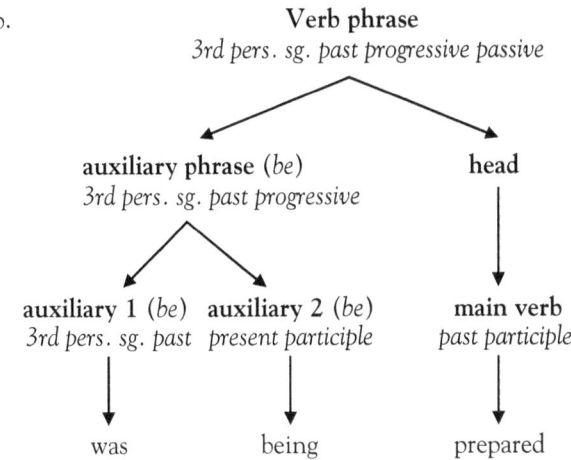

5.3 Auxiliary pro-forms

A particular feature of English verb phrase syntax is the omission (or **ellipsis**) of the main verb after an auxiliary. This is a sentence device in specific grammatical contexts to avoid the repetition of a main verb used immediately beforehand:

(22) a. Sonny **can** swim, but his girlfriend **can´t**.
 b. Christine **has** read a lot of crime fiction and her husband **has** too.

The gap left by the missing main verb acts as a back reference, rather like a pronoun in the case of a noun. It is the auxiliary, however, that mainly signals the 'pronoun' role, so to speak, and for this reason we call it here an **auxiliary pro-form**. What it refers back to is an **antecedent main verb**. This is always part of a preceding separate clause or sentence, which means that the following auxiliary pro-form is the predicator of its own separate clause, the **pro-form clause**. There are several different types of pro-form clause, some co-ordinate, like those in (22), and others subordinate. Two of the most common types of pro-form clause in spoken language are question and **answer tags** (see also SAGE, pp. 294ff.). The phrase diagram for an auxiliary pro-form, taking (22)b. as an example, is as follows:

(23)   **Verb phrase**
            3rd pers. sg. present perfect simple

       auxiliary (*have*)   **head**
       3rd pers. sg. present

                                    main verb (*read*)
                                    past participle (*read*)

            has   Ø

5.4 Two- and three-part verbs

We now come to prepositional and phrasal verbs. How do they fit into the general verb phrase pattern? Moreover, how do they affect sentence structure and functions? Here again, then, our consideration of the verb phrase will necessarily involve discussing features of sentence syntax.

5.4.1 Prepositional verbs

With prepositional verbs, as we said in 1.3.7, the accompanying preposition forms a semantic and syntactic unit with the verb, as in:

(24) a. Kelly's mother **looks after** the children during the week.
     b. I **waited for** Jamie outside the hairdresser's.
     c. The police **are looking into** the matter.
     d. They **looked at** the painting closely.

Further examples are *attend to, cater for, deal with, depend on, look at, wait on*, etc. (for a comprehensive overview see *LGSWE*, pp. 416–18).

There are several points to note regarding sentence syntax:

- a noun must always **follow** the preposition (i.e. in a simple declarative sentence);

- the noun following the preposition is sometimes called the prepositional object, but is functionally an ordinary direct object (**Od**);
- the preposition is part of the main verb unit, i.e. the preposition belongs syntactically to the verb (unlike the case with a prepositional phrase, where it forms a unit with the noun following).

The conception of the prepositional verb as a syntactic category is based on the meaning relationship between the verb and the preposition. So it is another good example of how syntax often reflects what are essentially semantic factors. Because of this we will briefly consider the meaning relations involved here and how they differ from the normal case of a preposition simply following a verb.

5.4.1.1 The semantics of prepositional verbs

Semantically, the significant point about prepositional verbs is that verb and preposition have a unified conceptual meaning that is usually more than simply the 'sum of the parts'. In other words, the meaning of the whole is not generally just 'verb meaning plus prepositional meaning'. It is an idiomatic combination. The idiomatic, or special, meaning is often clearly the case with both partners, exemplified by *look after* (= 'to tend, to take care of'), as in (24)a. But it may be mainly the preposition that deviates from its ordinary semantics, leaving the verb to retain more or less its usual sense. This is the case with *wait for*, as in (24)b. We find a third kind of semantic relation in (24)c., where *look into* to an extent retains the base semantics of both partners, but takes on an abstract or metaphorical sense specific to that individual prepositional verb. And finally, we might ask whether *look at*, as in (24)d., is really a prepositional verb at all, precisely because its combined meaning does appear to be the sum of the individual components of *look* + *at*. This is a fringe case which perhaps many would deny has any idiomatic sense to it. *Look*, certainly, means what it normally does. The preposition, however, is a borderline issue semantically: although normally locative (= 'in a particular place'), its 'directional' meaning is by no means unique to *look*, but is found with a whole series of verbs, such as *aim, shoot, fire* or *shout at*. On the other hand, it only takes on this sense with verbs that express a targeting of something or someone, indicating that it is strongly dependent for this meaning on the verb concerned. This is an open question, but for the purposes of this book we will regard such verbs as prepositional in nature.

5.4.1.2 Representation in phrase and sentence

In a phrase diagram prepositional verbs can be represented as follows, using as examples the verbs in (24)a. and (24)c.:

110 *Phrases and their structure (II)*

(25) a.

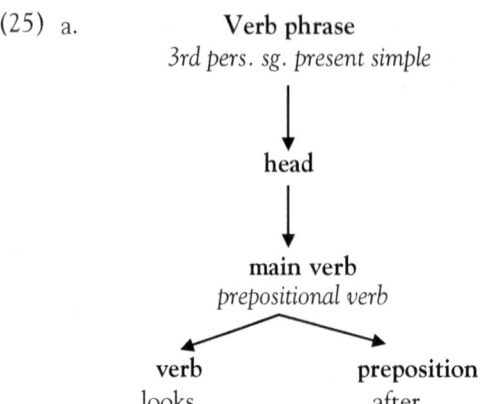

b.

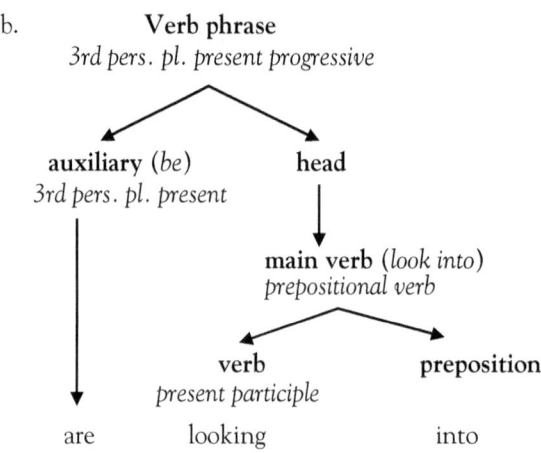

Functional analysis of the sentences in (24) is as follows:

	S	P	Od	A
(26) a.	Kelly's mother	**looks after**	the children	during the week.
b.	I	**waited for**	Jamie	outside the hairdresser's.
c.	The police	**are looking into**	the matter.	
d.	They	**looked at**	the painting	closely.

5.4.1.3 Prepositional verbs contrasted with prepositional phrases

Prepositions are very common in English, and it is important to see where they 'belong' if one wants to analyse sentences accurately. When we have identified a word as a preposition, we must then ask whether it forms a unit with the preceding verb (prepositional verb) or with the noun phrase following (prepositional phrase). This will of course depend on the meaning:

(27)
         S   P   A
a. She waited **on the street corner**. (= She stood on the street corner, waiting for something/somebody.)
         S   P   Od
b. She **waited on** the guests. (= She served the guests.)
         S   P   A
c. The cat has got **over the wall**. (= It has jumped or climbed to the other side.)
         S   P   Od
d. The cat **has got over** its illness. (= It is now healthy again.)

As indicated in bold type, the preposition and the noun belong together in (27)a. and (27)c., i.e. they form prepositional phrases (*on the street corner, over the wall*) functioning at sentence level as adverbials (**A**). In (27)b. and (27)d. the preposition belongs to the verb, i.e. here we have prepositional verbs (*wait on*, meaning 'serve with food and drink', and *get over*, meaning 'recover from'). A good test for the difference is substitution. Prepositional phrases allow us to replace the prepositions by others fairly freely, without changing the meaning of the verb or its relation to the noun following, e.g. *She waited at/by the corner* and *The cat got onto/off the wall*. But with prepositional verbs, this is either not possible at all (as with *get over*), or the range of possibilities is strictly limited and preposition substitution alters the meaning. If (27)b. is turned into *She waited with the guests*, for example, *waited* no longer has the sense of 'serve'. We might alternatively keep the meaning 'serve', and replace the preposition-noun sequence *on* + *the guests* by a suitable prepositional phrase, say, *in the restaurant*. We then get *She waited in the restaurant*. Although now ambiguous, the verb could still be interpreted as 'served'. But the verb–noun relation (*waited–restaurant*) has completely changed, semantically as well as syntactically, from what it was in the original (*waited–guests*).

5.4.1.4 Complex prepositional verbs

There is another type of prepositional verb which is followed by two nouns, one before, one after the preposition: *ask someone for something, blame someone/something for something, remind s.o. of sth., deprive s.o. of sth., congratulate s.o. on sth.*, etc. These are known as complex prepositional verbs, and have the pattern verb + noun + preposition + noun:

(28) a. An old man **asked** Jill **for** money.
     b. This house **reminds** me **of** St Pancras Station.
     c. The editor **congratulated** Harris **on** his new book.
     d. A fan **had mistaken** me **for** the famous singer.

First of all, sentence functions here need some clarification. Generally speaking, we can keep the idea of the prepositional object. This is the noun phrase following the preposition and functions as direct object (**Od**). The first noun phrase immediately after the verb is then the indirect object (**Oi**). In other words, the verbs here are ditransitive and the first noun phrase refers semantically to a receiver. This is most obviously the case when the verb refers to an act of communication or some kind of 'signalling', as in (28)a.–c. The verb *mistake*, as in (28)d., however, does not fit this semantic requirement. In cases like these what follows the preposition is not an object but an object complement (**Co**), and the first noun is then direct object (**Od**) (cf. 2.1.6). *Mistake* is thus a complex transitive verb:

	S	P_1	Oi	P_1	Od
(29) a.	An old man	asked	Jill	for	money.
b.	This house	reminds	me	of	St Pancras Station.
c.	The editor	congratulated	Harris	on	his new book.
	S	P_1	Od	P_1	Co
d.	A fan	had mistaken	me	for	the famous singer.

Again, we have an intrusion or postponement within the verb phrase and therefore mark both predicator parts with the subscript₁ to show that they belong together. The phrase diagram is the same as for ordinary prepositional verbs, but with the note below the verb slot that a **complex prepositional verb** is involved:

(30)

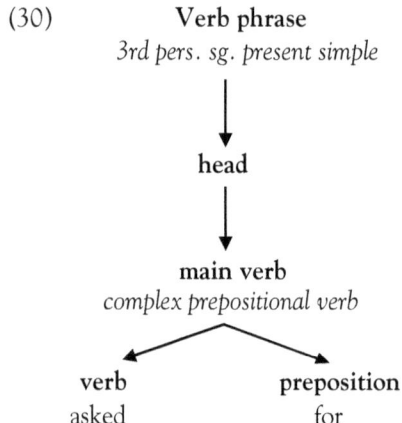

Other ditransitive examples of complex prepositional verbs are: *accuse s.o. of sth.*, *talk s.o. into sth.*, *persuade/convince s.o. of sth.*

Further complex transitive examples of complex prepositional verbs are: *regard sth./s.o. as sth., punish s.o. for sth., honour s.o. for sth., praise s.o. for sth., bother s.o. with sth., blame sth. on s.o.*, etc.

5.4.2 Phrasal verbs

A second kind of two-part verb is the phrasal verb. At first sight, phrasal verbs look exactly like prepositional verbs (for a comprehensive overview see *LGSWE*, pp. 407–13). Consider the following:

(31) a. She **took off** her coat.
 b. Bill **put up** his hand.
 c. I **have switched on** the light.
 d. You **must turn down** your stereo.

We meet the words *off, up, on* and *down* constantly as prepositions. However, they are not prepositions in this case. Prepositions must always **precede** a noun. Admittedly, the words that look like prepositions in (31) also precede nouns. Here, however, they could just as easily **follow** the nouns:

(32) a. She **took** her coat **off**.
 b. Bill **put** his hand **up**.
 c. I **have switched** the light **on**.
 d. You **must turn** your stereo **down**.

Stylistically, in fact, this is often the preferred position. Moreover, if the nouns are made into pronouns, the end position (or 'post-position') is compulsory. That is, for example, we say *She took it off* or *You must turn it down* (and not *She took off it or **You must turn down it*). This shows that *off, up, on* and *down* in (31) and (32) are **not** prepositions, but what we call adverb particles. When they combine with a verb, that verb is known as a phrasal verb. The verbs *take off, put up, switch on* and *turn down* are therefore phrasal verbs. Adverb particles belong to phrasal verbs in the same way that prepositions belong to prepositional verbs. That is, they are regarded as part of the verb phrase. Here the phrase diagrams for *take off* and *switch on* as they occur in (31) and (32):

(33) a.

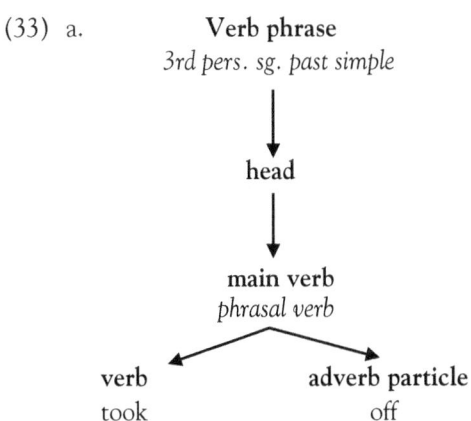

114 *Phrases and their structure (II)*

b.

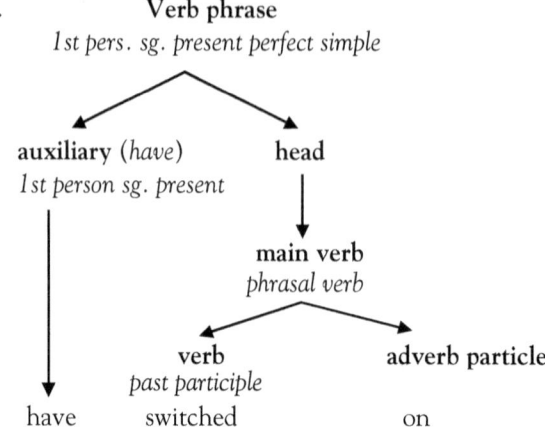

And in the sentence:

$\quad$ S $\quad$ P $\quad$ Od
(34) a. She **took off** her coat.

$\quad$ S $\quad$ P$_1$ $\quad$ Od $\quad$ P$_1$
b. She **took** her coat **off**.

That is, we have to account in the post-position also for postponement of the particle, using the subscript$_1$ to show that it belongs with the verb to the same predicator.

5.4.2.1 Intransitive phrasal verbs

Unlike prepositional verbs (which are always transitive), phrasal verbs can be transitive or intransitive. Those in our examples so far have all been transitive. We will now consider the intransitive variety:

(35) a. The plane **took off**.
   b. I **get up** around noon on Sundays.
   c. Caleb **came in** and **sat down** next to Francie.

Here, obviously, there is no risk of confusing the adverb particle with a preposition, as there is no noun following it. One must say, however, that in particular with verbs of motion, adverb particles generally have a concrete meaning of place or direction. And this is usually roughly identical with the meaning of an equivalent prepositional phrase in which the same word functions as a preposition. *Come in*, as in (35)c., is an example, and (36) shows a couple more:

(36) a. Caleb came **in(to) the room**. $\quad\Longrightarrow\quad$ Caleb **came in**.
   b. Grandfather walked **down the steps**. $\quad\Longrightarrow\quad$ Grandfather **walked down**.
   c. We swam **across the river**. $\quad\Longrightarrow\quad$ We **swam across**.

In this situation preposition and adverb particle are closely associated. In fact, the adverb particle can often only be understood on the basis of the equivalent prepositional phrase (here in brackets), which is either mentioned previously or implied in the particular context:

(37) a. Barry, please **come down** immediately (e.g. **down the ladder** you have just climbed).
b. The bus stopped and several people **got off** (= **off the bus**).
c. The little girl ran to one of the swings and **climbed on** (= **on**(to) **one of the swings**).
d. The cow came to the fence and **looked over** at us (= **over the fence**).

In cases like these we can speak of an ellipsis. That is, the noun following the preposition (the prepositional complement, as you will doubtless recall from Chapter 4, 4.2!) is omitted in a situation where it can be understood contextually. This converts the preposition immediately into an adverb particle, though the meaning is unchanged. We might say, in fact, that the meaning of the prepositional phrase is entirely shouldered by the preposition (which then, accordingly, loses its identity as a preposition).

5.4.2.2 Adverb particles only

As we have been saying, the majority of adverb particles are the same words as the corresponding prepositions. But there are one or two exceptions. The following are only particles. They do not occur as prepositions: *away, back, out, forward(s), backward(s), upward(s), downward(s)*. In some regional varieties of British and American English the particle *out* is in fact used as a preposition. It is not standard usage, however. To become prepositional in the standard language, *out* must join forces with *of*: the resulting combination *out of* is then regarded for syntactic purposes as a single preposition (or, more exactly, as a complex preposition, since it consists of more than one word).

5.4.2.3 The semantics of phrasal verbs

Adverb particles are important semantic building blocks, enabling speakers to form a great number of further lexical items by combining elements from a highly restricted range of base components. Common verbs like *bring, get, take* or *put* can be modified by particles such as *up, down, on, off, in, out*, etc., to generate an almost limitless number of separate items with distinct meanings: *take off, take on, take in, take out; put up, put on, put in, put off*, and so on (here again the LGSWE, pp. 407ff, provides you with a good overview of their use and distribution). Furthermore, each individual verb itself, due to the very general semantic nature of its components, can potentially fit a wide range of different contexts and so develop in daily usage a host of divergent meanings: *take off*, for instance, means to detach or remove one thing from another (clothes from oneself, or caps from bottles), to imitate other people, to leave a place hurriedly, or of aircrafts (and people in them), to rise from the ground in flight. Entities as diverse as guests (for the night), hands (in class), weapons (in battle) and sums of money (in business) can be *put up*; *put off* can mean extinguish (a light), distract someone from a task, postpone (a meeting), discourage (someone from doing something), and so on.

One can see from this diversity that phrasal verbs have large potential for all types and shades of concreteness or abstractness in their semantics. They can show highly subtle shades of differentiation between quite literal meaning at one end of the scale, and totally idiomatic or figurative at the other. *Taking clothes off (a line)* says precisely what the individual components mean, *taking clothes off (oneself)* is slightly more idiomatic, *taking off the queen* in the sense of impersonating her is totally so, and *taking off* as an aircraft does is somewhere in-between.

All this demonstrates again the intense connection between syntax and semantics and how, essentially, the former is the servant of the latter. Grammatical tools are basically implements of meaning.

5.4.3 Phrasal-prepositional verbs

These are **three-part** verbs. The second part is an adverb particle and the third is a preposition: *look forward to, look back on, get on with, go in for, put up with, set out for, get away with*, etc.:

(38)   *verb + adverb particle + preposition + prepositional object*
    a. The hikers   set   out   for   the next village.
    b. We   are looking   forward   to   our holidays.
    c. He   will not get   away   with   such behaviour.

Essentially, then, phrasal-prepositional verbs are a variant of prepositional verbs, and behave like them syntactically. They are *always* transitive and the third part, the preposition, *always* stays in the same position before a noun or pronoun – as we expect a preposition to do, of course. Phrase diagrams for (38)a. and b. as follows:

(39) a.

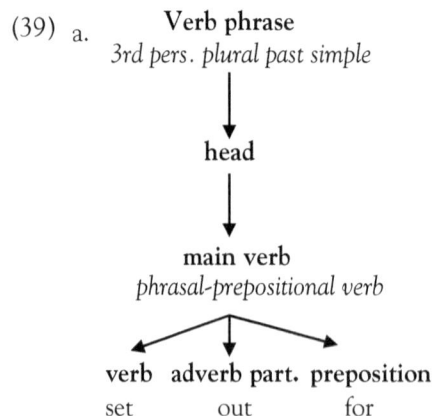

b.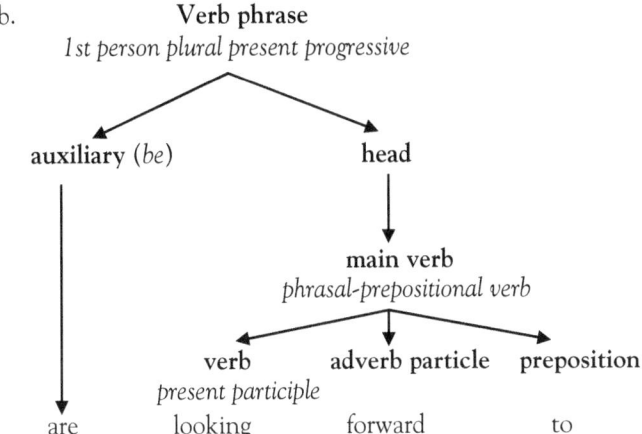

And in the sentence:

	S	P	Od
(40) a.	The boss	**backed out of**	the agreement.
b.	We	**are looking forward to**	our holidays.

We will also regard composite idioms of the pattern verb + noun + preposition as a variant of the phrasal-prepositional verb, e.g. *take care of, find fault with, pay attention to, take part in*, etc.:

	S	P	Od
(41) a.	Our son	**takes care of**	the garden.
b.	He	**pays attention to**	every detail.

Outwardly these bear the same structure as complex prepositional verbs and could also be analysed in the same way (see under 5.4.1.4 above). We prefer the analysis here, though, as there is very strong idiomatic cohesion between verb and noun. This is underlined by the lack of an article in the noun phrase and the fact that there are no substitution possibilities for the nouns in such expressions. Phrase diagrams for (41) would be the same as in (39)a., except that the adverb particle slot under main verb would be marked noun.

(42)   **Verb phrase**
       3rd pers. sing. present simple
                ↓
              head
                ↓
           main verb
       phrasal-prepositional verb
         ↙   ↓   ↘
       verb   noun   preposition
       takes care   of

5.4.4 Two- and three-part verbs in the passive

In the ordinary passive the active direct object function disappears. This means that there is no longer any noun to follow the preposition of prepositional verbs. Similarly, phrasal verbs that are transitive in the active voice lose the noun phrase following or preceding them when passivised. As a result, passive phrasal and prepositional verbs look the same, with nothing to distinguish the particle from the preposition. Compare the two active sentences in the following, i.e. (43)a. and c., with their respective passive versions in (43)b. and d.:

(43) a. David **switched on** the light.   [active phrasal verb]
     b. The light **was switched on** by David.   [passive phrasal verb]
     c. Professional serving staff **will wait on**
        the guests.   [active prepositional verb]
     d. The guests **will be waited on** by
        professional serving staff.   [passive prepositional verb]

The object noun phrases *the light* and *the guests* in (43)a. and c. are transferred forward into the subject position in (43)b. and d. (the passive versions), so that the object position falls vacant, so to speak. This does not change the particle status of *on* in (43)b., or preposition status of *on* in (43)d., of course. It is just that there is nothing overt to distinguish them syntactically. Not only the preposition is in fixed position after the verb: the particle is too, i.e. it cannot 'wander' anywhere. We cannot, for instance, say *The light was switched by David on*. Here are four more examples. The functional roles, as shown, are the same for all of them:

                    S   P-pass
(44) a. The stereo **must be turned down**.   [passive phrasal verb]
     b. Mrs Timms **was being looked after**.   [passive prepositional verb]
     c. All the guests **had been put up**.   [passive phrasal verb]
     d. The matter **is being looked into**.   [passive prepositional verb]

Complex prepositional verbs allow only the first noun (i.e. the one immediately following the verb) to become the passive subject. When the verb is ditransitive, this first noun is the active indirect object. In the passive, the direct object remains, as indeed it would when any ordinary ditransitive verb is passivised in this way (see 2.5.1):

(45) a. An old man **asked** Jill **for** money.   [active]
S P_1 Oi P_1 Od

b. Jill **was asked for** money by an old man.   [passive]
S   P-pass   Od   A

c. A teacher **accused** Nigel **of** cheating.   [active]
S P_1 Oi P_1 Od

d. Nigel **was accused of** cheating by a teacher.   [passive]
S   P-pass   Od   A

When the verb is complex transitive the first noun is the direct object, which in the passive, of course, becomes subject: this means that the active object complement (Co) then changes to passive subject complement (Cs):

(46) a. A fan **had mistaken** me **for** the famous singer.   [active]
S P_1 Od P_1 Co

b. I **had been mistaken for** the famous singer by a fan.   [passive]
S   P-pass   Cs   A

c. The police **blamed** the accident **on** Wendy.   [active]
S P_1 Od P_1 Co

d. The accident **was blamed on** Wendy by the police.   [passive]
S   P-pass   Cs   A

Phrasal-prepositional verbs are not usually found in the passive. Passive forms are either not possible at all, or, with the few that are possible, are usually avoided as being stylistically inelegant. Occasionally *look forward to* and *look back on* occur:

(47) a. The holidays **were looked forward to**.
    b. Schooldays **were looked back on**.

But the preference is always with the active version. In principle this is also the case with the noun-type phrasal-prepositional verbs like *take care of*, *find fault with*, *pay attention to*, *take part in*, etc. One, certainly, has a generally acceptable passive form, viz. *take care of*. But the rest, if they can be passivised at all, do not submit gladly:

(48) a. The garden **is taken care of** by our son.
    b. (*)The plan **was found fault with** by everybody.

120 *Phrases and their structure (II)*

A solution offering itself here, though, is to extract the noun from its idiomatic attachment within the phrase and treat it as an independent object. In some cases this is permissible (though in others it is certainly not, e.g. in c.):

(49) a. **Fault was found with** the plan by everybody.
     b. Great **attention has been paid to** detail.
     c. ***Part was taken in** the play by the whole class.

Exercises

Exercise 1

Analyse the underlined verb phrases using phrase diagrams:

1   I <u>had lost</u> my door-key.
2   The windows <u>were being cleaned</u>.
3   Charles said <u>you would be leaving</u> tomorrow morning.
4   Kelly <u>must have gone</u> to the cinema.
5   We <u>should have been staying</u> at a different hotel.
6   I <u>don't speak</u> Thai, but my wife <u>does</u>. [*Provide two separate phrase diagrams.*]
7   Chloe resented <u>being forced</u> <u>to give up</u> <u>seeing</u> Najeed. [*Provide three separate phrase diagrams.*]

Exercise 2

Analyse the following sentences functionally and state in each case whether prepositional phrases, prepositional verbs, or phrasal verbs are involved. Provide phrase diagrams for all two- and three-part verbs.

  1 Tom took off his shoes.
  2 The teacher came into the room.
  3 Terry's mother is looking after his children.
  4 Lynn jumped off the high diving-board.
  5 The teacher came in.
  6 The plane took off.
  7 Carla climbed down the ladder.
  8 I have put away the clean crockery.
  9 Our neighbours have been searching for their cat.
10 Carla climbed down.
11 We looked up the tree.
12 My daughter is waiting on the guests at the moment.
13 The boss congratulated them on their work.
14 The man was waiting on a street corner.
15 We looked up the word.

16 My son is looking forward to the game on Sunday.
17 The police have charged Fanshaw with murder.
18 The company blamed the low profits on the sales manager.
19 Joe got in the car and drove off.
20 The two cyclists had set out for Blandford that morning.

6 The multiple sentence

The simple sentence consists of just one clause. The multiple sentence, which we are going to introduce in this chapter, consists of two or more clauses. Clauses can be joined together in one of two ways: by **co-ordination** or by **subordination**.

6.1 Co-ordination

In the following, (1)a. and (1)b. are separate simple sentences. That is, each consists of one clause. (1)c. gives an example of how they can be joined together to form one sentence:

(1) a. Craig is a journalist.
     b. Millie works at a bank.
     c. Craig is a journalist **and** Millie works at a bank.

Each sentence in (1)a. and (1)b. becomes a clause of the same sentence in (1)c. The two clauses are joined by the word *and*, which belongs to the word-class conjunction. As we said in Chapter 1, 1.3.8, the task of a conjunction is to link clauses in a sentence. This link is both syntactic and semantic. That is, the conjunction not only combines potentially separate sentences, but also tells us how the second clause (the conjunction clause) relates in meaning to the first (the free clause). In the case of *and*, it is simply an addition of one thing to another. Other conjunctions are more profiled in meaning. For instance *but* expresses a contradiction between the clauses, and *or* an alternative:

(2) a. Craig is a journalist **but** Millie works at a bank.
     b. You can catch a bus from here **or** you can take the train from the main station.

In addition, conjunctions also affect the syntactic status of the two clauses in their relation to each other: *and*, *but* and *or* confer **equal** status on the two clauses. Potentially each one can stand alone as a separate sentence. All we would have to do is replace the conjunction by a full-stop. In a sense, therefore, the clauses are independent of each other. Underlining this is the fact that they can be swapped over, so that the conjunction clause becomes the free clause and vice versa:

(3) a. Millie works at a bank **but** Craig is a journalist.
  b. You can take the train from the main station **or** you can catch a bus from here.

This flexibility may be prevented by factors of meaning, however. Sometimes the order of reference to actions is fixed logically. For example, in the sentence *Jason got dressed and left the house*, the clause positions cannot be reversed. This has to do with semantic logic (and social custom!), however, and not with syntax. The compulsory sequence of mention would in fact apply even if the two clauses here were separate sentences: *Jason got dressed. He left the house.* Apart from this general semantic constraint, each clause can occur, syntactically speaking, in either position. This shows that the two clauses are essentially independent of each other and have equal status. (The importance of this point will become fully clear further below when we discuss clauses in the multiple sentence that have unequal status.)

Joining clauses of equal status is known as co-ordination, and the clauses themselves are called co-ordinate clauses. The conjunctions *and*, *but* and *or* are accordingly **co-ordinating conjunctions** (or simply **co-ordinators**). To these three we must add a fourth, *for*, discussed briefly below.

Multiple sentences consisting just of co-ordinate clauses, like those in (1)c., (2) and (3), are traditionally known as compound sentences.

6.2 Further aspects of co-ordination

6.2.1 *Ellipsis of subject and auxiliary*

When the subjects of co-ordinate clauses are identical in reference (i.e. refer to the same thing or person), the subject of the conjunction clause is usually left out, unless there is a need to emphasise it. (4)a. shows repetition for emphasis, (4)b. the generally preferred omission (with the omission sign Ø to mark the 'gap', followed by **S** to show what the missing element is):

(4) a. **He** cooked the meals and **he** did all the housework.
  b. **He** cooked the meals and Ø **S** did all the housework.

The omission of a grammatically necessary element like this is generally known as ellipsis. In (3)b., then, we have ellipsis of the subject in the conjunction clause, possible because of reference identity with the subject of the free clause. Ellipsis in co-ordinate clauses is also applied additionally to any auxiliary verbs that would otherwise be repeated. Here again the less usual included version in the first example and the preferred ellipsis in the second. (5)c. and (5)d. give further examples of **auxiliary ellipsis**:

(5) a. He **has** always cooked the meals and Ø **S has** done the housework.
  b. He **has** always cooked the meals and Ø **S** Ø ***aux*** done the housework.
  c. With her injury Kerry **can´t** play football or Ø **S** Ø ***aux*** go swimming.
  d. Somebody **will** come and Ø **S** Ø ***aux*** pick you up from the airport.

The ellipsis-markers are used here to show clearly what has been left out, but they are omitted in all examples following in the sections below.

6.2.2 Co-ordination of three or more clauses

When more than two clauses are co-ordinated, the conjunction, unless emphasised, usually occurs only between the last two. Previous clauses are separated by commas:

(6) a. He cooks the meals, does the housework and looks after the garden.
     b. With her injury Kerry can´t play football, go swimming or ride a bike.

A comma may also be placed, optionally, before the conjunction. But this is a semantic consideration. It is applied to emphasise the distinction between the two final clauses and tends to occur particularly with *or*:

(7) With her injury, Kerry can´t play football, swim long distances, **or** ride a bike.

Co-ordination by comma alone anticipates the later conjunction and must therefore express the same semantic link. If the connections do not share the same meaning, the comma solution is ruled out. Different conjunctions are then necessary:

(8) a. *Patrick loves the good life, must earn money, or win the lottery.
     b. Patrick loves the good life **and** must earn money **or** win the lottery.

This rule applies furthermore not just to adjacent clauses. All the clauses involved (i.e. in our examples all three) must stand in the same relation to each other. As this is generally ruled out with *but*, owing to the meaning of contrast, *but* does not participate in this kind of comma co-ordination:

(9) a. *She left the house, forgot the door key, but luckily met her husband by chance at the garden gate.
     b. She left the house, **but** forgot the door key, **but** luckily met her husband by chance at the garden gate.

Repetition of *but* can be avoided for stylistic reasons by substituting *and then* in the third clause, or using subordination, e.g., *Although she forgot the door key when she left the house, she luckily met* . . . .

6.2.3 Fixed position of co-ordinating conjunctions

A defining feature of co-ordinating conjunctions is that they are in **fixed position**. The conjunction clause, that is, cannot be placed first, i.e. we could not express (9)a. as (9)b.:

(10) a. They took a train **but** had no money with them.
　　 b. ***But** they took a train, they had no money with them.

The clauses themselves of course, as stated in 6.1, can exchange positions (*They had no money with them but took a train*), but the conjunction must always remain between them. As we will see later, this is a striking contrast to conjunctions involved in subordination.

6.2.4 The conjunction **for**

We have met the three main co-ordinating conjunctions: *and, but, or*. To these we can add a fourth, *for*. Note, however, the starred (*) sentence in (11)b.:

(11) a. We did not go on with our journey that afternoon, **for** we were very tired.
　　 b. *We were very tired **for** we did not go on with our journey that afternoon.

(11)b. is starred as unacceptable because it does not make sense to swap the two clauses over. With *for* a reason is given in the second clause for the semantic content in the first. That is, *for* is really a way of saying *because*, and will therefore logically not allow its clausal meaning relation (i.e. the element of causality) to be shifted to the other clause. However, as we have seen, flexibility in clause position is otherwise a feature of co-ordination. A further point is that *for* (unlike the other co-ordinators) will not allow subject or auxiliary ellipsis:

(12) a. We had had a hard journey and become very tired.
　　 b. *We had become very tired **for** had a hard journey.

These untypical characteristics of *for*, plus its semantic closeness to *because* and *as* (both subordinating conjunctions, as we will see further below) speak in favour of regarding *for* also as a subordinating conjunction. On the other hand, *for* has to remain between the two clauses. We cannot shift the conjunction clause together with its conjunction to the initial position, as we can with *as* or *because*:

(13) a. Because/As we were very tired, we did not go on with our journey that afternoon,
　　 b. ***For** we were very tired, we did not go on with our journey that afternoon.

So in this respect *for* behaves syntactically like a co-ordinating conjunction, and is usually therefore regarded as one.

6.2.5 Analysing compound sentences

We will now set about a full functional analysis of sentences containing co-ordinate clauses. First, some examples in their 'virgin state', so to speak:

126 *The multiple sentence*

(14) a. For his birthday we gave our grandson a bicycle and took him to the zoo.
  b. They took a train but had no money with them.
  c. The neighbours are probably on holiday, or have gone away for the weekend.
  d. With her injury, Kerry can't play football, go swimming or ride a bike.

The first point to bear in mind is that co-ordinating conjunctions are not parts of the clauses they introduce. If they were, the clauses could not change position. In analysis we will show this, and the equivalent syntactic status of co-ordinate clauses, by putting brackets around the separate clauses and leaving the conjunction outside:

(15) a. (For his birthday we gave our grandson a bicycle) and (took him to the zoo).
  b. (They took a train) but (had no money with them).
  c. (The neighbours are probably on holiday), or (have gone away for the weekend).
  d. (With her injury, Kerry can't play football), (swim long distances) or (ride a bike).

A full clause-internal functional analysis looks like this:

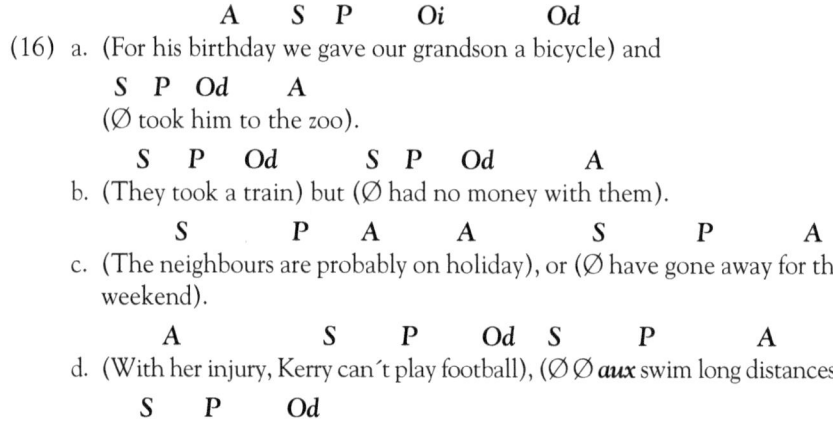

6.2.6 Co-ordination of phrases

However, co-ordinators link not only clauses, but also phrases:

(17) a. Dave and Sue are on holiday.
  b. Rana is going to buy a car or a motorbike.
  c. She was tired but happy.

We can regard most examples like these as having an ellipted co-ordinate clause (e.g. *She was tired but she was happy*), which is then simply reduced to a co-ordinated phrase. This is a theoretical consideration, however, and does not affect our formal analysis, which views the 'double phrase' as having a single function. The co-ordinate noun phrases in (17)a. and (17)b. and the co-ordinate adjective phrases in (17)c. each share the following functional slots:

(18) a. <u>Dave and Sue</u> are on holiday. [S]

    b. Rana is going to buy <u>a car or a motorbike</u>. [Od]

    c. She was <u>tired but happy</u>. [Cs]

6.3 Subordination

The second way of linking clauses produces an **unequal** relation between them, i.e., a hierarchy:

(19) a. Carla was actually in love with Roberto, **although** she was getting married to Paul.
    b. **When** Carla was getting married to Paul, she was in love with Roberto.
    c. **If** Carla gets married to Paul, she'll have to give up Roberto.

This is because here the conjunction clause is made into a functional part of the free clause, and thereby placed on a 'lower' level. This is known as subordination, with the conjunction clause as a **subordinate clause**, introduced by a **subordinating conjunction**. The free clause, as the 'dominant' partner in the relationship, is called the **superordinate clause**. In analysis, brackets are placed around the subordinate clause and its function is marked above the opening bracket. In (19) each of the subordinate clauses (or **sub-clauses** for short) functions in relation to its superordinate clause as an adverbial (**A**). In contrast to co-ordinating conjunctions, subordinating conjunctions are part of the clauses they introduce and are included within the bracket marking off the subordinate clause. The reason for this will become clear further below:

(20) a. Carla was actually in love with Roberto, [although she was getting married to Paul]. [A]
    b. [When Carla was getting married to Paul], she was in love with Roberto. [A]
    c. [If Carla gets married to Paul], she'll have to give up Roberto. [A]

Multiple sentences with subordinate clauses, like these, are known as complex sentences. Sub-clauses are also called **dependent clauses**, as they have a relation of **functional dependence** on the superordinate clause. Both this and the kind of function involved can be shown if we replace the sub-clause by a phrase of roughly similar meaning:

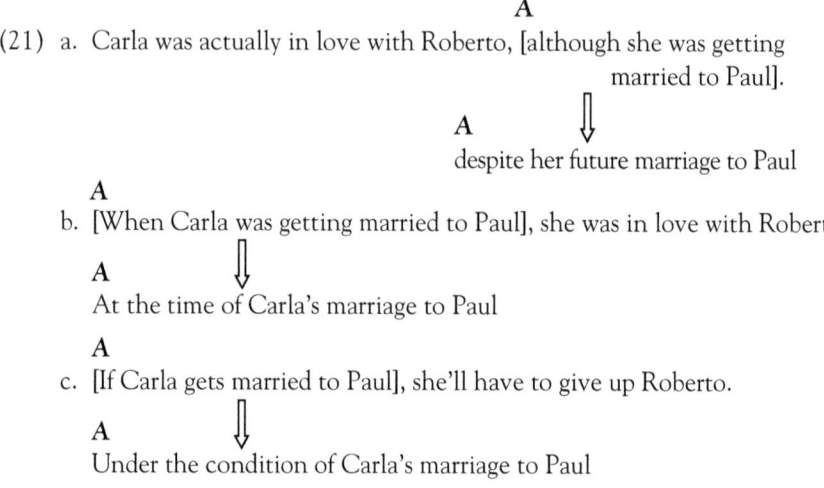

(21) a. Carla was actually in love with Roberto, [although she was getting married to Paul].
       despite her future marriage to Paul

   b. [When Carla was getting married to Paul], she was in love with Roberto.
      At the time of Carla's marriage to Paul

   c. [If Carla gets married to Paul], she'll have to give up Roberto.
      Under the condition of Carla's marriage to Paul

In replacing the sub-clause by a phrase, of course, we reduce our complex sentences to simple sentences. Note that it is then the former superordinate clause that remains as the core of the simple sentence:

(22) a. Carla was actually in love with Roberto, despite her future marriage to Paul.
     b. At the time of Carla's marriage to Paul, she was in love with Roberto.
     c. Under the condition of Carla's marriage to Paul, she'll have to give up Roberto.

Clause replacement in this way shows why we have to regard subordinating conjunctions as parts of their clauses. The conjunction has to be replaced too, as this signals the meaning relation of the sub-clause to the superordinate clause and also the nature of the syntactic link, i.e., the syntactic function of the clause. The conjunction is therefore part of the clause meaning, and must therefore be regarded as a syntactic component of the clause. Another indicator is the movement of the clause. As with co-ordinate clauses, many (though not all) sub-clauses can exchange position with their superordinate clauses. However, the conjunction then has to move too if the syntactic and semantic relation between the clauses is to remain the same:

(23) a. **Although** she was getting married to Paul, Carla was actually in love with Roberto.
  b. Carla was in love with Roberto **when** she was getting married to Paul.
  c. Carla will have to give up Roberto, **if** she gets married to Paul.

This is a further indication that the conjunction belongs to the clause.

6.3.1 Other functional roles of sub-clauses

Sub-clauses do not function just as adverbials. They take on the whole range of functional roles, except (naturally enough) those of predicator and indirect object. Here are examples of sub-clauses as direct object (**Od**), subject (**S**) and **subject complement** (**Cs**). The conjunctions associated with these roles are *that* and *whether*. In object clauses *that* can be omitted in more informal styles, as in (24)b. (the Ø symbol indicating the omission):

(24) a. We realised [**that** someone was following us].
       Od
  b. We realised [Ø someone was following us].
       Od
  c. Cathy asked [**whether** I would be at the conference].
       S
  d. [**That** Jake was out of work] did not bother him at first.
       S
  e. [**Whether** I would be at the conference] was uncertain.
       Cs
  f. The problem was [**that** Jake was out of work].
       Cs
  g. The big question is [**whether** I will be at the conference].

As we will see later, subject-clauses of this kind are more common with the sentence construction known as **extraposition** (see Chapter 7, 7.5.1).

Sub-clauses functioning as **object complement** (**Co**) do not involve conjunctions and will be dealt with later. This brings us to the general point that conjunctions do not by any means always play a role in subordination. There are other ways of subordinating clauses, as we will see further below. For the moment, though, we will stay with the conjunction as the prototype subordinator.

6.3.2 Sub-clauses as adverbials: semantic classification

It is common (though optional) to distinguish adverbial clauses according to meaning. We say, for instance, that *since* introduces an adverbial clause of time, *because* an adverbial clause of **reason**, and *unless* an adverbial clause of **condition**.

130   *The multiple sentence*

The following are further examples of common conjunctions introducing adverbial clauses, with the semantic specification given in brackets:

> *although, though* (**concession**); *if, in case* (**condition**); *when, while, after, before, as soon as* (**time**); *whereas* (**contrast**); *where* (**place**); *so that* (**purpose** and **consequence**); *so* (**reason** and **consequence**); *as, since* (**time** and **reason**).

Again we see the crucial role of conjunctions not simply as syntactic elements but also as semantic indicators. Semantic identification is particularly important, however, when there is no conjunction involved, as it is then often a little more difficult to see the nature of the meaning relations and thus also of the syntactic role of the sub-clause.

6.3.3 Subordinating conjunctions: points to note

Something to note in passing is that some conjunctions consist of more than one word, for example, *in case, as soon as, so that, provided that*, etc. These are sometimes referred to as 'complex conjunctions', but in behaviour and function they are exactly the same as their single-word colleagues. Another point to bear in mind is that words with varying uses and meanings may belong to more than one word-class. This applies to several conjunctions. For instance, *when, where, so* and *though* can also be adverbs; *that* occurs as a relative pronoun and demonstrative determiner; *after, before, as* and *since* double as prepositions. There is in any case a close connection between conjunctions and prepositions. Conjunctions that cannot themselves take on the role of a preposition generally have equivalent prepositional partners, for example, *although – despite*; *because – because of/due to/for*; *when – on/at*; *while – during*, etc. (As a reminder: conjunctions prototypically link clauses, whereas prepositions relate to a noun phrase.) The conjunction–preposition relation can be seen clearly in our operation above reducing clauses to phrases. Here for clarity are two further examples:

                  A
(25) a. Frank lost his job [**because** the factory closed].

           A   ⇓
           for this reason/**because of** factory closure.

           A
   b. It rained a lot [**while** we were on holiday].

           A   ⇓
           during our holiday

6.3.4 Relations between superordinate and subordinate clauses: further aspects

What we have seen so far is that sub-clauses fill most of the same sentence functions that phrases do: subject (**S**), direct object (**Od**), subject complement (**Cs**), adverbial (**A**), and to these, as indicated above, we can also add object complement (**Co**), though examples for this last one still have to be given (see Chapter 7, 7.4.3). Exceptions, as already pointed out, are the functions of predicator (**P**) and indirect object (**Oi**), neither of which are available for clausal roles. Furthermore, there are absolute parallels regarding what is optional and what is compulsory in particular sentences. Subject-clauses, of course, are always obligatory. Clauses complementing verbs (i.e. following the predicator) generally follow the same rules as phrases in the same functions. That is, whether clause complementation is obligatory or optional depends on the particular verb concerned:

(26)
         Od
  a. I knew [that I was wrong].
              Cs
  b. The question is [whether we have enough money].
             A
  c. She went to bed [because she was tired].
                 A
  d. Sylvia put the letter [where nobody could find it].

(26)a. and b. are part of compulsory patterns (**SPOd** and **SPCs** respectively). The same goes for (26)d., which has a compulsory adverbial slot, that is, with the obligatory pattern **SPOdA**. (26)c. has the same pattern, but here, as with most adverbials, the **A**-slot is optional. These factors affect traditional conceptions regarding the relative 'dependence' or 'independence' of the two clauses. A highly simplified traditional view of subordination explains the sub-clause as being 'dependent' in the sense that it cannot stand alone as a potentially separate sentence, whereas the superordinate clause (usually called the 'main clause', see below in 6.3.5) allegedly **can** stand alone and is therefore to be regarded as 'independent'. This is true of our example sentences in (19), (25) and (26)c. But it would not of course apply to any of those in (24) or (26)a., b. and d. Here the sub-clause fills an **obligatory function** of the superordinate clause, which as a result could not stand alone without the sub-clause. In the sense of the 'definition' the superordinate clause is therefore not 'independent' at all. Both clauses in these cases are dependent on one another. The superordinate clause is only potentially independent if the function of the sub-clause is optional. It is therefore better to ignore any traditional notion of subordination in terms of 'independent vs. dependent'. Two clauses are in a hierarchical relation to one another when one is a functional part of the other. This is the only valid general definition of subordination at sentence level.

132   *The multiple sentence*

A final point on the superordinate clause: in the sentences discussed so far the superordinate clause is what is traditionally known as the **main clause**. This designates it as the 'top clause', so to speak, in the clause hierarchy of the sentence. All superordinate clauses in our examples above are therefore main clauses. This may seem as if we have introduced a second term for the same thing. In the next section below, however, we come to complex sentences containing more than one subordinate clause. We will then see that the two concepts superordinate clause and main clause are not identical, and that we must distinguish between them.

6.3.5 Further clauses in the complex sentence

Our complex sentence examples so far have consisted of only two clauses, i.e. one main clause and a subordinate clause. Now we will add more clauses. The analysis here is a little more complicated, and raises one or two initial questions of orientation: where does one clause end and the next clause begin? And are there sub-clauses that themselves contain other sub-clauses?

6.3.5.1 Two sub-clauses

First of all some sentence examples with two sub-clauses, here again, to start with, in their unanalysed forms:

(27) a. We realised that someone was following us after we had been walking for about an hour.
   b. Frank has been out of work since he lost his job when the factory closed down.
   c. Although she went to bed because she was tired, Sally could not sleep.

As every clause has only one predicator (**P**), a useful first step is to identify the predicators in the sentence: this will show us the number of clauses it contains and will also give us a first point of orientation in determining their beginning and end. The next thing to be done is to decide which predicator represents the highest clause (the main clause) in the superordinate–subordinate hierarchy. Proceeding from there, we then identify the sub-clauses and put brackets around them. Phrase-substitution will help us:

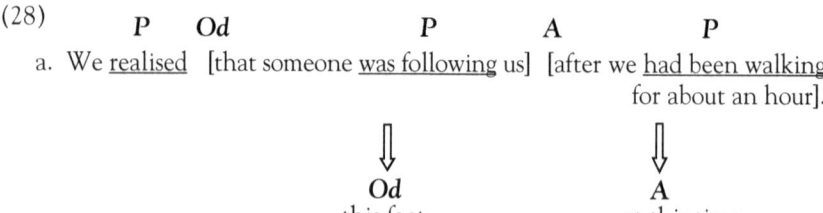

The multiple sentence 133

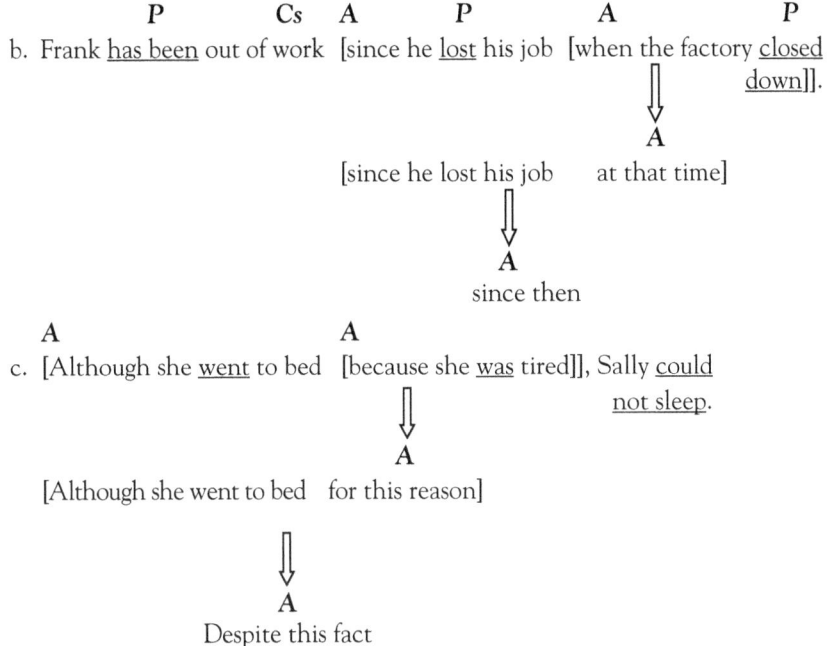

This is just a first analysis, in order to establish the core 'architecture' of each sentence (a full functional analysis, including the internal functions of the clauses, is given in the next section below). Each sentence contains three predicators, and therefore consists of three clauses. In (27)a., for instance, these are:

- Clause 1: we realised
- Clause 2: that someone was following us
- Clause 3: after we had been walking for about an hour.

We number the clauses just for the sake of clarity. Phrase substitution, as demonstrated in (28)a., shows, first, the length of each sub-clause and, second, its respective function. The resulting simple sentence *We realised* **this fact at this time** shows that the two substituting phrases are independent of one another. The replaced Clauses 2 and 3 are therefore also independent of each other, but both dependent, of course, on Clause 1. Clause 1 is therefore the main clause and subordinates Clauses 2 and 3 separately.

In (27)b. the three clauses appear to be in a similar arrangement:

- Clause 1: Frank has been out of work
- Clause 2: since he lost his job
- Clause 3: when the factory closed down.

134 *The multiple sentence*

There is a difference, however: here one sub-clause (Clause 2) subordinates the other one (Clause 3). In other words, Clause 2 contains Clause 3, as the phrase substitution in (28)b. shows. In this case there are two levels of subordination, one between Clauses 1 and 2, and another, 'deeper' one between Clauses 2 and 3. From a 'bottom-up' perspective we can see this as two rising levels of superordination: the immediate superordinate clause of Clause 3 is Clause 2. And the immediate superordinate clause of Clause 2 is Clause 1. So all three clauses are arranged in the **same hierarchy**. Clause 2 is a superordinate clause in relation to Clause 3, and a subordinate clause in relation to Clause 1. We can therefore say that this sentence contains two superordinate clauses, one of which (Clause 2) is subordinate to the other (Clause 1). It is the higher one, Clause 1, that is the main clause of the sentence. Here we can see why it makes sense to distinguish between the terms superordinate clause and main clause. A sentence may contain several superordinate–subordinate clause relationships, but only one of the superordinate clauses (the highest in the hierarchy) is the main clause.

6.3.5.2 Full internal analysis of clauses

After an initial survey of clause architecture, the functions inside the clauses have to be established in order to present the full picture. Each clause is now rather like a mini-sentence of its own, with separate internal functions that have nothing to do with anything outside that particular clause. A full analysis of the sentences in (27) looks like this:

        S   P   Od   S   P   Od A   S   P
(29) a. We realised [that someone was following us] [after we had been walking
        A
    for about an hour].
        S   P   A   A   S P   Od A   S
   b. Frank has been out of work [since he lost his job [when the factory
        P
    closed down]].
        A   S P   A A   S   P Cs   S   P
   c. [Although she went to bed [because she was tired]], Sally could not sleep.

6.3.5.3 Co-ordination in the complex sentence

Co-ordination may also play a part in complex sentences. Sub-clauses can be co-ordinated with one another and superordinate clauses as well:

(30) a. We thought that the team would win easily and get into the next round with no difficulty.
    b. As she was a complete stranger and didn´t know her way around the town, Kelly bought a detailed street map.

c. If a thunderstorm comes up you must take shelter or get on a bus home immediately.
d. You can come with us or stay at home until we get back.

In (30)a. the main clause (*We thought . . .*), has two co-ordinated sub-clauses (*the team would win easily* and *get into the next round*) as direct objects:

      S   P Od   S   P   A   Od P   A
(31) We thought [that the team would win easily] and   [get into the next round
      A
with no difficulty].

Note that the subordinating conjunction *that* counts as introducing each sub-clause separately, but is ellipted in the second one (along with the subject and auxiliary verb).

(30)b. has two co-ordinated sub-clauses (*As she was a complete stranger* and *didn't know her way around*) as adverbials:

    A   S   P   Cs   A P   Od
(32) [As she was a complete stranger] and [didn't know her way around the town],
      S   P   Od
Kelly bought a detailed street-map.

Here too the subordinating conjunction introduces the second sub-clause just as it does the first one, but is subject to ellipsis.

(30)c. has two co-ordinated superordinate clauses, both of which here are main clauses:

     A   S   P   S   P   Od   P   A
(33) [If a thunderstorm comes up] [you must take shelter] or [get on a bus home
      A
immediately].

Note that in this case we must bracket even the main clauses. This is because there are two of them and they are co-ordinated. What distinguishes them from the sub-clause is that the sub-clause has a function, here adverbial (**A**). This adverbial clause refers to **both** main clauses. In (30)d. we also have two co-ordinated main clauses. In contrast to the case in (30)d., however, the sub-clause refers only to one of the main clauses, i.e. is subordinated only to that particular one:

     S   P   A   P   A   A   S   P
(34) [You can come with us] or [stay at home [until we get back]].

136 The multiple sentence

6.3.5.4 Three or more sub-clauses

Finally, to complete the picture, we will add a sub-clause or two, making sentences longer and the arrangement of clauses more involved.

(35) a. Jamie had forgotten whether he had told Celia that if she met him in the pub with the rest of the cast after they had been rehearsing at the theatre, she should just ignore him and pretend that she had no closer relationship to him.
   b. As the sea was apparently quite calm in fine weather if you looked at it from a distance, we were surprised when we discovered that the water became quite rough as soon as we had left the harbour in our small yacht.
   c. Although Jane had never spoken to Drury while she was working at the hospital as an orderly before she took her final medical exams, she now found that she was soon talking to him in this new situation as if they had been close colleagues for many years.

We will apply the steps in analysis previously recommended. They are highly necessary in analysing sentences of this complexity. Taking (35)a. first, we will first focus on just counting the predicators to give us an idea of how many clauses the sentence contains:

(36) Jamie <u>had forgotten</u> whether he <u>had told</u> Celia that if she <u>met</u> him in the pub with the rest of the cast after they <u>had been rehearsing</u> at the theatre, she <u>should just ignore</u> him and <u>pretend</u> that she <u>had</u> no closer relationship to him.

As we have seven predicators, we can conclude that there are seven clauses, one of which, of course, is the main clause. Six clauses, then, are sub-clauses; some of these are probably also superordinate to others. To establish the clause arrangement, we can apply our substitution-by-phrase test. As before, this will also lead us to seeing clause functions more clearly:

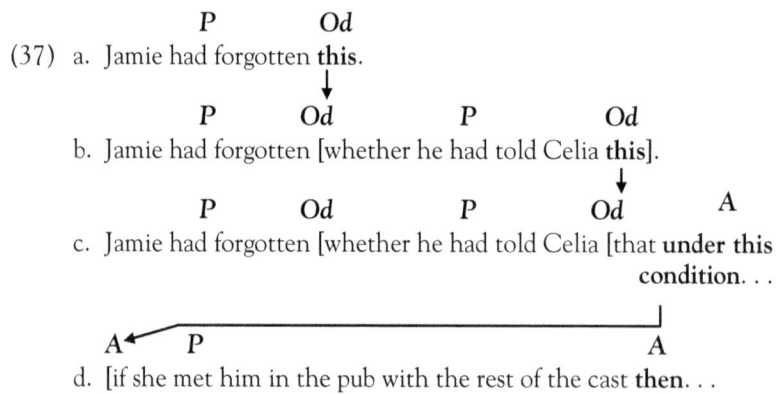

The multiple sentence 137

```
     A←         P
```
e. [after they had been rehearsing at the theatre]]...

```
     P₁       P₁           P    Od
```
f. she should just ignore him] and [pretend **this**]

```
     Od←      P
```
g. [that she had no closer relationship to him]]].

Transferring this architecture to the linear sentence and filling in the internal functions, we get:

```
         S          P    Od    S   P   Oi  Od  A S  P  Od     A
```
(38) Jamie had forgotten [whether he had told Celia [that [if she met him in the pub
```
         A              A   S         P                A
```
with the rest of the cast [after they had been rehearsing at the theatre]],
```
     S   P₁
```
she should
```
     A   P₁   Od         P    Od   S   P               Od
```
just ignore him] and [pretend [that she had no closer relationship to him]]].

We will not repeat the steps for (35)b. and c., but just give the final results of the analysis in (39)a. and (39)b.:

```
          A   S      P    A          Cs           A        A  S   P    A
```
(39) a. [As the sea was apparently quite calm in fine weather [if you looked at it
```
               A              S  P   Cs    A    S     P     Od     S
```
from a distance]], we were surprised [when we discovered [that the water
```
        P    Cs     A      S    P    Od             A
```
became quite rough [as soon as we had left the harbour in our small yacht]]].
```
       A       S  P₁  A   P₁      A      A   S     P         A
```
b. [Although Jane had never spoken to Drury [while she was working at the
```
          A         A     S   P             Od             S
```
hospital as an orderly [before she took her final medical exams]]], she
```
     A    P  Od  A       S    P       A       S   P₁  A
```
now found [that [whenever they met in the laboratory] she was soon
```
     P₁      A          A            A    S    P     Cs
```
talking to him in this new situation [as if they had been close colleagues
```
          A
```
for many years]].

6.4 Subordination without conjunctions

As already pointed out, conjunction clauses account only for a part of subordination. Two other types of subordinator can be added at this point: firstly, *wh*-words (as adverbs or pronouns), and on the other, non-finite verbs.

6.4.1 Wh-adverbs and -pronouns as subordinators

Like subordinating conjunctions, these belong to their sub-clauses, which as usual are bracketed and marked functionally in the following examples. The *wh*-words are italicised in bold script. They are discussed fully below.

                         Od
(40) a. I regretted bitterly [**what** I had said].
                     Od
    b. Mory had forgotten [**where** he had parked his car].
     S
    c. [**Why** she did not turn up at the meeting yesterday] is a mystery.
               Cs
    d. The question is [**who** we should invite to our party].

First of all one or two remarks on word-class:

- *what* in (40)a. introduces what is known as a **nominal relative clause** (see Chapter 12, 12.5 for a full explanation), and is classed as a **nominal relative pronoun**.
- *where* in (40)b. introduces an **indirect question** (or **interrogative clause**, see Chapter 12, 12.6), and is classed as an interrogative adverb.
- *why* in (40)c. is also an interrogative adverb introducing an indirect question.
- *who* in (40)d. also introduces an indirect question, though as an interrogative pronoun.

The contrast to conjunctions is that *wh*-words do not have a linking or introductory function alone (as do conjunctions), but in addition play a functional role in the clause. This is reflected among other things in the fact that they are adverbs and pronouns, which of course means that they represent internal elements of the clause. *Wh*-interrogatives, for instance, as in (40)b., c. and d., focus questions on semantic and syntactic components of the equivalent declarative sentence (see also Chapter 3, 3.1.2–3.1.4).

A full functional analysis of these sentences therefore looks like this:

      S   P   A   Od Od S   P
(41) a. I regretted bitterly [**what** I had said].
        S   P   Od A   S   P   Od
    b. Mory had forgotten [**where** he had parked his car].

```
              S A S     P            A    P   Cs
       c. [Why she did not turn up at the meeting] is a mystery.

              S       P    Cs  Od  S     P       A
       d. The question is    [  who we should invite to our party].
```

6.4.2 Non-finite verbs as subordinators

Non-finite verbs are gerunds, participles and infinitives (see Chapter 1, 1.3.3, and Chapter 5). Within their sub-clauses they function as predicators, just like finite verbs. But they also bring about subordination automatically. (This is because main clause predicates must always consist of a finite verb phrase):

```
                  S       P     Od    P      Od
(42)   a. Damian regretted   [leaving the company].
                S       P    Od   P    Od
       b. Clio wanted  [to teach history].
                 S        A    P   A      A  P       Od         A
       c. Our teacher once came into class [carrying a small dog in her arms].
```

Non-finite verbs and their clauses are dealt with in detail in the next chapter.

Exercises

Exercise 1

Analyse the following sentences functionally, putting square brackets around the separate clauses:

1. For our anniversary I am giving my wife a gold necklace and taking her to a concert.
2. Tomorrow we will probably just relax on the beach, or sit by the pool.
3. Donna left London early, but ran into a big traffic jam outside Dover and only just reached the ferry in time.
4. After your long illness, you must take proper rest, do no heavy work and not walk too far.
5. The children were extremely hungry, for they had not eaten since breakfast.

Exercise 2

Analyse the following sentences functionally:

1. Dan did not know that Connie was going to be at the party.
2. You should call my office if the package doesn´t arrive tomorrow.
3. Nobody had told us that we couldn´t buy tickets on the boat.
4. They got home late because the coach had been delayed by heavy traffic.

140   *The multiple sentence*

5   That the young couple had no money did not worry them at first.
6   When Kay was getting out of the car, she fell and hurt her ankle.
7   The big problem was that Sandy could not find a cheap flat near the university.
8   The walkers realised that if they did not get down the mountain before darkness fell, they would probably have to spend the night in the open.
9   Stomatos asked me whether I would lend him money if he did not get his pay at the end of that week.
10 Paula did not understand why the message had not been passed on after she had rung the firm and explained the situation with her sick child.

Exercise 3

Analyse the following sentences and identify the semantic specification of the clauses that are adverbial.

1   As Monday is a public holiday, this is a long weekend.
2   We should take jackets with us in case the weather turns cooler this evening.
3   Dinah has been working for the company since she left college.
4   As soon as she entered her house, she felt that something was not quite right.
5   Chris had parked in a side-street so that his car could not be seen from the house.
6   Though Jamie was new at the firm, he had been given a position of responsibility relatively quickly.
7   Luxury apartments have been built where the old theatre used to be.
8   While I was in the supermarket, my bicycle was stolen from the car-park at the rear.

7 Non-finite clauses in the complex sentence (I)
The infinitive

7.0 Non-finite clauses

In non-finite clauses the predicator consists solely of a non-finite verb. As said in Chapter 1, 1.3.3, there are three categories of non-finite verb: the infinitive, the participles and the gerund. In this chapter we examine these non-finite forms in detail. To re-cap, their main common characteristics are:

- They can occur without an overt subject, and in fact they generally do.
- When they do occur with a subject, they do **not** show concord (i.e. there are no inflections for subject–verb agreement, as there would be with a finite verb).
- They are not usually marked for tense. Their time reference is normally implied in the context, and is generally oriented to the tense form of the finite verb closest to them (very often the preceding catenative). Non-finites nevertheless have perfect tense forms. These are used to show 'pastness' when a time-level distinction has to be made clear between the non-finite verb and its nearest finite neighbour.
- Except for the infinitive, which has a progressive form, they are not marked for aspect either.
- With certain exceptions, non-finite verbs are functionally predicates in their own right, and form separate subordinate clauses.

Apart from these basic clausal considerations, a major syntactic issue addressed in this chapter is the question of which non-finite structures can actually accompany which kinds of superordinate clause. Compared with other languages, English makes particularly widespread use of non-finite verbs. Their distribution, however, is usually not open to random choice, but is fairly rigidly controlled by both semantic and syntactic factors. A central question here, especially for the EFL learner, is which kinds of non-finite structure can or must complement which individual catenatives.

7.1 The infinitive clause

An infinitive forms its own clause, whether it is alone or has complementation:

142 The complex sentence (I)

(1) a. We went to the café on the corner [to eat].
    b. We went to the café on the corner [to eat lunch].

In these examples the infinitive clause functions as an adverbial (**A**). Internally, the infinitive is the predicator (**P**) of the clause, which in (1)b. is complemented by a noun phrase as direct object (**Od**):

		A P
(2)	a. We went to the café on the corner	[to eat].
		A P Od
	b. We went to the café on the corner	[to eat lunch].

In other words, we analyse the infinitive clause in the same way as any finite subordinate clause. That is, we mark its external function with regard to the main clause and then turn our attention to the internal functions. Applying the internal clause analysis also to the main clause then, we get the following full picture:

	S P A	A P
(3)	a. We went to the café on the corner	[to eat].
	S P A	A P Od
	b. We went to the café on the corner	[to eat lunch].

The infinitive clause is an adverbial clause of purpose. We can see this just by adding *in order* to the infinitive:

	A
(4)	We went to the café on the corner [**in order** to eat].

More generally, though, we can establish sub-clause function by the same procedure as we used with finite clauses, i.e. by reducing the clause to a roughly equivalent phrase:

	A	
(5)	a. We went to the café on the corner	[to eat].
		A ⇓
	b. We went to the café on the corner	for this purpose.

As a further example, here is the infinitive clause as direct object (**Od**):

	Od
(6)	We wanted [to eat lunch].

Other functional roles are discussed in the sections following.

7.2 The infinitive clause as verb complementation

The infinitive is the most widely used non-finite form, especially after catenatives. It is nevertheless necessary to distinguish carefully (especially in EFL teaching and learning) between those main verbs that allow infinitive clauses to follow them and those that do not. A further question with those that do, is whether the infinitive is the only permissible sub-clause type, and if not, whether choice between two or more possibilities depends on further semantic or syntactic constraints (which is usually the case). Furthermore, infinitive complementation may involve the mandatory or optional presence of an object between catenative and sub-clause, or on the other hand rule it out. When an object does occur, the functional question arises as to what kind of object it is, for this varies according to the lexical nature of the verb. Finally, there are one or two cases where the infinitive is required without its introductory *to*-particle. All these factors depend on which main verb is selected as the catenative.

In summary, then, the issues are the following:

- Which main verbs allow complementation by the infinitive? Which of these require the 'bare' infinitive (i.e. without the *to*-particle)?
- Which of these verbs also occur with other types of non-finite complementation?
- Are there syntactic and/or semantic constraints on the presence or absence of a main-clause object?
- In the case of a main-clause object, is it a direct or an indirect object? How does this affect the function of the infinitive clause?

7.2.1 Catenatives followed by the infinitive: general overview

The following verbs take infinitive clauses as sub-clause complementation. Alternatives are indicated in brackets:

> *advise* (also gerund), *agree, allow* (also gerund), *appear, arrange, ask, attempt* (also gerund), *be* (also gerund), *begin* (also gerund), *care, cause, compel, consent, dare* (also gerund), *determine, encourage* (also gerund), *expect, fail, forbid, force, forget, hate, have* (= *cause*, without *to*, also past participle), *hesitate, hate, help, hope, intend* (also gerund), *instruct, invite, lead, learn, let* (without *to*), *like* (also gerund), *love* (also gerund), *make* (without *to*), *manage, mean* (also gerund), *need* (also gerund), *neglect, oblige, order, permit* (also gerund), *persuade, prefer* (also gerund), *prepare, promise, propose* (also gerund), *refuse, regret* (also gerund), *remember* (also gerund), *remind, request, seem, show how, start* (also gerund), *swear, teach* (also gerund), *tell, tempt, try* (also gerund), *urge, want* (also gerund), *warn*.

To these we must add verbs denoting acts of **sensory perception** (*feel, hear, notice, see, watch*, etc., all taking the infinitive without *to*). These combine alternatively with present participle clauses. The infinitive without *to* is dealt with in 7.4.1 below.

We will not for the moment go into the syntactic or semantic implications of the alternatives given. These are dealt with later in Chapter 8, 8.3.2.1.

7.2.1.1 Main verb + infinitive clause

In this pattern, the infinitive clause follows the catenative directly, i.e. without an intervening main-clause object:

(7)   S   P   Od   P   Od
     a. I had forgotten   [to post the letter].
          S   P   Od   P   Od   A
     b. Terry managed [to pass the exam this time].

The infinitive clause, as indicated, is the direct object of the main verb. Catenative verbs in this category follow only this pattern. They include:

> *agree, appear, arrange, attempt, begin, care, consent, determine, fail, forget, hesitate, hope, learn, manage, neglect, prepare, promise, propose, refuse, regret, remember, seem, start, swear, try.*

With these verbs, then, an intervening object between catenative and sub-clause is not possible. In most cases the monotransitive character is clear from the lexical nature of the individual verb. Sentences such as *We hesitated him to go or *I managed her to come, are obviously meaningless. The semantics of the verbs, that is, will not accommodate such a syntactic pattern. However, this is not necessarily the case with other members of the group. For example, *promise* and *refuse* can both be ditransitive from the perspective of their semantics. Syntactically, however, the ditransitive construction with these two verbs is allowed only in simple sentences. It is not possible when one of the objects is an infinitive clause. (8)a. is therefore permissible, but (8)b. is not:

(8)   a. The boss promised/refused his workers a pay-rise.
        b. *The boss promised/refused his workers to grant a pay-rise.

7.2.1.2 Main verb + object + infinitive clause

Verbs in this group require an object before the infinitive, i.e. in the main clause. Depending on the verb, this is either a direct or an indirect object. After a direct object the infinitive clause functions as an object complement. After an indirect object it functions itself as the direct object:

(9)   S   P   Od   Co   P   A
     a. Bad weather forced the boats   [to return to harbour].
          S   P   Oi   Od   P   A
     b. Mother told the children [to stay in the garden].

Functionally, then, we have two possible patterns here: one is ditransitive, the other complex transitive.

In the **ditransitive pattern** (9b.), the noun phrase following the verb takes on the semantic role of recipient. This is the case when the verb expresses an act of communication, such as an utterance, or some other form of 'giving and sending'. Examples are:

> *advise, allow, forbid, instruct, invite, order, permit, persuade, remind, request, show how, teach, tell, urge, warn.*

The **complex transitive pattern** (9a.) occurs with verbs that convey some other kind of force or influence affecting the noun phrase, e.g.:

> *compel, encourage, force, lead, oblige, tempt.*

7.2.1.3 With or without the intervening main-clause object

The verbs in this group can take either of the patterns presented in 7.2.1.1 and 7.2.1.2, depending upon the meaning intended:

```
         S   P         Od   P   Od
(10) a.  Ted wanted    [to marry Jane].
         S   P    Od    Co  P   Od
     b.  Ted wanted Jane    [to marry him].
```

When there is a main-clause object, most verbs here are complex transitive. But the ditransitive pattern can also occur, as in (11)b.:

```
         S      P           Od   P     Od
(11) a.  Charlene has asked    [to borrow Jake's car].
         S       P     Oi   Od  P    Od
     b.  Charlene has asked Tim  [to borrow Jake's car].
```

Verbs in this group include:

> *ask, dare, expect, hate, help, intend, like, love, mean, need, prefer, want.*

7.2.1.4 The infinitive clause as subject complement or adverbial

Subject complements, to re-cap, occur after verbs of 'being', 'becoming' and 'seeming' (e.g. *be, become, seem*). Some of the verbs within this group can take infinitive clause complementation. The infinitive clause then functions as subject complement:

(12) a.
       S   P   Cs P   A
Gerald appears [to be in Paris].

b.
    S   P   Cs P Od
Sonia came [to hate Ryan].

c.
     S   P   Cs P   A
My job is [to cook for the team].

As adverbials, infinitive clauses always express the meaning of purpose, and can invariably be expanded by *in order*:

(13) a.
      S   P   A   A   P   A
Gerald went to Paris [(in order) to be with Michelle].

b.
   A   P   Od   A   S   P   Od
[(In order) to achieve real success in this job], you need a lot of luck.

7.3 The subject of an infinitive clause

The subject of an infinitive is not usually stated as such explicitly, but is implied according to certain syntactic principles. Consider again our examples from (11) above, now repeated in (14):

(14) a. **Charlene** has asked to borrow Jake´s car.
b. Charlene has asked **Tim** to borrow Jake´s car

In (14)a. *Charlene*, the subject of the main clause, is also the implied subject of *to borrow*. Charlene, that is, intends to borrow Jake´s car herself. In (14)b. the intended borrower is *Tim*. Underlying this is the following rule:

- if there is a main-clause object preceding the infinitive, this is understood as the implied subject of the infinitive;
- otherwise, it is the main-clause subject which is understood as the implied subject of the infinitive (as in 14a.).

Putting it simply, then, the relation across the two clauses is **object–subject** when there is a main-clause object present (as in 14b.), and **subject–subject** when there is not (as in 14a.). The subject–subject relation applies also when the infinitive clause functions as an adverbial:

(15) a. **The driver of the car** braked suddenly to avoid a dog in the road.
b. To get there on time tomorrow, **we** should leave the house by 7 am.

In (15)a. the subject of both verb phrases (*braked* and *to avoid*) is *the driver of the car*. In (15)b. the subject of both verb phrases (*to get* and *should leave*) is *we*.

Violation of these principles leads to ungrammatical sentences:

(16) a. *Charlene has asked me to borrow my car.
     b. *To get away on time tomorrow, the car must be loaded tonight.

The object–subject rule designates *me* in (16)a. as the desired borrower of the car, but that is clearly not the intended meaning. Either the pronoun must be omitted (*Charlene has asked to borrow my car*, see analogy to (14)a., or the sub-clause must be finite, thus specifying subject relations: *Charlene has asked me whether she can borrow my car*. There is a similar deviant subject relation in (16)b., this time brought about by violation of the subject–subject rule: the syntax makes *the car* the subject of *to get away*, which clearly militates against semantic logic. The necessary amendment must introduce a contextually compatible subject into the main clause, e.g. *. . .we must load the car. . .*, or specify the same referent as subject of the sub-clause. One way of doing this is to make the sub-clause finite, e.g. in the form *If we intend to get away . . . .* Another is to put the verb in the main clause into the active voice: *. . . we must load the car . . . .*

It is also possible to specify infinitive subjects in syntactically overt form. This is discussed further in Chapter 12, 12.2.3.

7.3.1 Subject relations with infinitive clauses as subject complements

Subject-identity principles with clauses as subject complement are not always quite so straightforward as in the cases discussed so far. Let us return for a moment to the examples in (12) above, repeated here as (17):

(17) a. Gerald appears to be in Paris.
     b. Sonia came to hate Ryan.
     c. My job is to cook for the team.

In (17)a. and b. our subject–subject rule applies as we would expect from what was said in the preceding section: that is, in the absence of any objects, the **main-clause subjects** *Gerald* and *Sonia* are the **implied subjects** of their respective infinitive clauses. In (17)c., however, this is not so. Clearly, *my job* is not the implied subject of *to cook*. This has to do with the lexical nature of the verb *be*, which here means 'consist of' and confers the meaning of **equivalence** on the relation of subject to subject complement. Consequently (and in contrast to a. and b.), subject and subject complement can swap functions, allowing the infinitive clause to become the subject without changing the basic semantics of the sentence:

| S | P | Cs |
(18) [To cook for the team] is my job.

The message here is that the lexical nature of *be* suspends the subject-identity principles which normally apply to main verb complementation by infinitive clauses, even to those in the subject complement function. The unique character of *be* in this respect is further underlined by other factors: a gerund clause is also possible in the same meaning and function (*My job is cooking for the team*, see Chapter 8, 8.1), and likewise the construction we will meet further below as extraposition (see Chapter 12, 12.1). Neither of these alternatives apply to other verbs taking infinitive clauses as subject complements.

So where does this leave us as far as subject interpretation is concerned? The answer is that if syntactic principles of implication are absent, context and semantics ultimately decide. Certain references in the sentence may give more or less foolproof clues, it is true. In (18), for instance, the possessive determiner *my* (in *my job*) clearly indicates the speaker or writer as the subject of *cook*. However, signals such as genitives, possessives and other pointers may not be as obvious as this. Consider the following:

(19) a. The firm´s main strategy this year is to develop new markets abroad.
 b. Kate´s idea was to meet at the station.
 c. The best solution would be to play Morris and Kinley in midfield.

In (19)a. the s-genitive *firm´s* appears to indicate beyond all doubt that this noun is the subject of *develop*. Actually, however, it is additionally the lexis of *strategy* ('a course of action') that helps us to conclude this: *develop* equals a course of action 'belonging to' *firm*. The context of the sentence (in, say, discourse on company economics) and our world knowledge that this is the kind of thing companies do, are also factors flowing into our syntactic understanding of the subject relation. In (19)b. we can likewise assume subject relations from the genitive: the surrounding context, however, might tell us that *Kate* is not the only subject of *meet*, but that there are others involved in the plan. (19)c. is entirely dependent on context and/or co-text: whose 'solution' is being referred to here? Again, lexis (*play*, *midfield*) and general knowledge about team-sports and club decisions on player positions before a game also support our understanding of who or what the subject of the infinitive is.

Having considered all these internal and external factors involved in language meaning, we should now add that infinitive subjects can be specified as such syntactically. This is examined in the next section.

7.3.2 Overt subject specification in the infinitive clause

A subject can be introduced overtly into an infinitive clause using the preposition *for*:

(20) a. Kate´s idea was **for Tim and Mike** to meet at the station.
 b. **For us** to get away on time tomorrow, the car must be loaded tonight.
 c. The best solution would be **for the manager** to play Morris and Kinley in midfield.

The *for*-construction comes into play especially when the infinitive subject is different from what would otherwise be implied. (19)b., for instance, as we saw, implies that *Kate* is at least one of the subjects of *meet*. (20)a., by contrast, tells us a completely different story. In this version Kate is definitely not involved in the meeting. Her 'idea' is about a meeting between two other people. These therefore need to be marked as the subject of the infinitive. (20)b. is a further way of making the earlier deviant sentence in (16)b. grammatical. Without the overt introduction of *we* as the subject, the sentence is ungrammatical, as previously explained, since it then wrongly implies *the car* as the subject of the infinitive. The *for*-construction redresses the imbalance. (20)c., by contrast, can be felicitously interpreted in the same way as its predecessor, (19)c., without the *for*-construction. Context and 'experience', as explained in the previous section, would allow us to interpret (19)c. quite correctly in its intended sense. Subject-specification by *for* simply provides clarification beyond all doubt. In addition, it emphasises the subject, which could be important for contextual reasons within the discourse.

The *for*-construction occurs particularly frequently with extraposition (see below and Chapter 12, 12.1). But how can the *for*-construction be represented in functional analysis? This is still an open question in the theory. For the purposes of this book, we will give two possible alternatives:

```
           S         P    Cs  A                     P        A
(21) a. Kate's idea was   [ (for Tim and Mike) to meet at the station].
           S         P    Cs    S           P        A
     b. Kate's idea was   [for Tim and Mike to meet at the station].
```

The first solution, in (21)a., integrates *for* as a preposition into a prepositional phrase, doing better justice to standard syntactical patterning, but on the other hand failing to capture the subject role of the noun phrase. In (21)b. the preposition *for* is not treated as a preposition, but as a kind of eccentric 'conjunction', whose job is simply to introduce the sub-clause. The noun-phrase *Tim and Mike* can then accordingly be marked as what it essentially is, i.e. as the subject of the infinitive. Tendentially, this is the solution we prefer.

7.4 Some special cases in complementation by infinitive clause

Complementation by the infinitive is subject to one or two special conditions with certain kinds of catenative: these concern the use of the 'bare' infinitive (i.e. without *to*), restrictions on the catenative use of verbs in certain lexical fields, and also the preference for passive constructions with some catenatives.

7.4.1 The infinitive without to

The bare infinitive is encountered most widely with modal auxiliaries (*You must see that film; My father can **speak** several languages*). But there are certain catenatives that also require it in the pattern verb + object + infinitive clause:

- Verbs of sensory perception (such as *feel, hear, notice, see, watch*, etc.):

        S   P   Od   Co P   A

(22) a. We saw the man   [swim across the river].

         S   P   Od   Co P   A

      b. Katie heard someone   [come up the stairs].

The meaning in these cases is that the whole of the action expressed by the infinitive verb was perceived, including its end. In (22)a., that is, the onlookers saw the man swim from one riverbank to the other, while in (22)b. the subject *Katie* perceived that the person on the stairs started at the bottom and arrived at the top. The semantics are important, since the same verbs can be complemented by participles, though then with a different meaning (see Chapter 9).

- The verbs *let* (= *allow*), *make* (= *force*), and *have* (= *cause/order*):

        S   P   Od   Co P   A

(23) a. We do not let guests   [smoke in the house].

        S   P   Od   Co P   A

     b. Hunger made the children   [hurry home].

7.4.2 Verbs of knowing and thinking

Verbs from the semantic field of mental states and activities have a restricted range of infinitive complementation: they can only be combined with the infinitives of *be* and *have*, and only with an intervening object (functioning as **Od**):

(24) a. Yorkshire police knew Bradley to be violent.
     b. The committee considered these two candidates to have the best qualifications.
     c. Many guests assumed the man in the dark suit to be the bridegroom.

Infinitive structures in these cases are stylistically elevated. More neutral are the equivalent finite clauses with the conjunction *that*. The infinitive versions are more commonly used with the catenatives in the passive, especially when the agent is generalised, or clearly indicated in the context, and can therefore be left unstated:

(25) a. Bradley was known (by Yorkshire police) to be violent.
        Yorkshire police knew that Bradley was violent.
     b. These two candidates were considered (by the committee) to have the best qualifications.

The committee considered that these two candidates had the best qualifications.
c. The man in the dark suit was assumed (by many guests) to be the bridegroom.
Many guests assumed that the man in the dark suit was the bridegroom.

7.4.3 Catenatives in the passive

Passive constructions are popular with catenatives in certain contexts. This is usually because, as generally in passive usage, action and patient are profiled and the agent is unknown or unimportant. An additional motive, especially with commands, requests and other forms of communicated obligation, is that the passive has a softening effect. It emphasises the responsibility of the patient, but does so without mentioning the agent as the authority behind the communication:

(26) a. Passengers are kindly requested to remain seated during the flight.
b. Visitors to the private zoo were forbidden to feed the animals.
c. You have been asked to report to the controller, Mr Simms.

However, there are also considerable restrictions on catenative passivisation:

- Monotransitive catenatives **cannot** be put into the passive, i.e. the infinitive clause cannot function as a passive subject:

(27) The authorities tried to stop the demonstration.
⇒*[To stop the demonstration] was tried by the authorities.

- Ditransitive catenatives allow the passive. Only the active indirect object, however, can become the passive subject. This is because the active direct object is the infinitive clause, and as just seen in (27), infinitive clauses are ruled out as passive subjects:

```
            S         P        Oi       Od
(28) a.  The Institute asked Empson  [to give a lecture].    [active]

            S       P-pass      A         Od
     b.  Empson was asked by the Institute [to give a lecture].  [passive]

            S
     c.  *[To give a lecture] was asked of Empson by the Institute.
```

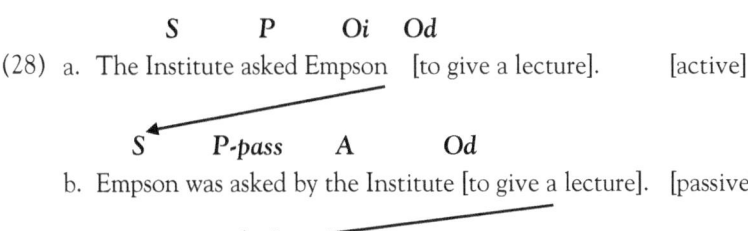

- Many complex transitive catenatives allow the passive, but there are some that do not. The chief factors in the distinction are lexical, and are explained below. We will look at the syntax first. As with the passivisation of all complex transitive verbs, the active direct object becomes the passive subject, while the active object complement functions as passive subject complement:

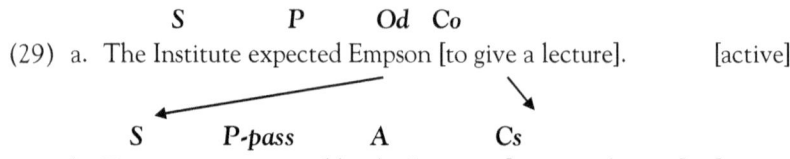

(29) a. The Institute expected Empson [to give a lecture]. [active]

b. Empson was expected by the Institute [to give a lecture]. [passive]

Complex transitive catenatives that allow the passive include: *compel, encourage, expect, force, help, intend, lead, mean, oblige, tempt*. Semantically, most of these convey a force or directive influence acting on the referent of the object noun phrase. The verbs that do not allow the passive express wishes and similar emotional dispositions: *hate, like, love, need, prefer, want*. None of the verbs followed by the infinitive without *to* can passivise in that form; however, three of the sensory perception verbs (*feel, hear* and *see*), plus *make*, permit passive versions (though with the addition of *to* to their infinitives):

(30) a. A man was seen to enter the building just after midnight.
 b. A car was heard to pass the house.
 c. The cinema-goers were made to wait outside in the pouring rain.

7.5 The infinitive clause as subject

So far we have been looking at the infinitive clause when it complements catenatives. We will now turn our attention to its function as the subject of the main clause:

```
        S   P   Cs    P    A          Cs
```
(31) a. [To get rich] was always my greatest ambition.
```
        S   P      Od       A    P    Oi       Od
```
 b. [To see his relatives in poverty] gave Shelley a bad conscience.

The initial position of the subject clause, as here in (31), is found in formal styles, but is not generally favoured in neutral or everyday language. The tendency in this case is to place the infinitive clause in final position, especially if it is an element in the sentence that is being introduced into the particular text or discourse for the first time. This is because medial and final positions in English sentences are generally rather more profiled or accentuated than initial positions (more is said on this point below in 7.5.1). The construction needed here to shift the clause into final position is known as extraposition, and is explained briefly in the next section.

7.5.1 Extraposition

With extraposition, the subject clause occurs in final position as the 'real', or **logical**, subject (marked as **S-log.**), and is represented at the beginning of the sentence by a grammatical 'dummy' subject in the form of *it* (marked as **S-gramm.**):

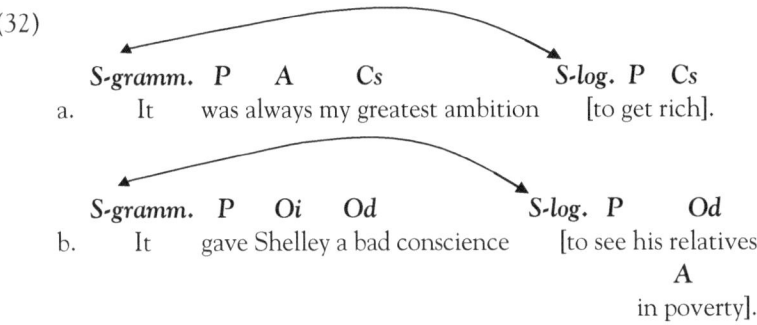

(32)
| | S-gramm. | P | A | Cs | S-log. | P | Cs |
a. It was always my greatest ambition [to get rich].

| | S-gramm. | P | Oi | Od | S-log. | P | Od |
b. It gave Shelley a bad conscience [to see his relatives
                                                    A
                                                    in poverty].

It might be thought of as thoroughly against the rules of functional analysis to have two subjects in a sentence. However, these are not really two subjects, but merely two subject positions for the **same** functional element. The **S-gramm.** as a 'dummy' subject simply fills what would otherwise be a syntactically impermissible gap in the initial sentence position, upholding the prescribed basic S-P-O-structure of an English sentence, and as a kind of cataphor foreshadowing full subject-reference in the **S-log.** position to which it points forward (see also SAGE, pp. 267 and 481).

Extraposition is particularly common with *be* as the main verb, particularly so as the construction is almost mandatory with adjective phrases as subject complements (see also Chapter 9):

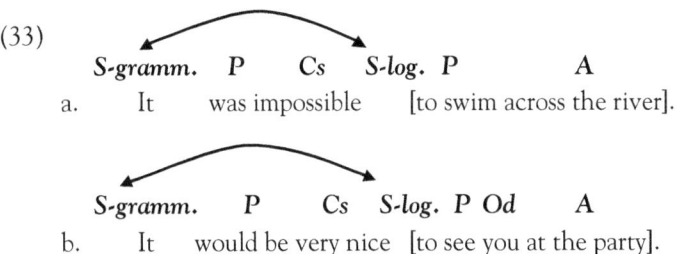

(33)
| | S-gramm. | P | Cs | S-log. | P | A |
a. It was impossible [to swim across the river].

| | S-gramm. | P | Cs | S-log. | P | Od | A |
b. It would be very nice [to see you at the party].

Extraposition is taken up again in Chapter 10.

7.6 Semantics: implicative meanings of catenatives with infinitives

Quite a number of catenatives with infinitive complementation show a systematic semantic relation between main verb and sub-clause: the infinitive act is implied as taking place. To indicate this **implicative relation** we use the symbol → (= 'implies'):

(34) a. Rangers managed to score in the last minute.
   → Rangers scored in the last minute.
   b. The police forced the car to stop.
   → The car stopped.
   c. Brian happened to meet Sandra in the bar.
   → Brian met Sandra in the bar.

Implicative relations are logical semantic relations between two elements. If we call these two elements X and Y and X implies Y (X → Y), then it is logically impossible for X to be true and Y to be false. Applied to our examples, that is, saying that *Rangers managed to score* means *Rangers scored*; if *The police forced the car to stop* is true, then *The car stopped* must also be true.

Other examples of implicative catenatives like those shown in the examples are *bother, dare, remember* and *take care*.

An important point is what happens when the catenative is **negated**. In all cases the implication is then destroyed (*not-X ↛ Y*). With many of them, however, a **negative implication** then additionally replaces the destroyed positive one (*not-X ↛ Y*, and also *not-X → not-Y*):

(35) a. Rangers did not manage to score in the last minute.
   → Rangers did not score in the last minute. (*not-X ↛ Y*, and also *not-X → not-Y*).
   b. The police did not force the car to stop.
   ↛ The car stopped. (*not-X ↛ Y*).
   c. Brian did not happen to meet Sandra in the bar.
   → Brian did not meet Sandra in the bar. (*not-X ↛ Y*, and also *not-X → not-Y*).

In (35)b., the negative of (34)b., the implication of (34)b. that the car stopped is no longer given. We do not know now whether the car stopped or not. But in (35)a. the statement that *Rangers did not manage to score* . . . not only destroys the implication *Rangers scored* . . . in (34)a., but replaces it by the negative implication *Rangers did not score* . . . . A similar negative implication occurs in (35)b. Whether a negative implication arises or not depends on the individual catenative: *happen*, when negated, as in (35)c., leads to a negative implication, like *manage*. So also do *bother, dare, remember* and *take care*, when negated. Verbs of perception, however, to name a further example, behave like *force*, i.e. their negatives are not implicative:

(36) a. I saw the three men enter the bank.
    → The three men entered the bank.
  b. I did not see the three men enter the bank.
    ↛ The three men entered the bank.

The negation of (36)a., then, leaves it quite open whether the three men (from the point of view of the speaker) entered the bank or not.

Some catenatives in the positive form have negative implications:

(37) a. I forgot to post the letter.
    → I did not post the letter. (X → not-Y).
  b. Fred refused to move his car.
    → Fred did not move his car. (X → not-Y).
  c. They failed to reach the valley before nightfall.
    → They did not reach the valley before nightfall. (X → not-Y).

Here the effects of negation, again depending on the individual catenative, either just cancel the implication, or, in doing this, additionally bring about a positive one:

(38) a. I did not forget to post the letter.
    → I posted the letter. (not-X ↛ not-Y, and also not-X → Y).
  b. Fred did not refuse to move his car.
    ↛ Fred did not move his car. (not-X ↛ not-Y).
  c. They did not fail to reach the valley before nightfall.
    → They reached the valley before nightfall. (not-X ↛ not-Y, and also not-X → Y).

It is important to remember that the implicative relation applies only to some of the catenatives taking infinitives. Others are **non-implicative**, e.g. *agree, ask, decide, hope, invite, try,* etc.

We will come back to the concept of implicative meaning later in Chapter 8, 8.3.2 when we discuss catenatives that are complemented by both infinitives and gerunds.

7.7 Tense and aspect

As these fields of grammar are morpho-semantic rather than syntactic, thorough discussion of them would go beyond the scope of this book. Nevertheless, certain points of tense and aspect use with infinitives have effects on syntax and need mentioning briefly.

There are two tense forms with the infinitive, the neutral or **base form**, and the **perfect infinitive**. There is additionally an **aspect distinction** in both, i.e. a simple form and a progressive form respectively (for more on the notions of tense and aspect, see SAGE, pp. 312ff.):

Base form simple	Base form progressive	Perfect infinitive simple	Perfect infinitive progressive
to eat	to be eating	to have eaten	to have been eating

7.7.1 Tense

The perfect infinitive expresses pastness or completion, and can be regarded as both a 'perfect' and a 'past' infinitive in one form:

(39) a. Barry seems to have met Sylvia yesterday.
    (Past tense meaning: It seems that Barry **met** Sylvia yesterday).
  b. Barry seems to have met Sylvia several times already.
    (Present perfect meaning: It seems that Barry **has met** Sylvia several times already).

At this stage, it is important to emphasise a general point: unlike their finite counterparts, non-finite verbs do not have a direct grammatical time relation to the moment of speech. Their time orientation is expressed indirectly: that is, it is understood as being oriented to the tenses of catenatives or other main verbs present in the context. In this sense, non-finites are grammatically tenseless. The following examples show this principle with the infinitive:

(40) a. Barry seems to like Sylvia.

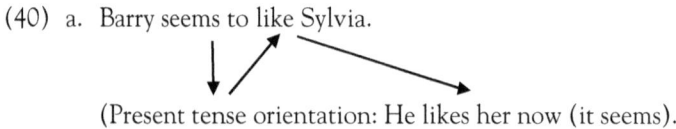

  (Present tense orientation: He likes her now (it seems).

  b. Barry seemed to like Sylvia (when they first met).

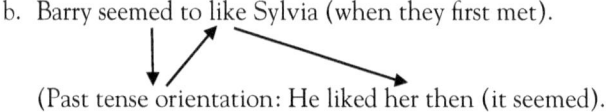

  (Past tense orientation: He liked her then (it seemed).

Here we see how the infinitive retains the same form in (40)a. and b., even though it refers to the present in the first and the past in the second. The difference in time orientation between the two sentences is signalled through the tense distinction in the catenative alone. The infinitive tense only changes when it is oriented to a time **prior** to that of the catenative. This is the case in (39) above, now explained in (41):

(41) a. Barry seems to have met Sylvia yesterday.

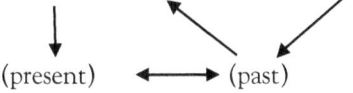

   b. Barry seems to have met Sylvia several times already.

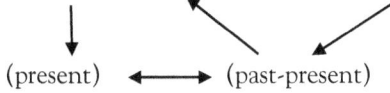

We cannot say *. . . *seems to meet*. . . here because in contrast to the case in (40) catenative and infinitive do not share the same time-level. The *before*-relation of infinitive to catenative requires the perfect infinitive to signal this. In (39)–(41) the finite equivalents are the past tense and the present perfect. In the following, the equivalent is the past perfect:

(42) Barry seemed to have met Sylvia the week before/several times already.

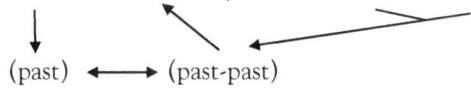

(= It seemed that Barry had met Sylvia the week before/several times already.)

The perfect infinitive thus serves, as it were, as an 'all-purpose' past and perfect tense. It can function like this as it is not speaker-time-related, but merely shows the discrepancy in time orientation between catenative and infinitive. Separate infinitive forms for past and past perfect tenses are therefore unnecessary. As it does not show the full range of tense distinctions of a finite verb, the infinitive can be called **defective** in that respect.

7.7.2 Aspect

Whereas the infinitive is defective (i.e. 'limited') regarding tense, it manifests the same aspect relations as a finite verb. The non-progressive forms of the infinitive are **perfective** in meaning, i.e. semantically equivalent to finite simple forms. They express an action as a whole, completed entity. By the same token, the progressive infinitives are semantically equivalent to finite progressive forms: they are **imperfective**, and express an action as ongoing, i.e. in the course of occurrence, at a given or implied point of time:

(43) a. The builders have promised to do the job by next Friday.
(= They have promised to complete the job by next Friday.)
b. The builders have promised to be doing the job by next Friday.
(= They have promised to start the job by next Friday.)
c. She seems to have run away when she saw the tiger.
(= It appears that she saw the tiger and then ran away.)
d. She seems to have been running away when she saw the tiger.
(= It appears that she was already in the course of running away and the sight of the tiger interrupted this.)

7.7.3 Voice: the passive

To complete the picture, we should add that there are passive forms of the infinitive. These behave semantically and grammatically like the passive forms of finite verbs. The progressive forms of the passive infinitive exist in theory, but in practice are avoided because they sound awkward. The question marks in the table indicate their borderline character.

Passive base form simple	Passive base form progressive	Passive perfect infinitive simple	Passive perfect infinitive progressive
to be eaten	(?) to be being eaten	to have been eaten	(?) to have been being eaten

(44) a. This house is to be sold.
b. It seems to have been re-painted last year.

Exercises

Exercise 1

Analyse the following sentences in terms of sentence functions:

1 Grandmother wants to do the shopping.
2 Grandmother wants you to do the shopping.
3 Des asked Frank to give him a cigarette.
4 Carrie would like Jason to come to her party.
5 Carrie has invited Jason to come to her party.
6 I was expecting my brother to arrive on the afternoon flight from Toronto.
7 The heavy rain forced us to take cover in an old barn.
8 My boss has persuaded me to do overtime this Saturday.
9 The children had been told to stay off the grass in the garden.
10 For years Katie was considered to be the best singer-songwriter in London.
11 I refused to let her drive my car.

12 Sam did not manage to get the job with Lloyd's.
13 MacDowell's plan is to cross the Sahara by jeep.
14 It is MacDowell's plan to cross the Sahara by jeep.
15 It was generous of them to give so much money to charity.
16 She had sat down on the terrace with a cup of coffee to relax after a long day at the office.
17 It became difficult for us to steer the boat as the sea got rougher outside the harbour.
18 On the way home we stopped to have a drink at a roadside café.
19 In the dusk I noticed two figures climb over the garden fence and hide in the bushes.
20 I have been reminded to tell you not to forget to feed the cat while my parents are away.

Exercise 2

Identify and correct the errors in the following:

1   *We promised Mum to be back in time for tea.
2   *The tourist guide recommended to visit the Old Palace in the hunting park.
3   *Dave asked me to take my CD home with him.
4   *To go to the coast tomorrow, breakfast should be early.
5   *Delia offered Nathalie to drive her to the station.
6   *It is not allowed to smoke in this building.
7   *Mrs Frinton invited to come to her house for dinner the next day.
8   *The police inspector made all the suspects to line up against the wall.
9   *I assume my guests to arrive tomorrow.
10 *It was attempted by the firm to sack all the strikers.

Exercise 3

State the differences in meaning between the a. and b. sentences in the following, and say how those differences arise. Provide possible contexts. How are implicative meanings involved in 3. and 4.?

1   a. Clint saw Samantha crossing the road.
    b. Clint saw Samantha cross the road.
2   a. Smoke seems to have filled the room when they opened the window.
    b. Smoke seems to have been filling the room when they opened the window.
3   a. Kylie managed to reach the village by nightfall.
    b. Kylie did not manage to reach the village by nightfall.

4 a. I heard the stranger threaten the barkeeper.
   b. I did not hear the stranger threaten the barkeeper.
5 a. Simon intended to be cooking the meal by the time Chloe returned.
   b. Simon intended to cook the meal by the time Chloe returned.
6 a. Scragg happened to meet Mullery at the station.
   b. Scragg happened to have met Mullery at the station.

8 Non-finite clauses in the complex sentence (II)
The gerund

8.0 The gerund

The gerund is an *-ing*-form. It refers to actions, and especially to activity **fields**, in much the same way as a noun does:

(1) a. **Jogging** became her great passion.
    b. Jill hates **shopping**.
    c. Their favourite evening activity was **reading**.

There is also a passive gerund with the *-ing*-form of *be*, plus the past participle of the full verb, e.g. *Jenny likes **being asked** difficult questions*.

Gerunds are not only noun-like in meaning. They also fill the same sentence functions as noun phrases, as we can see from these examples: subject in (1)a., direct object in (1)b. and subject complement in (1)c. For this reason, the gerund is traditionally called a 'nominal' verb form. Modern linguists, though, tend to regard this view as an oversimplification: the infinitive, after all, can take on the same functions, yet it is not seen as particularly 'nominal' in character. Secondly, like any other non-finite verb, the gerund always has a predicator function. It forms a subordinate clause even when it is alone, as in the sentences in (1). And this demonstrates its **verbal** character, underlined by the fact that within its own clause it can take its own verbal complementation:

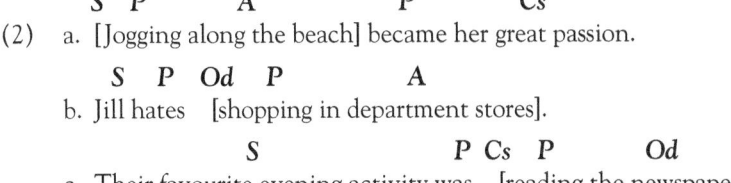

(2) a. [Jogging along the beach] became her great passion. (S P A / P Cs)
    b. Jill hates [shopping in department stores]. (S P Od P / A)
    c. Their favourite evening activity was [reading the newspaper]. (S / P Cs P Od)

On the other hand, stressing the 'nominal' label does have a certain justification to it, particularly when the gerund is contrasted with the present participle. The latter is also an *-ing*-form, but as we will see later has no 'nominal' character at all syntactically. Secondly, even though infinitive clauses can also be noun-like, gerunds are especially (and more or less exclusively) so. In addition to what might be called their 'classical' sentence functions as subjects and objects, gerunds

- occur clausally as the complement of a preposition (*a brush for cleaning shoes*); can be the first or second element in a **compound noun** (*swimming-pool*; *shark fishing*);
- can be preceded in their clauses by the *s*-genitive or a possessive determiner (*I do not like Jane´s driving my car*); and
- can take on a complete noun-like character as an **actional nominal** (*I do not like Jane´s driving of my car*).

A major consideration in the sections following is how the gerund is used in sentences and with what kinds of meaning. A particular issue, as with infinitives, is the part played in catenative complementation. Which main verbs are followed by gerunds, as opposed, say, to infinitives, or can be complemented by either type of clause depending on certain other grammatical and semantic conditions? This question also poses a teaching problem in EFL which teachers are well advised to grasp first of all theoretically.

To start with, however, we will consider the syntax of the gerund clause, both internally and externally, in detail.

8.1 The gerund clause

To repeat what was indicated above, the gerund at sentence level is always clausal. Even when not further complemented, it functions as predicator and introduces a subordinate clause. This is shown if we go back to the sentences in (1) and analyse them fully:

(3) a. S P   P   Cs
         [Jogging] became her great passion.
         S P   Od   P
     b. Jill hates [shopping].
         S   P Cs   P
     c. Their favourite evening activity was [reading].

As with all subordinate clauses, replacement by an equivalent phrase (e.g. *this*, *this activity*, etc.) will demonstrate the functional relation to the main clause:

(4) a. S   P   Cs
         This became her great passion.
         S P   Od
     b. Jill hates **this activity**.
         S   P Cs
     c. Their favourite evening activity was **this**.

By far the most common sentence functions of the gerund clause are those shown here, i.e. as subject, direct object and subject complement. Gerund clauses do not generally occur as adverbials: adverbial *-ing*-clauses are almost always present participle clauses (see Chapter 9). For semantic (and also stylistic) reasons gerund clauses are rarely indirect objects, though this is not impossible:

	S	P	Oi	P	Od	Od
(5)	The company	has given		[building the new warehouse]	top priority.

Gerunds have a strong attraction to prepositions, and frequently appear as parts of prepositional phrases (*on arriving, without saying goodbye, by breaking the door open*, etc.). This is a phrase-level function which will not concern us in detail at this point (see more in Chapter 10). Gerunds following prepositions do occur in sentence-level functions, however, when the prepositions are attached to prepositional verbs:

(6)   a. S — They   P — decided   Od — on   P — [promoting   Od — her   A — immediately].

b. S — We   P — look   Od — forward   P — to   Od — [meeting   A — you   A — here next month].

c. S — Terry's parents   P — congratulated   Oi — him   Od — on   P — [passing   Od — the exam].

d. S — The club   P — fined   Od — Sanchez   Co — for   P — [insulting   Od — other players].

A word of explanation here: ordinary prepositional verbs (*decide on*), and phrasal-prepositional verbs (*look forward to*) are complemented by direct objects (called in this case prepositional objects). The verbs *congratulate someone on something* and *fine someone for something* are complex prepositional verbs (see Chapter 5, 5.4.1.4, and *SAGE*, p. 380). These are mainly ditransitive, as in (6)c., but can also be complex transitive, as in (6)d. In the first case, the element after the preposition is the direct object, and in the second the object complement (also a comparatively rare function of the gerund).

The most frequent types of main verb complementation in which gerunds occur, as we said above, are those of subject, direct object and subject complement. And it is these that we will focus on in the next sections. First of all, though, let us shift the perspective briefly to the 'inner life' of a gerund clause, and consider one particular internal function more closely: the subject of a gerund predicator.

8.1.1 Subject matters

As with other non-finite verbs, the subject of a gerund is usually implied. It can be generalised or specific:

(7)   a. Reading is a great educator.
      b. Drinking all that wine was a bit stupid.
      c. Running so fast had made him breathless.

In (7)a. it is the activity itself that is in the foreground, and the subject, understood as 'anyone', or 'people in general', is unimportant. As the gerund can focus on actions, it lends itself very easily to generalised references of this kind. The other examples point to specific subjects. With (7)b., certainly, we could only know who did the drinking from the situation of utterance or a preceding reference: a speaker with a headache, say, talking about the party she attended the night before. But the grammar of the sentence itself contains no actual clue to this. Subject implication, here, then, depends entirely upon context. (7)c., by contrast, tells us quite concretely who had been *running*, even though it is unstated in the gerund clause: it is the person 'made breathless', i.e. the *him* referred to in the main clause. This illustrates a general principle of **concrete subject implication**: unless otherwise indicated (see further below), the implied subject of a gerund is usually considered to be identical with a semantically appropriate noun phrase occurring in the main clause. This principle is seen at its clearest when the gerund clause is in the object position, i.e. follows the catenative. We will therefore turn our attention now to this case, and come back afterwards to subject-position clauses like those in (7).

8.1.1.1 *The subject of the gerund clause in object position*

With gerund clauses following catenatives, the principle just stated translates into an invariable syntactic rule: the **subject of the main clause** is almost always **the implied subject of the gerund**. As with the infinitive, that is, we have **subject–subject congruity**:

(8)   a. My brother hated playing rugby.
      b. Kiara does not remember ordering this computer.

In (8)a. *My brother* is the subject of both *hated* and *playing*; in (8)b. the same applies to *Kiara* as regards *remember* and *ordering*.

However, this may not be the intended meaning. Let us now assume, as a variant, that *my brother* hated it when **someone else** played rugby, and that what *Kiara* does not *remember* is that not she but **I** ordered the computer. In cases like this, when gerund subject and main clause subject diverge, the gerund subject must be made explicit. Traditionally this is done by inserting the subject between catenative and gerund, as a **genitive noun** or possessive determiner:

(9)   a. My brother hated **his girlfriend´s** playing rugby.
      b. Kiara does not remember **my** ordering this computer.

However, as this is regarded nowadays as rather formal and elaborate style, genitives and possessives are usually replaced, more neutrally, by an **object noun** or pronoun:

(10) a. My brother hated **his girlfriend** playing rugby.
　　b. Kiara does not remember **me** ordering this computer.

On the surface, this appears to be a direct parallel to the **Od** + sub-clause pattern with the infinitive:

```
                           Od         Co
```
(11) a. My brother hated   **his girlfriend**   [playing rugby].
　　b. Kiara does not remember   **me**   [ordering this computer].

The version in (9) speaks against this analysis, however. Syntactically, genitives and possessives are determiners, which means that they really have their place inside the sub-clause. This also reflects the semantic relations better. Semantically, *his girlfriend* and *me* in (10) are not objects of the main verb, and the latter does not create a genuine complex–transitive relation between an object and a sub-clause. What was respectively 'hated' and 'not remembered' were actions, not people. The persons involved feature simply as agents. For these reasons we will favour the following functional version for both (10) and (11):

```
         S        P    Od   S           P   Od
```
(12) a. My brother hated   [**his girlfriend(´s)** playing rugby].

```
         S        P          Od   S      P    Od
```
　　b. Kiara does not remember   [**my/me** ordering this computer].

8.1.1.2 The subject of the gerund clause in subject position

We will now return to consideration of examples like (7)c. and add two more for good measure:

(13) a. Running so fast had made him breathless.
　　b. Working overtime at weekends has exhausted me.
　　c. Smoking so heavily is going to kill Lucy.

Here we have essentially the same principle operating as in (8), but reversed. As the gerund clause is now the subject of the main verb, its own implied subject in the main clause must be the object, i.e. here it is the **object of the main clause** that is the implied subject of the gerund. Here, in other words, we have **subject–object congruity**: *him* is the implied subject of *running*, *me* of *working* and *Lucy* of *smoking*, respectively.

Let us now look at the case discussed in the previous section of what we will now call **subject divergence**. Here, with examples like those in (9)–(12), the gerund subject diverges in reference from the main clause object. So, again, the gerund subject must be made explicit: a genitive noun or possessive determiner is introduced, as previously, before the gerund:

(14) a. **The children's** running so fast surprised their parents.
b. **My** working overtime at weekends bothers my wife.
c. **Lucy's** smoking so heavily disturbs her family.

Reduction to an ordinary noun or pronoun is possible here in informal varieties of English (cf. 11):

(15) a. **The children** running so fast surprised their parents.
b. **Me** working overtime at weekends bothers my wife.
c. **Lucy** smoking so heavily disturbs her family.

But there is still a general preference in standard varieties for the genitive/possessive versions, as in (14), when the gerund clause begins the sentence as it does here.

Another question that arises with gerunds in initial position involves minor violations of the congruity rule, which, in some cases and with some speakers, seems to be less stringently applied than it does when the gerund clause follows the main verb. Consider:

(16) a. (*) Working overtime at weekends bothers my wife.
b. (?) Running so fast made the children's faces red.
c. (?) Smoking heavily affected Lucy's heart.
d. (?) Driving across the mountains ruined Freddie's tyres.

(16)a. is correct on the reading that *my wife* is the gerund subject. It is grammatically wrong, however, if it is meant in the same way as (15)b., since then there would be a discrepancy between the implied subject and the main clause object. On the same grounds, (16)b., c. and d. would also be ungrammatical (especially so as there is no alternative reading possible as with (16)a.). The subjects of *running*, *smoking* and *driving* are intended, respectively, to be *children*, *Lucy* and *Freddie*, even though these are actually not the heads of the main clause object noun phrases. What these sentences say, strictly speaking, is that *the children's faces* were 'running', *Lucy's heart* was the smoker and the *tyres* on Freddie's vehicle did the driving: all nonsensical and unintended, of course. But we give the examples question marks here rather than stars as, in our estimation, though doubtful for some speakers, they are not impossible for others.

8.1.2 Extraposition of the gerund clause in subject position

To re-cap: with infinitive clauses in subject position, extraposition is more or less mandatory (see Chapter 7). Gerund clauses, however, as our various examples so far show, can be quite readily placed in initial position. Nevertheless, extraposition is frequently used with gerunds, especially in informal language, to give emphasis:

(17) a. It was very restful lying on the beach.
  (= Lying on the beach was very restful.)
 b. It will be fun running over the dunes.
  (= Running over the dunes will be fun.)
 c. It's not very nice sitting out here in the rain.
  (= Sitting out here in the rain is not very nice.)

As a reminder: extraposition moves the clause concerned (here the gerund clause) into final position, where it remains the logical subject (**S-log.**); the initial position is then occupied by the 'dummy' subject *it* (the **S-gramm.**):

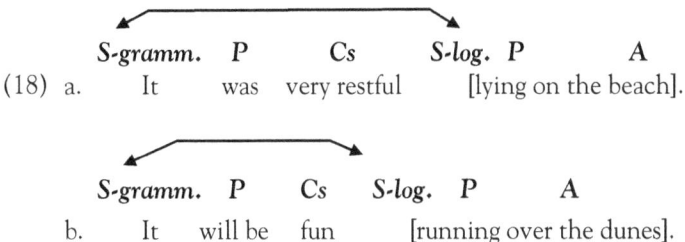

	S-gramm.	P	Cs	S-log. P	A
(18) a.	It	was	very restful	[lying on the beach].	
b.	It	will be	fun	[running over the dunes].	

In standard usage, extraposition with gerunds is confined to sentences with *be* as main verb. In informal varieties, though, other main verbs can also occur:

(19) a. It had made him breathless, running so fast.
 b. It is going to kill Lucy, smoking so heavily.
 c. It has exhausted me, working overtime at weekends.

Stylistically, to emphasise the point, sentences like these are felt to be colloquial. When spoken, they usually include a slight pause before the gerund, shown in writing by a comma. The pause suggests that the gerund reference has been mentioned before and is now being repeated as a kind of clarifying afterthought.

8.2 The semantics of the gerund

The use of the gerund has certain semantic implications that can affect the syntax. Here are a couple of general remarks on what the gerund as a form means:

- an **activity** in a general sense: *cooking, reading, swimming, playing chess, shopping for clothes, hiking in the hills*. Because of this the gerund often figures strongly in the expression of habits: *Jill doesn't enjoy shopping for clothes; Reading the paper is something I do every day*;
- an **event** on a specific occasion: *Meeting Kenny at the fair last Saturday was a coincidence.*

In both of these uses there is a strong tendency for the gerund to indicate that the event referred to is in one sense or another a factual experience and actually takes or took place:

(20) a. I hate jogging (I've done it a couple of times and disliked it).
  b. Jill doesn't enjoy shopping for clothes (although she is forced to do it occasionally).
  c. Meeting Kenny at the fair last Saturday was a coincidence (= We met Kenny at the fair last Saturday and it was a coincidence).

As a result, gerunds are attracted to contexts that we call **factive**, i.e. ones containing expressions that **presuppose** (symbol ») the truth or factual status of other things referred to (see SAGE, pp. 496f.). Typical factive verbs are catenatives like *resent, regret* and *appreciate*:

(21) a. Our neighbours resent us buying a bigger car (= ... resent the fact that we bought ...).
    » We bought a bigger car.
  b. Tom now regrets leaving the firm last year (= ... regrets the fact that he left ...).
    » Tom left the firm last year.
  c. We appreciate your coming to see us (= ... appreciate the fact that you have come ...).
    » You have come to see us.

These verbs express a feeling, comment or attitude in relation to an act that happened beforehand (and is consequently referred to in the gerund). They only make sense if the act actually did take place. **Non-factive** verbs, by contrast, do not show this **presuppositional** relation:

(22) a. Our neighbours think we have more money (*... think our having ... /*... the fact that we have ...).
  b. Tom now says he left the firm last year (*... says leaving .../*... the fact that he left ...).

Significantly, gerunds are not possible in these cases. Non-factive verbs cannot generally take gerunds as complementation, whereas factive verbs usually do. This is not a hard-and-fast rule, and there are several exceptions. Nevertheless, it is a general principle.

By no means all factive verbs express comments or feelings:

(23) a. Billy gave up smoking.
    » Billy smoked beforehand.
  b. We resisted being tempted by their offer.
    » We were tempted by their offer.

As their factive presuppositions are of a slightly different kind from those in (21), the catenatives *give up* and *resist* do not allow gerund paraphrase by *the fact that*. Nevertheless, since they refer to acts operating on other events or processes, the previous occurrence of the latter is logically presupposed. Presuppositions of (23)a. and b., respectively, are *Billy smoked* and *We were tempted*. Other verbs of this lexical type are *cease, stop, go on, continue*. Related to these are verbs that carry **negative presuppositions** such as *take up, start* and *begin*. Here, that is, the gerund in a sentence like *Billy started smoking* is presuppositionally motivated by the fact that the action expressed must **not** have occurred beforehand. Other verbs occupy a kind of middle position in that they presuppose the contextual presence of a risk or plan of the gerund action occurring: *avoid, postpone, prevent, risk, save*, etc.

Adjectives (chiefly evaluative in lexical nature) can also be factive and attract gerunds, as in (24)a., for example. Those in (24)b., by contrast, are not factive, and do not allow the gerund:

(24) a. Richardson's leaving the meeting early was regrettable/inconsiderate/ unwise.
 b. *Richardson's leaving the meeting early was likely/true/impossible.

Catenatives taking the gerund are listed below. Those that in addition can have infinitive complementation are commented on individually. We will then return to the concept of factivity in contrasting gerund and infinitive meanings (see 8.3.2.2 below).

8.3 The gerund clause as catenative complementation

As indicated at the beginning of the chapter, a particular issue in the syntax of non-finite verb forms, and one especially relevant to applied linguistics and EFL/ESL, is the question of which individual catenatives are complemented by which kind of non-finite structure. Just as some main verbs are followed by the infinitive, so others need the gerund; others again take either form of complementation, but according to certain systematic conditions, sometimes grammatical in nature and sometimes semantic. A third alternative often given in the case of verbs taking gerunds is the finite clause introduced by the conjunction *that* (referred to here as *that*-clauses). The purpose of this section is to examine these issues and (where possible) explore any systematic factors involved in the selection of appropriate catenative complementation.

8.3.1 Catenative + gerund

The following verbs require the gerund as non-finite clausal complementation. Some among them additionally allow a *that*-clause:

admit (also *that*), *anticipate* (also *that*), *avoid*, *deny* (also *that*), *defer*, *delay*, *enjoy*, *dread* (also *that*), *can´t endure*, *entail*, *excuse*, *finish*, *give up*, *can´t help*, *imagine* (also *that*), *involve*, *it´s no good/no use/worth/not worth*, *keep*, *mind*, *miss*, *postpone*, *prevent*, *put off*, *recollect* (also *that*), *resent* (also *the fact that*), *resist*, *risk*, *save*, *suggest* (also *that*), *can´t stand*, *tolerate*.

8.3.2 Catenative + gerund or infinitive

The following verbs can have gerund **or** infinitive clauses as non-finite complementation. Where indicated they additionally allow a *that*-clause:

advise, agree (also *that*), *allow, attempt, bear, begin, consider* (also *that*), *continue, decide* (also *that*), *go on, hate, intend, like, love, mean* (also *that*), *need, permit, prefer, propose* (also *that*), *recommend* (also *that*), *regret* (also *that*), *remember* (also *that*), *remind* (also *that*), *start, stop, try, understand* (also *that*), *want, warn* (also *that*).

With these verbs the choice of complementation is oriented to one of the three following factors:

- Lexical semantics: the catenative has different meanings, and these require different complementation-types. In the following we distinguish between the 'gerund meaning' and the 'infinitive meaning' of individual catenatives.
- Syntax: considerations of grammar determine the choice (e.g. presence of a main clause object, possible conversion of the catenative into a prepositional verb, and so on).
- The choice is essentially free, though subject in some cases to certain collocational restrictions.

Gerunds and (where possible) *that*-clauses are usually semantically equivalent, though there are one or two exceptions. Certain syntactic factors may rule a *that*-clause out. Complementation types are discussed for individual verbs in the sections following. Section divisions correspond to the three main criteria just presented.

8.3.2.1 Gerund or infinitive according to meaning

Verbs in this group are: *consider, bear, go on, hate, like, love, mean, prefer, propose, regret, remember, stop, try, understand, want.*

(I) CONSIDER, BEAR, GO ON:

- *Consider*:

(25) a. The boss had considered giving Daly a different position.
    o Catenative meaning with gerund: 'think about'.

- *that*-clause also possible: . . . *had considered that he might give* . . . .
- Restriction: modal verb (*would*, *might*, etc.) necessary in sub-clause.

(25) b. The interviewers considered her to be unsuitable for the job.

- Catenative meaning with infinitive: 'believe/regard as'.
- Pattern: object + infinitive.
- Restriction: usual only with the **stative** verbs *be* and *have*.
- Passive catenative or *that*-clause more common: . . . *was considered to be* . . .; . . . *considered that he was unsuitable* . . . .

- *Bear*:

(26) a. She couldn´t bear people touching her.

- Catenative meaning with gerund: 'stand/tolerate'; factive: *People touched her and she couldn´t bear it.*
- Restriction: usual only with negated *can/could* in main clause.
- Related meaning with negated verb and no modal, but passive sense (see also *want* under (vi) below):
- The consequences don´t bear thinking about (= . . . *are too awful to be considered*).

(26) b. She couldn´t bear people to touch her.

- Catenative meaning with infinitive: also 'stand/tolerate', but infinitive non-factive: *People didn´t touch her, because she couldn´t bear it (and therefore prevented it)*.
- Pattern: infinitive, object + infinitive.

- *Go on*:

(27) a. The speaker went on talking about America.

- Catenative meaning with gerund: 'continue'; factive: *The speaker had been talking about America and continued to do so.*

(27) b. The speaker went on to talk about America.

- Catenative meaning with infinitive: 'changed the topic': *Having talked about Canada, the speaker went on to talk about America.*
- Pattern: infinitive.

(II) HATE, LIKE, LOVE, PREFER:

- *Hate, like, love:*

(28) a. I loved/hated going on that boat trip last week.
b. Simon likes relaxing by the pool.

- Catenative meaning with gerund: *hate* = 'strongly dislike', *like* = 'enjoy'; factive: attitude towards a single action, as in (28)a., or towards a habit/regularity, as in (28)b.

(28) c. Simon loves/hates to talk while he is resting.
d. Simon likes to relax by the pool.

- Catenative meanings with infinitive: *hate/love* retain the same meaning, but are only used in this combination for habits. Additionally, the infinitive in British English (though less so in American) always confers a non-factive sense, suggesting that occurrence of the action or state is 'theoretically possible' but rare, e.g. *Simon hates to talk while he is resting (and therefore refuses to admit visitors during such phases)*. Because of this more 'theoretical' connotation, the infinitive is used with conditionals: *I would love to see you on Saturday, but I won't promise anything as I would hate to disappoint you.*
- The verb *like* can also have this connotation, e.g. *Simon likes to relax by the pool, but rarely gets the chance to do so.*
- A second common meaning with the infinitive is 'want/think something good/advisable'. (28)d. could then mean, for instance, *Simon always relaxes by the pool, as he thinks that's the best place to do so.*
- Pattern: infinitive, object + infinitive.

- *Prefer:*

(29) a. I preferred cycling to walking.

- Catenative meaning with gerund: 'do both actions but like one of them more'; factive.

(29) b. I preferred to cycle rather than walk.

- Catenative meaning with infinitive: 'want/choose one action and reject the other'; non-factive.
- Pattern: infinitive, object + infinitive.

(III) REMEMBER, REGRET:

- *Remember:*

(30) a. Shane remembered sending off the package.

- Catenative meaning with gerund: 'recall to mind afterwards'; factive.
- *that*-clause also possible: . . . *remembered that he had sent off* . . . .

(30) b. Shane remembered to send off the package.

- Catenative meaning with infinitive: 'think of in advance and then do'; non-factive.
- Pattern: infinitive.

- *Regret*:

(31) a. Sheila regretted breaking up with Robbie.

- Catenative meaning with gerund: 'be sorry about afterwards'; factive.
- *that*-clause also possible: . . . *regretted that she had broken up* . . . .

(31) b. We regret to tell you that you have failed the test.

- Catenative meaning with infinitive: 'be sorry about the message following'; non-factive.
- With the infinitive *regret* is used purely as a set-phrase accompanying the introduction of bad news.
- Pattern: infinitive.

(IV) MEAN, PROPOSE:

- *Mean*:

(32) a. A job like hers means travelling all over the world.

- Catenative meaning with gerund: 'involve/have as a consequence'.

(32) b. I did not mean to travel so far.

- Catenative meaning with infinitive: 'intend'.
- Pattern: infinitive, object + infinitive.

- *Propose*:

(33) a. She proposed going to the cinema.

- Catenative meaning with gerund: 'suggest'.

(33) b. She proposed to go to the cinema.

- Catenative meaning with infinitive: 'intend'.
- Pattern: infinitive.

(V) STOP, TRY:

- *Stop*:

(34) a. She stopped talking to her next door neighbour.

- o Catenative meaning with gerund: 'cease/give up/discontinue', e.g. *Because of the conflict she did not talk to her next door neighbour any more.*

(34) b. She stopped to talk to her next door neighbour.

- o Catenative meaning with infinitive: 'break off/interrupt an (unnamed) action in order to do the action expressed by the infinitive, e.g. *She interrupted her walk home so that she could talk to her next door neighbour.*
- o Pattern: infinitive.
- o The syntax here is different from that of the gerund version. The main verb is not really used as a catenative. It is intransitive, and followed by an adverbial clause of purpose:

```
         S       P        A        P              A
```
(34) c. She stopped   [(in order) to talk to her next-door neighbour].

- *Try*:

    - o We deal here with the infinitive version first, as this is the most common of the two structures:

(35) a. We tried to push the car.

- o Catenative meaning with infinitive: 'attempt the infinitive action', e.g. *We tried to push the car, but it was too heavy for just the two of us to move.*
- o Pattern: infinitive.

(35) b. We tried pushing the car.

- o Catenative meaning with gerund: 'do something in order to achieve a further state or action', e.g. *We pushed the car as an attempt to start it.*
- o Factive, i.e. we actually did push the car, as a means to achieve something else. Could be paraphrased as *We tried to start the car by pushing it.*

(VI) UNDERSTAND, WANT:

- *Understand*:

(36) a. I can't understand Jane reacting like that.

- o Catenative meaning with gerund: 'see the reason for'; factive.

(36) b. I understood Jane to be in Barcelona.

- o Catenative meaning with infinitive: 'think that something is the case'.
- o Pattern: object + infinitive. Usually only with the verb *be*, both as full verb and auxiliary, and also with utterance verbs like *say*. In this respect like verbs of 'thinking', see Chapter 7, 7.4.2. A *that*-clause would be less elevated and more neutral in style: *I understood that Jane was in Barcelona*.

- *Want*:

(37) a. The car wants washing properly.

- o Catenative meaning with gerund: 'need'. Informal usage. The main clause subject is in this case not the subject, semantically speaking, but the object of the gerund. An alternative way of expressing this would be to say that the gerund meaning is passive. However, we cannot actually use the passive of the gerund here: **The car wants being washed*. This kind of meaning and syntax occurs also with *bear* (see under (i) above) and *need* (see 8.3.2.4 below).

(37) b. I want the car to be washed properly.

- o Catenative meaning with infinitive: 'wish/desire'.
- o Pattern: infinitive, object + infinitive.

8.3.2.2 Factive vs. implicative meaning

An important semantic point made above (see 8.2 and example (21)) is that gerunds usually indicate actions and states as **facts**, and therefore tend naturally to combine with catenatives that are factive, i.e. that presuppose (symbol ») the occurrence of the event or state referred to by the gerund:

(38) a. Our neighbours resent us buying a bigger car.
  » We bought a bigger car.
  b. Tom now regrets leaving the firm last year.
  » Tom left the firm last year.

Catenative + infinitive combinations, by contrast, are always non-factive: that is, there is **no** presupposition of the infinitive act occurring:

(39) a. Our neighbours appear to dislike us.
  ≯ Our neighbours dislike us.
  b. Tom wanted to leave the firm last year.
  ≯ Tom left the firm last year.

However, many catenative + infinitive structures, though all non-factive, indicate a certain kind of 'hidden meaning' of their own. This is what we called implicative meaning (symbol →), see Chapter 7.6:

(40) a. Tom has managed to find a new job.
    → Tom has found a new job.
  b. We happened to meet Tom in the pub.
    → We met Tom in the pub.

Implicative and factive meanings appear to have certain similarities. Let us compare the factive verb *regret* with the implicative verb *manage*:

(41) a. We regret selling the house.   [factive, i.e. X » Y]
    » We sold the house.
  b. We managed to sell the house.   [implicative, i.e. X → Y]
    → We sold the house.

Both sentences 'say' that *we sold the house*. That is, they both contain the same hidden meaning. But there is a significant difference in the respective relations to the main verb:

- In terms of time, presupposed elements **precede** what the main verb refers to, and are assumed to be the case prior to the utterance. The main verb and the sub-clause verb are independent of each other in their meanings:
  We sold the house and then regretted it.
- Implied elements **follow on** logically from the meaning of the main verb, i.e. they are actually part of that meaning:
  The sale of the house was what we managed.

Implicative meaning is therefore based on the semantic dependence of the sub-clause verb on the main verb. Factive meaning, on the other hand, is based on the semantic independence of the two verbs. This contrast is shown clearly in the **negation test**. When a factive catenative is negated, the sub-clause verb (= the gerund) remains positive and the presupposition stays the same. When an implicative catenative like *manage* is negated, the sub-clause verb is negated as well, and the positive implicative meaning is replaced by a negative one:

(42) a. We do not regret selling the house.   [presupposition same as positive,
    » We sold the house.   i.e. not-X » Y]
  b. We did not manage to sell the house.   [implication now also negative,
    → We did not sell the house.   i.e. not-X ↛ Y, and also not-X →
                                              not-Y]

As we saw in 7.6, not all implicative verbs behave like *manage* when negated. The implications of the positive form, however, are always cancelled by negation. By contrast, active presuppositions remain unaffected when the factive verb is negated: indeed, this is a requirement, since even the negated version only makes sense against the background of the presupposition. For example, *We regret selling the house* and *We don't regret selling the house* both presuppose that *We sold the house* is true.

With catenatives taking gerunds or infinitives as semantic alternatives, the two meanings very often show a factive–implicative contrast:

(43) a. Brian remembered calling Maisie last Tuesday.
        [factive: He called Maisie and remembered this afterwards.]
    b. Brian remembered to call Maisie last Tuesday.
        [implicative: He called Maisie (since he remembered beforehand that he had to do it).]
    c. Timpson went on growing very rich.
        [factive: He continued a process which had already begun.]
    d. Timpson went on to grow very rich.
        [implicative: He grew rich (later).]
    e. I did not like entering the cave alone.
        [factive: I entered the cave and then felt uncomfortable in there.]
    f. I did not like to enter the cave alone.
        [implicative: I did not enter the cave (because I didn't think it a good idea to do so alone).]

Again, this is a tendency only, and not a rule. Apart from anything else, of course, infinitive-bearing catenatives are by no means all implicative. Nevertheless, this is an interesting systematic dimension of semantic difference between the two complementation types with the same verb, and is yet another illustration of the deep intertwining of syntax and meaning.

8.3.2.3 Gerund or infinitive according to grammar

Verbs in this group select infinitive or gerund not according to semantics, but on syntactic grounds.

(I) PERMIT, ADVISE, RECOMMEND, ALLOW:

When there is an object (generally indirect) in the main clause, the infinitive is required:

(44) a. The company does not allow **people to smoke** inside the building.
    b. My friends **advised me to call** the police.

And in terms of functions, for the sake of clarity:

           S   P   Oi   Od P   A
(45) a. The company does not allow people   [to smoke inside the building].

          S   P Oi Od P   Od
     b. My friends advised me   [to call the police].

The infinitive remains even when the catenative is passivised and the main clause object is thus lost:

          S   P-pass   A   Od P   A
(46) a. People are not allowed (by the company)   [to smoke inside the building].
          S   P-pass   A   Od P   Od
     b. I was advised (by my friends)   [to call the police].

What this rule essentially boils down to is that the infinitive is required when the agent of the non-finite clause (i.e. the direct object) is referred to: *people, friends* (45)/(46).

When there is no object in the active main clause (i.e. when there is no reference to the agent of the non-finite clause), the gerund is required:

(47) a. The company does not allow **smoking** inside the building.
     b. My friends advised **calling** the police.

And functionally:

          S   P   Od P   A
(48) a. The company does not allow   [smoking inside the building].
          S   P   Od P   Od
     b. My friends advised   [calling the police].

Catenative passivisation is possible here as well, with the gerund clause becoming the subject:

          S P   A   P-pass   A
(49) a. [Smoking inside the building] is not allowed (by the company).
          S   P   Od   P-pass   A
     b. [Calling the police] was advised (by my friends).

This grammatical gerund/infinitive rule is important in the pedagogical context of a widespread error among EFL/ESL students, especially those with a European native language background:

(50) a. *To smoke is not allowed inside the building.
     b. *It is not allowed to smoke inside the building.

(50)a. and b. show the same error in different syntactic forms. (50)b. is the extraposition version of (50)a., and occurs with particular frequency. The use of the infinitive here is ruled out by the omission of the sub-clause agent. Only the gerund is possible: *Smoking is not allowed inside the building*. By the same token, sentences like **It is not recommended to eat too much fat*, or **It was not advised to walk in the town after dark* are similarly deviant, and require gerund clauses: *Eating too much fat is not recommended; Walking in the town after dark was not advised*.

(II) WARN, AGREE, DECIDE, REMIND:

This is a different case. These verbs can combine with prepositions to become prepositional verbs; as far as they have non-finite complementation, they then require the gerund:

(51) a. The lifeguard warned us *against* bathing near the rocks.
 b. The two major parties agree *on* developing renewable energy.
 c. We decided *on* going by train.

Otherwise the infinitive is necessary:

(52) a. The lifeguard warned us not to bathe near the rocks.
 b. The two major parties agree to develop renewable energy.
 c. We decided to go by train.

8.3.2.4 *Gerund or infinitive with little semantic or syntactic distinction*

There are no syntactic or major semantic differences between gerund or infinitive complementation after the following verbs: *attempt, begin, continue, dread, intend, need, start*. Nevertheless, there are one or two nuances of meaning to distinguish in the usage.

(I) ATTEMPT, BEGIN, CONTINUE, INTEND, START:

When there is an object (generally indirect) in the main clause, the infinitive is required:

(53) a. Our neighbour began mowing his lawn.
 b. Our neighbour began to mow his lawn.
 c. We will not attempt installing the new boiler until the spring.
 d. We will not attempt to install the new boiler until the spring.

Basically, (53)a. and b. and (53)c. and d. are interchangeable. However, there are contextual preferences, depending mainly on the type of action expressed by the non-finite verb. The more neutral form is always the infinitive. The gerund is chosen for **process-like** actions, especially when intensity and duration are stressed. In fact, we could insert the words *the process of* in (53)a. and c.: *Our neighbour began the process of mowing . . .*; *We will not attempt the process of installing . . . .*

The infinitive is also much preferred with stative verbs and passive forms:

(54) a. Faraday began to be more considerate towards other people.
 b. (?) Faraday began being . . . .
 c. After a short time in the jungle, we began to be assaulted by clouds of flies.
 d. (?). . . we began being assaulted . . . .

Similar conditions apply to *start, continue* and *intend*.

(II) DREAD:

This is a slightly different case. The basic meaning of *dread* (= *be very afraid*) is the same in each case, but the infinitive is restricted to certain collocations with verbs denoting 'mental visions', such as *think, imagine, envisage*, etc. Otherwise the standard form is the gerund:

(55) a. I dread to think what might happen to the roof in a storm.
 b. Cathy dreaded meeting Paul in the town.

Infinitive collocations such as that in (55)a. lend to the basic lexis of *dread* the connotation *dare not*, making it implicative in a negative sense: *I do not think . . .* (*because I am afraid of imagining the consequences*). With the gerund, *dread* might be called factive in the same sense that we applied the term to verbs like *avoid* and *risk*. (55)b. expresses 'meeting Paul in the town' as a given possibility (i.e. as a presupposition) that 'Cathy' was afraid of.

(III) NEED:

In this case there is no difference at all in terms of catenative meaning, nor indeed in the choice of gerund vs. infinitive as such. Equivalence, however, depends on the morphological distinction of passive vs. active. The following sentences mean the same:

(56) a. Your hair needs to be cut.
 b. Your hair needs cutting.

(56)b. shows the same construction and meaning as example (37)a. above with *want*. That is, the main clause subject *your hair* is from the semantic perspective the direct object of the sub-clause verb *cutting*. As with *want*, we might alternatively express this by saying that the gerund in (56)b. has passive meaning.

The complex sentence (II) 181

In fact the semantic equivalence to (56)a. (with the passive infinitive) seems to suggest this strongly. Rather curiously, however, we cannot replace the active gerund by the passive gerund here: **Your hair needs being cut*. So which is the most likely interpretation? The same question will arise later when we discuss the **false subject** construction with the infinitive (see 12.2). But we will leave the issue open here, and simply say that the active gerund following *need* is understood

- **either** in a passive sense;
- **or** in an active sense, but with the main clause subject interpreted as the gerund direct object.

Whichever explanation we favour, though, the facts of the case with example (56) are clear: the two sentences are only identical in meaning if the infinitive version is in the passive voice and the gerund version in the active voice.

8.4 Questions of tense and aspect

Tense and aspect, as morpho-syntactic categories, are not major concerns in a book of this kind (for more see, for example, SAGE), but they are relevant peripherally to the syntax of non-finite verb forms, as we saw previously with the infinitive. Time relations involved in gerund use therefore deserve a little attention here.

The gerund has two tense forms (the base form and the **perfect**), and in the perfect also an aspect distinction, as there is a **perfect progressive form**:

Base form	*Perfect simple*	*Perfect progressive*
eating	having eaten	having been eating

The passive equivalents here would be *being eaten* (see the beginning of this chapter) and *having been eaten*. The passive form of the perfect progressive (*having been being eaten*) is felt to be clumsy, and is usually avoided for stylistic reasons.

As with the infinitive, the **perfect forms** indicate pastness or completion, usually in relation to the catenative, but also with reference to other elements in the sentence. As the base form can also express this temporal relation there is a considerable degree of overlap, making the perfect largely redundant. In a few contexts, it is nevertheless necessary. Before discussing these, we will look briefly at time reference with the base form.

8.4.1 Temporal semantics of the gerund base form

As has already been said, the base forms of non-finite verbs are tenseless, morphologically and semantically speaking. They take their time reference from factors of context, including especially and typically the tenses of catenatives or other co-occurring main verbs (see also Chapter 7). This general principle is illustrated in the following gerund examples:

(57) a. I'm going to enjoy swimming in the ocean for a change.
 b. Walking in the woods on Sunday was a rather wet experience.

From the *going-to* form in (57)a. it is clear that the gerund is future-oriented, while in (57)b. it follows from the past tense of the main verb that *walking* refers to a past action. This would also normally be underlined by particular contexts of utterance, here perhaps a general discussion of a future plan in the first instance, and conversation on 'past weekend experiences', say, in the second.

An additional time factor can be implied in the lexical character of individual catenatives. Consider the following:

(58) a. Cathy regrets going to the party   (= Cathy **regrets** that she **went** . . .).
 b. I remembered seeing Tom on the beach   (= I **remembered** that I **had seen** . . .).

The finite versions in brackets indicate explicitly that each catenative is oriented to a later time than its respective gerund. The time-level distinction comes about in part lexically, as the catenative itself entails a retrospective view of the gerund action. A further factor is the systematic factive character of gerund meaning (see 8.2 above); the occurrence of the gerund action is presupposed as a fact, underlining the retrospective meaning of the catenative and thus the priorness of the gerund action temporally.

8.4.2 Temporal semantics of the perfect gerund

The **perfect gerund** explicitly introduces the meaning of pastness or completion, usually in relation to the catenative, but also with reference to other elements in the sentence. It therefore fits as an alternative to the base form in examples like those in (58):

(59) a. Cathy regrets having gone to the party.
 b. I remembered having seen Tom on the beach.

There is no grammatical necessity for the perfect gerund here, however, because the base form (as we have seen) does the job nicely on its own. The use of perfect forms where base forms express the same is regarded in general as a little stilted, and in neutral style is normally avoided. The (58) versions, then, would be preferred to those of (59). In contexts like these, the perfect gerund is therefore a redundant form. In other situations, however, the priorness interpretation of the base form may be ruled out if the catenative–gerund relation is not retrospective, or other time factors in the sentence contradict it. Use of the perfect gerund is then essential for the past meaning. Compare the following:

(60) a. I remember Paul leaving the meeting when Sanderstone arrived.
 b. I remember Paul having (already) left the meeting when Sanderstone arrived.

(60)a. and b. mean different things. The time clause introduces a further temporal relation into the sentence that has to be interpreted additionally. Did Paul leave before or after Sanderstone´s arrival? In (60)a. it was afterwards. In (60)b. it was beforehand, i.e. Paul had already left when Sanderstone arrived. This can be made clear by adding *already*, as indicated in the brackets. Here we need the distinguishing effect of the perfect because of the clausal addition.

The perfect may also be needed when the relation between catenative and gerund action is not retrospective, as in (61)a. and b., or is ambiguous in that respect, as in (61)c.:

(61) a. They anticipated eating at 9 o´clock.
      b. They anticipated having eaten at 9 o´clock.
      c. He resented spending his money on trivial amusements.
      d. He resented having spent his money on trivial amusements.

(61)a. and b. obviously point to distinct objects of anticipation: in the first case that the subjects would begin to eat at the stated time, and in the second that they would then already have done so. In (61)c. it is left open whether the subject´s resentment already arose during the act of spending or did not actually occur until after it. (61)d. comes down clearly in favour of 'afterwards'. It therefore has a disambiguating function with respect to the possible retrospective interpretation of (61)c.

8.4.3 The question of aspect

As seen above, differences in aspect are not shown morphologically in the base form of the gerund. That is, if we take as an example the base form *running*, there is no progressive equivalent **being running*. On the other hand, one might think that as an *-ing*-form the gerund already carries progressive meaning, and that it is actually a 'simple form' that is missing. However, this is not so. Semantically, in fact, gerunds are usually construed as perfective, that is, as carriers of simple form meaning, denoting actions as a whole. This does not rule out imperfective interpretations (i.e. progressive meaning). Indeed, we have just discussed a possible progressive reading of (61)c. Imperfective meaning, however, is chiefly determined by the semantic nature of the catenative or other elements of context which suggest being 'in the middle of' an ongoing action. Even then, there may be an alternative perfective interpretation, as also with (61)c.

In principle, then, the base form of the gerund will accommodate imperfect interpretation, but its 'default value' is perfective. (61)a., for instance, clearly means . . . *anticipated that they would eat* (= *begin to eat*) *at 9 o´clock*. The imperfective version . . . *would be eating at 9 o´clock* (indicating *eat* as in progress at the stated time) could only be rendered with the gerund by the addition of an appropriate adverbial phrase, e.g. *They anticipated being in the middle of eating at 9 o´clock*.

With the perfect gerund, this is a different matter. Here we do have aspect differentiation:

(62) a. I regret having spoken to Rodney (= I regret that I spoke . . .).
      b. I regret having been speaking to Rodney (when you called) (= I regret that I was speaking . . .).

In finite terms, then, the simple form of the perfect gerund (*having spoken*) is equivalent to the past simple, while the progressive form of the perfect gerund (*having been speaking*) corresponds to the past progressive. There are two things to point out here: firstly, for stylistic reasons the finite progressive is often preferred to the perfect progressive gerund, which can sound stilted and is in any case 'a bit of a mouthful'; secondly, the base form can replace *having spoken* in (62)a. (*I regret speaking . . .*), but not *having been speaking* in (62)b.: *I regret speaking to Rodney when you called*. This links to the point made previously that base form gerunds are usually construed as perfective. The imperfective variant is the perfect progressive gerund, i.e. the missing base form progressive is compensated for by using the perfect progressive (where this is possible) or, alternatively, using a finite progressive, as illustrated in the brackets in (62)b. In other words, to repeat the point, the imperfective partner of the base form gerund is the perfect progressive: as long, that is, as the base form is retrospective in the given context. Compare:

(63) a. She remembered going down the stairs when she heard the noise in the kitchen.
      (= She heard the noise in the kitchen and then went down the stairs.)
      b. She remembered having been going down the stairs when she heard the noise in the kitchen.
      (= She was already in the process of going down the stairs when she heard the noise.)

A context for (63)a. might be that the subject was upstairs when she heard a noise below and then went down to investigate. (63)b. is a framework situation. The subject is already on the way down when she hears the noise (and, say, then runs back upstairs to her mobile phone to call for help). A more common way of expressing this (only (63)b., though!) is simply in a *that*-clause with the progressive: *She remembered that she was going down the stairs when . . .*).

8.5 The action nominal

Gerund clauses can often be expressed alternatively by noun phrases in which the *-ing*-form is kept. The resulting full noun phrase is known as the **action nominal**:

(64) a. **Driving the car** is Martin's job.   [gerund]
      b. **The driving of the car** is Martin's job. [action nominal]

Assuming for the sake of simplicity that we have converted (64)a. to (64)b., we can say that the sub-clause in (64)a., along with the gerund in predicator function, has been lost. In the action nominal version, the *-ing-*form has simply become the head of a noun phrase, reducing a complex sentence in (64)a. to a simple sentence in (64)b. The direct object of the gerund in (64)a. (*the car*) is now expressed in a postmodifying prepositional phrase with *of*.

With that we now pass from sentence to phrase level, and in doing so really go beyond the scope of this chapter. However, there are certain systematic relations (i.e. regular contrasts and similarities) between the gerund and the action nominal that deserve a brief word of explanation, and this is an appropriate place to compare them.

A first point concerns meaning. In principle the two constructions mean the same. However, the action nominal is often chosen to give emphasis to the action itself. It is also stylistically more elevated and is often found in formal or official contexts, for instance on notices relating to public behaviour. If the agent is generalised or unmentioned, the definite article precedes:

(65) a. The hunting or harming of wildlife in this wood is prohibited by law.
 b. The sailing of model boats on the lake is not allowed.

As the action nominal profiles the action itself and its procedure more than the gerund, it is the action nominal that is invariably chosen for reference to the manner in which something occurs. The gerund, on the other hand, is usually taken to express the fact that something occurs. Subject specification with an action nominal requires an *s-*genitive noun or possessive determiner, which is also one of the gerund options, of course:

(66) a. I did not like Jerry´s riding of the horse. He was not very gentle with it.
   [action nominal: *the way in which he rode it*]
 b. I did not like Jerry´s riding the horse. Celia should have ridden it. It was her turn.
   [gerund: *the fact that he rode it*]

As both constructs can be used with intransitive verbs, there may be ambiguity, e.g. if we leave out mention of 'the horse' in (66).
 (67)a. can then mean either (67)b., or (67)c.:

(67) a. I did not like Jerry´s riding.
 b. I did not like the way that Jerry rode. [action nominal interpretation]
 c. I did not like the fact that Jerry rode. [gerund interpretation]

This ambiguity only occurs here also because both gerunds and action nominals can be preceded by genitives and possessive determiners. However, only the gerund allows reduction to a noun or object pronoun, whereas only the action nominal allows a definite article before it:

(68) a. I did not like the riding.
 [action nominal interpretation only: *the way the rider rode*]
 b. I did not like Jerry riding.
 [gerund interpretation only: *the fact that Jerry rode*]

To sum up, here is an overview of the syntactic contrasts between the two forms:

Gerund	Action nominal
Verbal predicator in sub-clause.	Noun phrase.
Can be preceded by *s*-genitive noun/possessive determiner, or ordinary noun/object pronoun: but **not** by the definite article: **The driving cars.*	Can be preceded by *s*-genitive noun/possessive determiner, or definite article: but **not** by an ordinary noun or object pronoun: **Alan driving of cars.*
Can occur with nothing preceding it. *Driving cars.*	Always needs a determiner: *Alan's/The driving of cars*, but **not** **Driving of cars*.
Patient of action as direct object: *Alan's driving the car.*	Patient of action connected by *of*-phrase: *Alan's driving of the car.*
Can be further described (modified) by adverbs: *Alan's driving the car dangerously.*	Can be further described (modified) by premodifying adjectives: *Alan's dangerous driving of the car.*
Can be formed from stative verbs: *John's realising the problem.*	Cannot be formed from stative verbs: **John's realising of the problem.*
Has a perfect form: *Alan's having driven the car.*	Has no perfect form: **Alan's having driven of the car.*

Exercises

Exercise 1

Analyse the following sentences in terms of sentence functions:

1 We didn't mind missing the film on Saturday.
2 Repairing old cars is Frank's favourite pastime.
3 Saul didn't like his little sister borrowing his bike.
4 Berkdale's leaving the company at this time has caused a sensation.
5 The chairman can't bear people criticising him.
6 She doesn't remember lending the book to anyone.
7 Your saying those things to Ruth really upset her.
8 Clara was looking forward to seeing her parents again.
9 Her worst nightmare was driving in heavy traffic.
10 The teacher accused Phil of cheating in the test.

Exercise 2

Fill in the gaps, using the gerund or infinitive forms of the verbs in brackets. Any nouns or pronouns in the brackets indicate the subject of the verb:

1   Some maths teachers do not permit ……. (*their pupils, use*) pocket calculators.
2   Tony suggested ……. (*we, consult*) a child therapist in London.
3   Somehow Paul can never avoid …….. (*upset*) people, although he never means ……. (*do*) so.
4   You may not remember …….. (*meet*) me at the party, but you definitely liked ……. (*listen to*) my jokes.
5   As Kate did not like ……. (*enter*) the building alone, she put off ……. (*go in*) until other police officers arrived.
6   If you need ……. (*see*) a particular doctor at the clinic, it could mean ……. (*wait*) for some time.
7   Let us now stop ……. (*talk*) about Scottish history and go on …… (*look at*) the present condition of the country.
8   Tony and Geoff are considering ……. (*go*) to Morocco for their holidays, but as Geoff hates ……. (*be*) in the sun all day, I have discreetly advised ……. (*they, try*) Finland instead.
9   I don´t deny ……. (*watch*) Chelsea on certain occasions, but I much prefer … (*see*) Arsenal play, and will go on ……. (*support*) them as usual, even if they do badly.

Exercise 3

State the differences in meaning between the a. and b. sentences in the following, and provide possible contexts.

1   a. He stopped to buy flowers on his way home.
    b. He stopped buying flowers on his way home.
2   a. They tried to open the windows, but without success.
    b. They tried opening the windows but without success.
3   a. We regret to inform guests that there will be no meals this evening.
    b. We regret informing guests that there will be no meals this evening.
4   a. What do you propose to do?
    b. What do you propose doing?
5   a. I didn´t remember calling the Sampsons.
    b. I didn´t remember to call the Sampsons.

9 Non-finite clauses in the complex sentence (III)
The participles

9.0 The participles

We now come to the participle, our third type of non-finite verb form after the infinitive (Chapter 7) and the gerund (Chapter 8). There are two main types: the present participle, an *-ing*-form like the gerund (e.g. *painting*), and the past participle, with a regular form ending in *-ed* (e.g. *painted*), and a variety of irregular forms. These differ individually from one another depending on the particular verb concerned.

With all regular verbs, the past participle is always formally identical with the past tense. Some irregular verbs also have the same form for past tense and participle (*buy* is given as an example below); more usually, however, irregular past participles have their own distinct forms:

Infinitive	*Past tense*	*Past participle*
walk (*regular*)	walked	walked
buy (*irregular*)	bought	bought
do (*irregular*)	did	done

A major phrase-level function of the participles is as **morphological formatives**, i.e. they contribute to the construction of composite finite verb phrases (see also Chapter 5, 5.1). In this role the present participle is instrumental in forming the progressive, and the past participle in constructing the perfect tense and the passive voice:

(1) a We are **painting** the kitchen door.
 b. We have **painted** the door.
 c. The wall is going to be **painted** too.

Both participle types feature in perfect and passive progressives, though the past participle in the perfect progressive and the present participle in the passive are solely forms of *be* (i.e. *been* and *being* respectively):

(2) a. We have **been painting** the kitchen door.
    b. The door is **being painted**.

Participles also occur

- as adjectives premodifying nouns (*a **satisfying**/**cooked** meal*);
- as adjectives functioning at sentence level as Cs (*The meal was **satisfying**/**cooked***);
- as predicators of clauses postmodifying nouns (*a meal **satisfying** all our needs/**cooked** to perfection*);
- as predicators of clauses in the phrase function of adjectival complement (*happy **lying** here on the beach*).

All these cases are dealt with fully in Chapters 10 and 11 on Complex phrases.

What interests us in this chapter are participles used in a similar way to that described in the two preceding chapters on gerunds and infinitives: that is, as predicators introducing sub-clauses at sentence-level:

(3) a. **Taking** her child tightly by the hand, Claire left the room.
    b. The king entered the scene **followed** by three servants.

With certain exceptions, participle clauses are not closely tied to particular main clause verbs. Subject to constraints of meaning, they can appear with almost any verb in the main clause. This syntactic independence means that they are not generally part of the main verb complementation, and the main verb therefore does not have a catenative relationship to the participle. In this respect participles differ from a large body of usage with gerunds and infinitives, where the individual main verb, as we have seen, can have a strong determining effect on the type of non-finite clause following it. In the case of participles, this kind of relationship is confined mainly to verbs of perception, as we will see further below.

9.1 The present participle and its clause

As the present participle and the gerund have the same form, they are easily confused with one another. However, they are syntactically and semantically very different, and should be carefully distinguished.

Participle clauses at sentence-level are always adverbial in function. Within its own clause, the participle functions just like other non-finites, i.e. as predicator:

```
           A  P      Od      A       A        S  P   Od
(4) a.   [Taking her child tightly by the hand], Claire left the room.
           S   P         A        A   P        Od
    b.   A man came into my office  [carrying a large briefcase].
```

It is the adverbial function that distinguishes participle clauses syntactically from gerund clauses. Gerund clauses function in the same way as noun phrases, i.e. as **S, Oi, Od, Cs** or **Co**. They are also 'attracted' to prepositions, as we will see when we come to discuss prepositional phrases. But they can rarely be adverbial clauses. Participle clauses, on the other hand, are only adverbial in function. This also points to the fact that present participles and gerunds differ radically from each other in terms of meaning, as we will see further below.

The adverbial function accounts for the basically flexible position of the participle clause, which in principle can precede or follow the main clause, as shown in the examples.

9.1.1 Subject relations

In their subject relations, participles are similar to other non-finites. The subject of the participle is generally implied, and in sentences like those in (4) is understood as identical with the main verb subject:

(5) a. [↓Taking her child tightly by the hand], Claire left the room.
    (S)←——————————————————S

b. A man came into my office [↓carrying a large briefcase].
   S————————————→(S)

The presence of a direct object in the main clause, as in the example in (4)a. and (5)a., does not alter this basic principle:

(6) a. Joe greeted Dick [↓standing on one leg].
       S——Od   →(S)

b. I washed the dog [↓using the garden hose].
   S——Od   →(S)

This does change, however, when the participle clause becomes part of the main verb complementation and a catenative relation arises:

(7) a. Joe saw Tim [↓going into the lift].
       S   Od→(S)

b. I noticed the dog [↓playing with the garden hose].
   S   Od→(S)

In this case it is the main clause object that is understood as the subject of the participle clause. Even here, though, the sense may allow a non-catenative interpretation as an alternative, in which case the subject–subject relation kicks in. This is unlikely in (7), but certainly possible, giving (as alternatives) the respective meanings *Joe saw Tim as Joe was going into the lift* and *I noticed the dog as I was playing with the garden hose*. The ordinary way of avoiding such ambiguity is to start with the participle clause when the subject–subject meaning is intended:

(8) a. [↓ Going into the lift], Joe saw Tim.
        (S) ←――――――― S   Od

   b. [↓ Playing with the garden hose], I noticed the dog.
        (S) ←――――――――― S   Od

We deal with catenative cases and their possible ambiguities later in the chapter, in particular when we take a more detailed look at 'perception constructions' like those in (7). What we wish to emphasise for the moment is that in the absence of a catenative interpretation the implied participle subject **must** be identical with that of the main verb. If this is obviously not the case, the sentence is ungrammatical:

(9) a. *Raining heavily, we ran for shelter.
     b. *Losing control of the sails, Daly's yacht turned on its side.

These examples show what are called **misrelated** or (rather less formally) 'dangling' participles. The grammar clashes with the sense, often creating, as here, a grotesque or comical effect: people do not 'rain heavily', nor do yachts lose control of themselves, though in fact that is what these sentences express according to their syntax. As we will see in the following section, there is a certain tolerance of misrelated participles in a few closely defined cases. Generally, though, if the subjects of the two clauses are distinct, we have to change the syntax.

9.1.1.1 Variant subjects

One way of restoring balance and correctness to the sentences in (9) is to replace the participle clause by a finite one:

(10) a. As it was raining heavily, we ran for shelter.
     b. Daly's crew lost control of the sails and the yacht turned on its side.

Another solution is simply to add the separate subject to the participle clause.

(11) a. We ran for shelter, the rain pouring down heavily.
     b. Daly's crew losing control of the sails, the yacht turned on its side.

As this operation is not possible with pronouns, the *it* in (10)a. has to disappear and the wording must be changed accordingly. Participle clauses with their own subjects are traditionally called **absolute**. Stylistically, they have a literary character and do not occur outside formal contexts. In more neutral style the participle subject is introduced via the preposition *with*:

(12) a. We ran for shelter, **with** the rain pouring down heavily.
　　 b. **With** Daly´s crew losing control of the sails, the yacht turned on its side.

With often carries a causal note, as suggested in (12)b. It is used especially to underline causality when particular circumstances are responsible for something:

(13) a. With Charles and Julia getting married, we won´t be going on holiday this year.
　　 b. They felt forced to sell the house, with developers buying up the land around them.

This is a strong tendency also with stative verbs (see below).

Misrelated participles are acceptable in certain kinds of comment clause which have the character of set phrases:

(14) a. He´s dissatisfied with his performance, judging by the look on his face.
　　 b. Considering how long she has been learning French, her pronunciation is poor.
　　 c. Strictly speaking, you need a special pass to enter the building.

Informally, they are also tolerated in certain impersonal constructions, when the subject is referred to elsewhere in the sentence, or with passives when there is a clear link to a stated or implied *by*-agent:

(15) a. The gas-tap must be installed using special equipment (= by someone, using . . .).
　　 b. When leaving the house, it occurred to me that I had not phoned Ellen.

9.1.2 Semantics of the present participle

The present participle has the same basic imperfective meaning as the finite progressive form. This is not surprising: after all, the present participle is actually used in forming the progressive (see also above).

9.1.2.1 The framework situation

Taking the finite progressive briefly as our starting-point, we can say that it expresses an act as **ongoing**, i.e. in the course of occurrence, at an implied or stated point of time. Aspect works together with tense. The tense used (e.g. present or past) tells us where the relevant point of time is located (i.e. in the present or in the past). Thus the sentence *I am writing a letter*, for example, means that the act of writing is ongoing 'now', at the moment of speaking. 'Now', in other words, is a point of time implied as being inside the act of writing, or, as we might alternatively put it, as 'falling' or intruding into the event contour:

(16)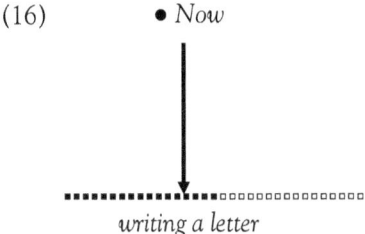

This **framework situation**, as we call it, is crucial to an understanding of imperfective meaning (see also SAGE, pp. 313ff.). The act referred to in the progressive forms a kind of 'frame' into which the implied point of time falls. This time point could be overtly stated (e.g. *at 10 pm*), or implied in an interrupting act in the simple form (e.g. *. . . when Jenny called*), or given as a combination of both:

(17)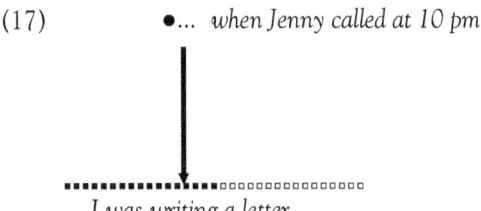

In essence, the present participle has the same aspectual meaning and can be represented in the same way:

(18) a. Copeland hurt his arm **playing** tennis.
      (= . . . when/while he was playing . . .)
   b. She tore her dress **getting** out of the car.
      (= . . . when/as she was getting . . .)

And as a framework diagram:

(19)

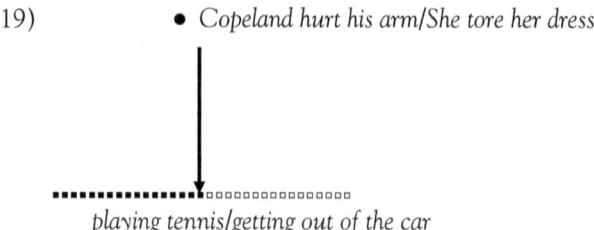

In fact, participles can appear with time conjunctions, especially in more formal style, to emphasise this time-frame sense (. . . *while playing tennis*; . . . *when getting out of the car*). The basic framework meaning is not necessarily always given in this strict sense. It can often glide over into a more general sense of 'ongoingness' and suggest a **parallel action** to the activity or state expressed in the main clause. In this case it may then imply 'throughout':

(20) a. Bryant left for work still wearing his carpet slippers.
 b. Be careful climbing those cliffs!
 c. Passengers must remain seated going through the tunnel.

Through this reference to accompanying actions, participles typically express a more detailed 'break-down' of the main clause action, often conveying a meaning of manner or **attendant circumstance**:

(21) a. Mac spends all his time training dogs.
 b. She sat at a corner-table drinking coffee and reading the paper.
 c. On the TGV we had to travel from Karlsruhe to Paris standing in the corridor.

Parallel actions can additionally take on **instrumental** overtones:

(22) a. We emptied the tank using a hand-pump.
 b. Lying flat on his stomach in the undergrowth, Jason observed the bears unnoticed.
 c. They crossed the rest of the desert riding on camels.

Despite this, however, participle clauses are usually regarded primarily as adverbial clauses of time (if specification is required), since the prominent meaning is the simultaneous or parallel one. We have already seen that participles can appear with conjunctions. These can in fact specify other meanings of the clause in addition to the time factor in the participle:

(23) a. Although wearing a suit, I was not admitted to the hotel restaurant. [concession]
　　b. If intending to cross the Channel by ferry this weekend, travellers must be prepared for long delays. [condition]

9.1.2.2 Verbs with a point-telic meaning

Point-telic verbs refer to **momentary** actions, such as *arrive, break, drop, hit, leave*, etc. They represent a kind of 'border-crossing', so to speak, from one state to another, e.g. with *break* from 'whole' to 'broken' in one moment of time (on the concept of 'telic' and other verbal action types, see also SAGE, pp. 298–300). In present participle form they can create a meaning of **sequence**:

(24) a. Dropping all their tools, the burglars escaped in panic.
　　b. He dived too strongly into the shallow pool, hitting the bottom and breaking his arm.
　　c. Arriving at the station almost too late, we rushed straight to the barrier at Platform 9 ¾.

The sequence of acts is understood as being in the order in which they are mentioned. Public media commentaries make considerable use of point-telic participles, where appropriate, as they can 'economise' on language volume. The resulting sentences, though, are often incomplete (i.e. without a main clause):

(25) a. Rover Boy there jumping the fourth slightly ahead of Time Out and What's Up, but landing awkwardly and losing ground as Time Out challenges strongly on the far side.
　　b. The Queen leaving the plane now in front of Prince Philip and coming down the gangway to greet the Mayor of Berlin.

9.1.2.3 The present participle of stative verbs

Stative verbs do not normally appear in the progressive form, as they do not denote actions, but express states and acts of perception (see also SAGE, p. 324). Consequently, we might not expect them to occur in the present participle form either. However, they do, though usually with a special meaning. A stative present participle typically conveys a **causal** relationship, particularly in initial position:

(26) a. Thinking the banknotes were forged, Ray contacted the police.
　　　 (= As he thought . . .)
　　b. Trusting the salesman's promise, we bought the car immediately.
　　　 (= Because we trusted . . .)
　　c. Feeling rather ill, I drove to the local doctor's surgery.
　　　 (= As I was feeling . . .)

196 *The complex sentence (III)*

In general, this semantic relation also remains when the participle clause follows. However, some stative verb participles in this position can alternatively convey the parallel ('accompanying') meaning:

(27) a. Ray contacted the police thinking the banknotes were forged.
     (= When he contacted ..., he thought ...)
   b. I drove to the local doctor's surgery feeling rather ill.
     (= During the drive I felt ...)
   c. We bought the car immediately, trusting the salesman's promise.
     (= When we bought the car, we trusted ...)

A lot depends here on the individual verb and whether its lexical meaning is amenable to the idea of an 'accompanying circumstance'. Sometimes, as in (27)a. and b. with *think* and *feel*, the parallel meaning is furthered especially when there is no pause (and in writing no comma) before the sub-clause.

As indicated above (see 9.1.1.1), a separate participle subject introduced by *with* strongly underlines causal meaning; and this is particularly so with stative participles:

(28) a. With Jonathan being out of work, we won't be going on holiday this year.
   b. The house in the town is very convenient, especially with Cathy having no car.

9.1.3 Catenatives followed by the present participle

Catenative use with the present participle is focused largely on verbs of sensory perception, like *see, hear, feel, notice, watch*, etc. A main clause object is always present. The participle clause has its usual adverbial function:

```
          S     P       Od         A  P                    A
(29) a. Ginny heard her husband  [playing with their children].
          S  P     Od   A        P       Od          A
     b. We felt the plane     [gathering speed on the runway].
```

Note again what was said about subject relations and catenatives in 9.1.1: here the direct object of the main clause is the implied subject of the participle.

9.1.3.1 The choice between participle and infinitive

Verbs of perception are complemented not only by present participles, but alternatively by the infinitive without *to* (see Chapter 7, 7.4.1). The difference is linked to the aspectual semantic distinction between simple and progressive forms:

(30) a. Hannah watched Charlotte **swim** across the river.
     (= Charlotte swam across the river and Hannah watched this.)

b. Hannah watched Charlotte **swimming** across the river.
      (= Hannah watched Charlotte as Charlotte was swimming across the river.)
   c. Jamie saw Ron **eat** a sandwich.
      (= Ron ate a sandwich and Jamie saw this.)
   d. Jamie saw Ron **eating** a sandwich.
      (= Jamie saw Ron as Ron was eating a sandwich.)

The infinitives in (30)a. and c. show the simple form meaning of **completion**, i.e. the **whole** act was perceived in each case: Charlotte swam from one river bank to the other and Ron ate the whole sandwich. The present participles, on the other hand, only express the respective acts as in progress, i.e. there is no entailment in (30)b. that Charlotte actually reached the other river bank, nor in (30)d. that Jamie ate all of the sandwich. This basic distinction leads to a common preference for the participle when the process of the action or its manner of occurrence is in focus, while the infinitive tends to stress a whole 'occasion' of the action or the fact that it occurred:

(31) a. I´ve heard Maria sing. (= I´ve experienced her performance.)
     b. I´ve heard Maria singing. (= I´ve experienced her technique and style.)
     c. We´ve watched the horses race. (= their behaviour over the whole length of a race.)
     d. We´ve watched the horses racing. (= the style and speed of their gallop.)

Note that although participle clauses are adverbial after verbs of perception, infinitive clauses function as object complements:

```
           S       P       Od      Co P         A
(32) a. Hannah watched Charlotte [swim across the river].
           S     P  Od  Co P      Od
     b. Jamie saw Ron   [ eat a sandwich].
```

This is because they do not refer to the circumstances of perception (an adverbial relation), but to part of its object.

9.1.3.2 Other kinds of catenative

Other catenatives commonly taking participle complementation are similar to acts of perception, though they do not strictly denote them. These are verbs referring to other types of 'intrusive' experience like *catch, come across, discover, find, leave*, etc.:

(33) a. I came across Craig and Bryant lying on the beach.
     b. A passer-by has found the body floating in the lake.
     c. The children left Mr Tulliver mowing his lawn.
     d. My wife caught the dog eating grapes from the table.

Another group consists of causative verbs such as *get*, *have* and *keep*:

(34) a. You always keep people waiting!
b. I had/got the car running again in no time.

One or two intransitive verbs belong here also, e.g. *remain*, *stay*, and *get* in the sense of 'become':

(35) a. Several passengers remained standing in the train.
b. Julia stayed sitting on the couch.
c. We must get moving as quickly as possible.

Exceptionally, the participle clauses here function as complements, rather than as adverbials:

```
         S    P       Od     Co  P        A         A
(36) a.  I   had got  the car  [running again]  in no time.
         S    P       Cs  P              A
     b.  We must get     [moving] as quickly as possible.
```

9.1.4 Questions of tense and aspect

Tense and aspect forms of the present participle are identical to those of the gerund (see Chapter 8, 8.4). There is a base form and a perfect form, with the aspect distinction **simple–progressive** in the perfect only. The perfect is known traditionally as the **perfect participle**:

Base form (present participle)	Perfect participle (simple)	Perfect participle (progressive)
eating	having eaten	having been eating

As with the other non-finite perfects, the perfect participle indicates pastness or completion, generally speaking relative to the time level attached to the main verb and manifested in its tense form. It is equivalent, that is, to the finite past tense, the finite present perfect, or the finite past perfect, depending on context. As might be expected, perfect participle clauses are adverbial in function, like their base form equivalents:

```
            A        P       Od      S  P      A        A
(37) a. [Having mown the lawn], I went into the house for a drink.
        (= After I had mown the lawn, . . .)
            S   P     A          A       A      P      Od       A
     b. We settled cosily into our theatre seats, [having deposited our coats in the
        cloakroom].
        (= . . ., after we had deposited . . .)
```

In terms of time reference, the perfect participle and the present participle are quite distinct. Unlike the case with the gerund, that is, there is no time-semantic overlap between base form and perfect. This is because the present participle (due to its 'progressive' meaning) always expresses an action parallel to that of the main verb. The aspect relation thus implies also a 'same-time' tense relation. To express '**beforeness**' we therefore always need the perfect participle form. A further point is that in the perfect, as has been said, there is an aspect distinction. Unlike the present participle, which by its very nature can only have imperfective (i.e. 'progressive') meaning, the 'beforeness' of the perfect participle will naturally admit both perfective and imperfective meanings, and therefore both aspects, simple and progressive:

(38) a. I don't really feel like any food now, **having been eating** for most of the afternoon. (= . . . as I have been eating . . .)
 b. **Having been cooking** when you called yesterday, I did not hear the phone. (= As I was cooking yesterday . . .)

A further point that we can see from (38) is that the perfect participle can be used to express causal meaning, or at least causal overtones. The conjunction *as* makes this clear in the finite paraphrases. This is a contextual (and/or lexical) connotation. It is not part of the participle meaning as such, but results simply from the close nature of the time relation between the two clauses. Causal meaning is essentially decided by the overall semantic relation between the two clauses, i.e. whether what they respectively refer to can be regarded logically as causally linked or not. Despite the heavy role of context here, though, perfect participles are very often favoured when causal meaning has to be expressed, especially if a stylistically less direct and rather more incidental and nuanced reference to causality is intended.

9.1.4.1 Voice: the passive

Passive forms of the present participle are (as one might expect) identical to those of the gerund. The passive perfect participle, though grammatically possible, is usually avoided for stylistic reasons of awkwardness. This is indicated by the question mark in brackets:

Passive present participle	*Passive perfect participle (simple)*	*Passive perfect participle (progressive)*
being eaten	having been eaten	(?) having been being eaten

9.1.5 Present participles as adjectives

This is phrase-level syntax and belongs, strictly speaking, in Chapter 4. However, a note is appropriate here as we have been talking in this chapter about the base meaning of the present participle, and it is the meaning which makes the participle available for an adjectival role. The present participle occurs as an adjective premodifying nouns, i.e. in attributive position, as it is called traditionally:

> *freezing rain, standing passengers, a flying object, blossoming flowers, a smiling face.*

The participle refers to an action performed by or happening to the noun-referent and can be paraphrased by a relative clause, e.g. *freezing rain* = *rain that is freezing*. This shows that even as an adjective the participle keeps a certain verbal identity in semantic terms: on the other hand, it also loses some of its force as a verb. It cannot be complemented. We cannot, for instance, say **a flying through the air object*. It therefore does not have a predicator function here and is not clausal. True, it can be further described by an adverb, but this must precede the participle in the same way that adverbs precede adjectives: *quickly freezing rain* (not **freezing quickly rain*). Furthermore, the participle cannot be used semantically in this way simply to refer to any action that the noun-referent is performing. We cannot normally call a girl who is eating, e.g., **an eating girl*. The participle must signify a characteristic, a form of context-typical behaviour, placing the noun it describes in a certain 'category': *standing passengers* are those in buses and trains who are not seated, *freezing rain* is a certain type of rain, and so on.

On the other hand there are restrictions on adjectival use. There are no comparative and superlative forms, and participles cannot be used **predicatively** (i.e. complementing verbs) in the sense of adjectives (**The object looked flying*). A participle following *be* is quite simply regarded as forming a progressive: *The faces were smiling.*

Participles used in this part-verb and part-adjective role just described can best be regarded as 'verbal adjectives'. However, some of these, mainly with abstract meanings, have lost their verbal character completely over time, and have developed lexically into full adjectives. Examples like *boring, comforting, interesting, worrying*, etc., behave grammatically as normal adjectives: they can be compared (*more/less worrying*) and occur predicatively: *The story seemed interesting at first, but turned out rather boring.*

9.1.6 Distinguishing the present participle from the gerund

As was said at the beginning of the chapter, it is analytically important to make a clear distinction between the present participle and the gerund. As they share the same form and both function as predicators in their own sub-clauses, they can easily be confused. In clausal terms, however, they have very different functions and meanings, as we have shown, and should therefore be kept apart conceptually. Below, in table form, is a summary of the contrasts.

Present participle clauses – Sentence functions	Gerund clauses – Sentence functions
Adverbial (A): *Lennie lay on the couch reading.*	**Subject (S):** *Reading improves one's mind.*
Never subject, object, or complement.	**Direct object (Od):** *I like reading.*
	Subject complement (Cs): *My favourite pastime is reading.*
	Never adverbial (apart from the exceptional case of *go shopping/swimming/jogging,* etc.)

Present participle meaning	Gerund meaning
Imperfective: refers to an ongoing action accompanying the main clause action or interrupted by it: *Grumbling profusely, the janitor unlocked the school doors. I saw Billy crossing the street (*and going into a drugstore).*	**Perfective:** refers to an action or state as a whole: *I remember Billy crossing the street and going into a drugstore.* **Factive** in tendency: complements many catenatives that presuppose prior occurrence of the gerund action: *Tom regretted buying the house. Geraldine hated studying economics.*

As we will see later, there are also clear distinctions at phrase level.

9.2 The past participle and its clause

In function, past participle clauses are similar to present participle clauses, i.e. they are mainly adverbial. As clauses, they also have an accompanying (or parallel) meaning, and the same kind of subject relation:

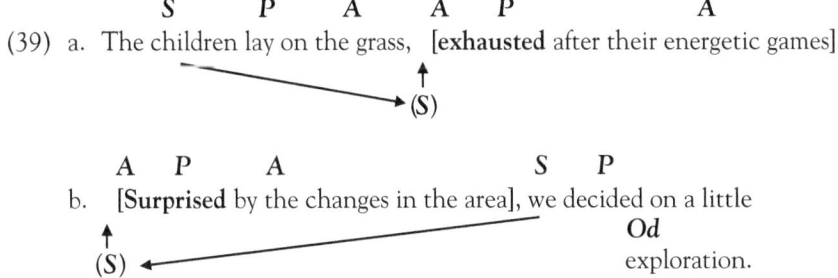

(39) a. The children lay on the grass, [**exhausted** after their energetic games].

b. [**Surprised** by the changes in the area], we decided on a little exploration.

However, there is an important contrast between the individual semantics of the two participles themselves:

- the present participle is active (in terms of voice), and imperfective (in terms of aspect);
- the past participle is generally passive (in terms of voice), and always perfective (in terms of aspect).

The past participle, in other words, expresses a state (and not an action) as an 'accompanier' to the reference in the main clause. The state, however, **results** from a previous action and therefore can be said to imply one. With transitive verbs, the implied subject of the past participle is the patient of this implied action. The past participle thereby confers a passive sense on the participle clause, and in many (if not most) cases can be understood as a kind of 'passive participle' shortening an implied passive construction. This is underlined by the fact that paraphrase by a finite verb usually requires the passive form:

(40) a. **Re-decorated** in brighter colours, this room would be ideal for children.
(If it is re-decorated ...)
b. Jeremy's bicycle stood against the fence, **covered** by a sheet of plastic.
(... , and had been covered ...)

The 'beforeness' element in examples like these can often be expressed alternatively by a perfect participle: but notice that here also we need a passive form: *Having been decorated ...* ; *... having been covered.*

Passive meaning, then, is strongly associated with the past participle. However, there is not always a direct and automatic link to the passive in syntactic terms. The most prominent semantic factor in the past participle is the state itself. As we will see further below, there are cases where this cannot really be said simply to derive from a passive verb form alone. Apart from this, past participle use also extends to a small number of intransitive verbs. With these, there is no passive meaning at all. The term 'passive participle' is therefore not 100% appropriate, and is thus better placed in inverted commas, as we have done. The semantics of state, however, always apply when the past participle occurs.

9.2.1 Specification of adverbial meaning

Like present participles, past participles are usually regarded as forming adverbial clauses of time, with manner and circumstance as further (and sometimes overlapping) possibilities. Greater specification can be brought about by appropriate conjunctions:

(41) a. **When** freshly painted, furniture must be placed in the drying room.
[time]
b. Children under 10 are not allowed in the pool, **unless** accompanied by an adult.
[condition]
c. **Although** just serviced, the car has broken down again.
[concession]

9.2.2 Variant subjects and the with-solution

When the participle clause has its own subject, this must be named. As with present participles, absolute clauses like this (see 9.1.1.1 above) have a formal or literary ring to them, and in more neutral style are usually introduced by *with*:

(42) a. The cases safely stowed in the luggage compartment, we took our seats.
    b. With our cases safely stowed in the luggage compartment, . . .
    c. Sadie climbed into the boat, her hair thrown over her shoulder.
    d. Sadie climbed into the boat, with her hair thrown . . . .

This is especially favoured when causal overtones are involved:

(43) a. With the famous tower closed for repair, Blackpool has attracted fewer visitors this summer. (As the famous tower is closed . . .)
    b. The team is much less effective with Braeburn and Dawley injured. (. . . , as Braeburn and Dawley are injured.)

9.2.3 Catenatives followed by past participles

Catenative constructions are not widespread with past participles. They are confined to a handful of verbs with particular meanings; among these are verbs of perception, plus one or two other semantic types with specific and often idiomatic uses. There is always an object present in the main clause (which, again, is the implied subject of the participle). Noteworthy here is that the participle clause is not adverbial, but functions as an object complement (**Co**).

9.2.3.1 Shortened passive infinitives

In this case the past participle is truly a 'passive participle', and actually does replace a passive construction. This occurs, firstly, with verbs that we might call **volitional** in meaning, i.e. those such as *like* and *want* that express forms of demand or desire:

(44) a. I would like the food (to be) delivered on Saturday morning, please.
    b. The boss wants this package (to be) sent off immediately.

As the infinitives in brackets indicate, either the passive infinitive can be used in full, or alternatively be reduced to the past participle alone. Other catenatives belonging to this group are *desire*, *require* and *prefer*.

A second catenative group consists of verbs of perception:

(45) a. Peter listened to a joke told by Marie about politicians.
    b. Joey saw his favourite team beaten by Leicester City in the Cup last week.

We dealt above with verbs of perception followed by the present participle or the infinitive without *to* (see 9.1.3.1). The difference, to re-cap, is aspectual, with the present participle as the imperfective partner (= finite progressive form), and the infinitive as the perfective one (= finite simple form). The examples in (45) are the passive versions of active infinitive clauses, i.e.:

(46) a. Peter listened to Marie tell a joke about politicians.
   b. Joey saw Leicester City beat his favourite team in the Cup last week.

The past participles in (45), that is, have the same perfective meaning as the active versions with the infinitive in (46). A point to note here is that the alternatives with passive infinitives, as in (44), are not an option in (45). This is because the active infinitive clause with a verb of perception needs an infinitive without *to*, and this has **no passive equivalent**. We cannot say **Peter listened to a joke be told . . .* , or **Joey saw his favourite team be beaten . . . .* Reduction to the past participle is therefore mandatory here.

Functional analyses are as follows:

```
         S    P      Od         Co P            A
(47) a. The boss wants this package [sent off immediately].

         S    P      Od              Co P        A              A          A
     b. Joey saw his favourite team [beaten by Leicester City in the Cup last week].
```

As was said above, it is important to note here that the participle clause is functionally an object complement. This corresponds to the active interpretations with the infinitive, e.g.:

```
       S    P      Od            Co P        Od              A            A
(48) Joey saw Leicester City [beat his favourite team in the Cup last week].
```

The same functional labelling of the sub-clause would apply also to an active rendering of (47)a., such as *The boss wants you to send off this package immediately*.

Catenatives with **causative** meanings also fit this pattern. As they have one or two further syntactic characteristics of their own, we deal with them in a separate sub-section immediately below.

9.2.3.2 Causative constructions

The verbs *have* and *get* occur with the past participle in what semantically speaking are **causative constructions**. The pattern *to have something done* means 'to order something to be done/to arrange for something to be done':

(49) a. I **had** my car **washed** at a service station.
   b. The couple next door **are having** their garden **re-designed**.

The sub-clause active equivalents, like the examples discussed in 9.2.3.1, use the infinitive without *to*:

(50) a. I had (somebody at) the service station wash my car.
   b. The couple next door are having a landscape architect re-design their garden.

Again, as the infinitive without *to* has no passive form (**I had my car be washed* . . .), reduction to the past participle is the only permissible passive equivalent.

Get features in the same construction with a similar meaning, though with the added connotation of 'manage' or 'make an effort to achieve':

(51) a. You must get your hair cut.
     b. I'll get the job done by the end of the week.

Agent relations here can vary according to context. In (51)a. the case is the same as with *have*, i.e. the task expressed by the participle is not performed by the subject of the main verb. In (51)b., however, the agent is identical with the subject of the main verb. *Have* does not allow this interpretation. This makes no difference to the functional syntax, though.

Another meaning of the same construction with *get* and *have* is 'to experience something negative', often with the connotation of the subject being careless or otherwise partly responsible:

Zadie had her mobile phone stolen on a train; *Tom got a fishbone stuck in his throat*.

Finally, there are one or two fixed idiomatic expressions with *make* that follow the same pattern: *to make something/oneself heard/understood/felt*. Examples:

Because of the howling wind we could not make ourselves understood; *The influence of the new law is slowly making itself felt*; *John wants to make his voice heard in the art world*.

Functional relations are the same as for the examples in the previous section:

```
        S  P   Od  Co P               A
(52) a. I had my car [washed at a service station].
          S     P     Od      Co P
     b. You must get your hair [cut].
```

9.2.4 Past participles as adjectives

Like present participles (see 9.1), past participles can take on the role of an adjective: *boiled potatoes, chopped wood, locked doors*. In addition to this attributive position (i.e. before nouns, as noun phrase premodifiers), they also occur, like most adjectives, in predicative position, following intransitive verbs:

(53) a. In storms walkers get lost on the moors.
     b. All the shops in the city centre remained closed after the riots.

In these cases the participles have no verbal character and therefore no predicator function. Consequently, they do not form sub-clauses, but remain as adjective phrases at main clause level. Like any other kind of adjective phrase in the same position, the participles here function as subject complements:

206   *The complex sentence (III)*

```
             A         S        P Cs         A
(54) a. In storms walkers get lost on the moors.

                      S                    P    Cs        A
     b. All the shops in the city centre remained closed after the riots.
```

The 'state' meaning of past participles makes them particularly suited to an adjectival role, so much so, in fact, that distinguishing between verbal and adjectival character is difficult in certain cases. This is especially so after the verb *be*. The following are ambiguous in both meaning and syntax:

(55) a. The eggs were fried.
     b. The park gate is closed.

These may mean, firstly, that the respective subject is described as being in a particular condition, e.g. the eggs on the plate were in a fried state (and not raw or scrambled), and the park gate was not open but shut, so that nobody could enter. Here *be* is a full verb followed by an adjective as **Cs**:

```
             S             P      Cs
(56) a.  The eggs         were   fried.
     b.  The park gate    is     closed.
```

The other interpretation involves an action: someone fried the eggs and someone closes the gate, e.g. *The eggs were fried in this pan*; *The park gate is closed punctually every day at 6 pm*. In this case *be* is an auxiliary verb forming the passive:

```
             S             P-pass
(57) a.  The eggs         were fried.
     b.  The park gate    is closed.
```

It is important to note that this ambiguity arises only with *be*. No other verbs can take on the role of an auxiliary in passive constructions. *Get* in (54)a., for instance, must be viewed as a full lexical verb with the meaning of *become* (hence the subject complement following).

9.2.4.1 'Are we finished now?': *adjectival past participles with 'active' meaning*

The answer to the question is 'Not quite, but almost'. Finally, we must include a remark on past participles with an 'active' meaning. First, though, a note of explanation and reminder: all past participles discussed so far have been those of transitive verbs. This is logically so, as the kind of state meaning we have been talking about is 'passive' in nature, even when the participle is an adjective: *fried eggs*, that is, are eggs that *have been fried*, and a *closed gate* is one that *has been closed*. In other words, the entity that the participle describes is (or was) the patient of an action and the potential subject of a passive verb (as pointed out at the beginning of the chapter). However, there is a handful of adjectival past participles, formed mainly from intransitive verbs, which convey an 'active' meaning. The noun involved here is the potential subject of an active verb and refers, classically, to the agent of an action:

(58) a. Mel and Frampton, as it turned out, were **escaped** convicts.
       (= convicts who had escaped from prison.)
    b. Davis used to work here, but is now **retired**. (= He doesn't work anymore.)
    c. Our dog is **well-behaved**. (= It behaves well.)
    d. I was busy cooking, but I am now **finished**. (= I have finished cooking.)

(58)d. is a rare transitive example, and can only occur in this sense predicatively. The others are intransitive. Further examples (also intransitive) are the following: *fallen apples, a faded colour, an advanced student, an experienced guide, a departed soul*. Most of these potential subjects refer to the **experiencer** of an action, rather than the agent. But we will not pursue that point here. In their adjective roles, most of these participles can be used either predicatively or attributively, but one or two are restricted: *fallen* and *escaped*, for instance, are generally avoided in predicative position, while *finished* in attributive position takes on passive meaning (*a finished product*). A common predicative-only example is *gone*, as in *My money is gone*.

Exercises

Exercise 1

Analyse the following sentences in terms of sentence functions:

1 Wiping his forehead with a handkerchief, the gardener put down his spade.
2 A woman was sitting at the bar sipping a cocktail.
3 Shouting angrily, the couple pursued the bicycle thief out of the park.
4 Cleo got onto the train thinking it was the 4.30 to Hendon.
5 Seeing the water boiling, I turned off the gas.
6 When walking up to her front-door one evening, Soraya heard a loud noise coming from behind the house.
7 With our only van broken down, we unfortunately can't make home deliveries.
8 Although bored by the disc-jockey, Cindy and Clive stayed dancing at the club for another two hours.
9 The singer returned to the stage followed by his band.
10 Astonished by the scene at the bank, we just stood there, staring at the police cars.
11 With their sirens blaring, four fire engines raced into the park.
12 Sue always has her hair done by the stylist in Market Street.
13 You cannot use the country club dining room unless invited by a member.

Exercise 2

State the differences in meaning between the a. and b. sentences in the following, and say how those differences arise. Provide possible contexts.

1. a. Brett saw Connie climbing a tree.
   b. Brett saw Connie climb a tree.
2. a. Kay noticed Alex talking to Marie.
   b. Talking to Marie, Kay noticed Alex.
3. a. Leaving the building, I realised I had no key.
   b. Having left the building, I realised I had no key.
4. a. Sophie was missed at the office.
   b. Sophie was missing at the office.
5. a. We don´t like our dog barking at night.
   b. We don´t hear our dog barking at night.
6. a. The housework is done quickly.
   b. The housework is done already.
7. a. Tony went to Gail holding a glass.
   b. Gail went to Tony holding a glass.
8. a. Sheila´s hobby is singing.
   b. Sheila´s hubby is singing.
9. a. I´ve often seen Robby riding badly.
   b. I´ve often seen Robby ridden badly.
10. a. The ticket-office was closed 10 minutes after we joined the queue.
    b. The ticket-office was still closed 10 minutes after we joined the queue.

10 The complex phrase (I)
The complex noun phrase

10.0 The complex phrase

We now leave subordination at sentence level and come to subordination at phrase level. Sub-clauses at phrase level are parts of phrases. That is, they do not have a functional relationship to a clause or sentence, but to the head of a phrase. A clause inside a phrase makes that phrase into a complex phrase. Here are three examples:

(1) a. The man **sitting next to Jane** spilt his coffee over her.
     b. Jane was sure **that he did it on purpose**.
     c. She left without **saying a word**.

In (1)a. we have a present participle clause as postmodifier in a noun phrase, in (1)b. a *that*-clause as adjectival complement, and in (1)c. a gerund clause as prepositional complement. Notice these clauses are **not** directly related to their respective sentences. It is only the particular phrase as a whole that has a sentence function:

the man sitting next to Jane ⟶ noun phrase functioning as subject (**S**) of *spilt*.

sure that he did it on purpose ⟶ adjective phrase functioning as subject complement (**Cs**) following the verb *be*.

without saying a word ⟶ prepositional phrase functioning as adverbial (**A**).

The clause itself, of course, will have its own internal sentence functions, just like any other sub-clause:

```
              P       A
(2)  a.  ... sitting next to Jane ...
              S  P   Od      A
     b.  ... that he did it  on purpose ...
              P    Od
     c.  ... saying a word ...
```

210   *The complex phrase (I)*

However, a preliminary word on analysis conventions is necessary here. In just a sentence-functional analysis, we will indicate clauses subordinated at phrase level by slants or backslashes (/ /), and show the head of the phrase by an arrow (◢◣).

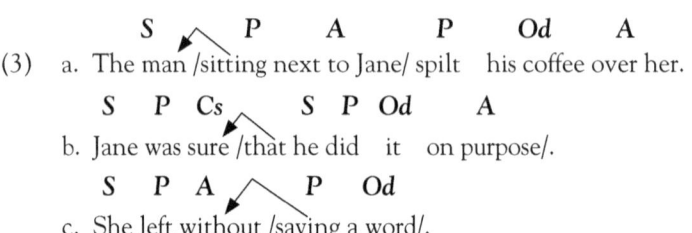

(3) a. The man /sitting next to Jane/ spilt his coffee over her.
    b. Jane was sure /that he did it on purpose/.
    c. She left without /saying a word/.

Note that this is not a full internal analysis of phrases. It is a functional sentence and clause analysis which is basically of the kind we have been doing in the previous chapters. We are introducing the slant convention here to distinguish sub-clauses at phrase level from those at clause level (for which we will continue to use square brackets, as we have done so far). A more detailed analysis of phrase functions, as shown in Chapter 4, is best done separately. This point will be taken up again later in the chapter.

10.0.1 *The complex noun phrase*

Clauses in the noun phrase always belong to the postmodification, i.e. they always follow the head (see Chapter 4, 4.1 for these terms). They can be finite (e.g. a relative clause or *that*-clause) or non-finite. Common types of finite clause are relative clauses and, with nouns of a certain semantic kind, *that*-clauses. Non-finite clauses are usually participle or infinitive clauses:

(4) a. The strange girl **who Jenny had noticed on the train** was standing outside the café.
    b. Jenny had a vague idea **that the girl was in some kind of trouble**.
    c. Two boys **playing football in the street** saw Mrs Belford leave her house.

The clauses in bold type are part of the same phrase as the noun which they follow. The noun is the head of the phrase, but in its relation to the postmodification it is traditionally called the antecedent:

The complex phrase (I) 211

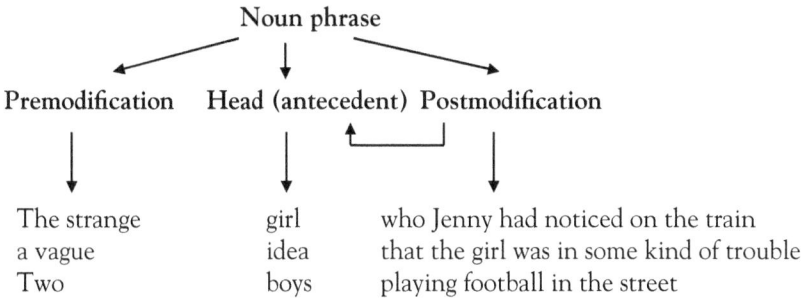

The strange	girl	who Jenny had noticed on the train
a vague	idea	that the girl was in some kind of trouble
Two	boys	playing football in the street

If we were analysing the sentences in (4) just in terms of sentence and clause functions, we would do this in the way that we showed above in (3):

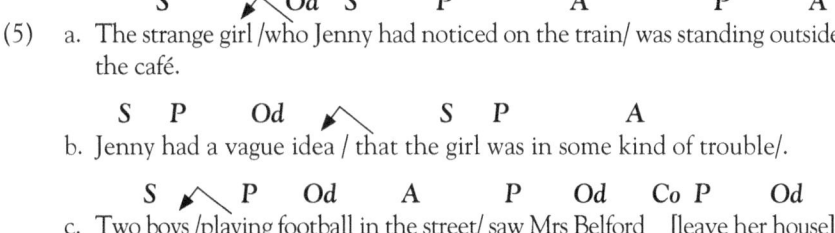

(5) a. The strange girl /who Jenny had noticed on the train/ was standing outside the café.

   b. Jenny had a vague idea / that the girl was in some kind of trouble/.

   c. Two boys /playing football in the street/ saw Mrs Belford [leave her house].

We will now look in detail at the different types of postmodifying clause.

10.1 Postmodifiers: the relative clause

The relative clause is the most widespread kind of finite clause postmodifying nouns. The subordinating element is the relative pronoun, which has the same reference as the antecedent and links the clause with it. The relative pronoun represents the antecedent, so to speak, in the relative clause. But it has its own sentence function inside the relative clause. It is important to realise this. Any kind of clause inside a phrase has its own separate internal sentence functions, as already shown in (5). There are more examples further below. First, though, a consideration of relative pronouns.

10.1.1 Relative pronouns

English has several distinct relative pronouns. The main ones are *who*, *which* and *that*, selected first and foremost according to semantic criteria:

- *who* refers to persons;
- *which* to things and animals;
- *that* to persons, things and animals.

Selection involves certain syntactic criteria, usually in the form of restrictions on the use of individual pronouns to certain clause positions or functions. These are dealt with in the course of the discussion below.

Points of usage that can be noted here already are the following:

- relative pronouns are used regardless of number and gender;
- *that* is less formal than the other two pronouns; it is especially colloquial in the subject function of the relative clause;
- *who* has an object form *whom*, regarded as formal in style; *who* generally replaces it in more neutral language;
- there is a genitive relative pronoun, *whose*, expressing a genitive relation to the antecedent; syntactically speaking, it is a relative determiner, since a noun must accompany it, and it premodifies this noun;
- animals referred to as *he* or *she* (because speakers are individually familiar with them, or wish to treat them in this way) can also take the relative pronoun *who*.

A particular characteristic of English relative clauses is that the relative pronoun can be left out. The 'gap' resulting from this omission of the pronoun is usually referred to as the **zero relative pronoun** (marked ø in sentence analysis). It can occur with all three relative pronouns:

(6)   a. The strange girl **who** Jenny had noticed on the train . . .
         ⟶ The strange girl *(ø)* Jenny had noticed on the train . . .
     b. The car **which/that** I bought last month . . .
         ⟶The car *(ø)* I bought last month . . .

The zero relative pronoun is also subject to certain restrictions. Stylistically, it is generally confined to speech and informal language. The major syntactic condition is that it can only occur as an object or complement of the relative clause, or with prepositions. In other words, omission of the regular relative pronoun is **not** permissible when it is the subject of the clause. Examples illustrating this are given in the next section.

10.1.2 Sentence functions of relative pronouns

Relative pronouns occur in nearly all the functions in which nouns occur, **except** as indirect object (see below). The most common functions are as subject, object or (when accompanied by an independent preposition) as part of an adverbial. The examples in (7) and (8) focus entirely on the relative pronoun, showing its function and indicating possible alternative pronouns in brackets (zero = ø):

                         S
(7)   a. Mandy did not know the person /**who** (**that**) had sent her the flowers/.
                Od
     b. The car /**which** (**that**, **ø**) I am going to buy/ is not yet in the showroom.

                                           Od
   c. Tony and Christine are the people /**who** (**whom, that**, ø) we see most
      often socially/.
                          A
   d. That is the house /**in which** my father was born/.

(7)d. is an example of a **prepositional relative clause**. There will be more to say on this in the next section.

Relative pronouns can also function as subject and object complements, though they are not that common:

                           Cs
(8) a. The kind of man /**that** (**which**, ø) Simon had become/ shocked us profoundly.
                          Co
    b. I will not repeat the names /**that** (**which**, ø) the boss called you/ in his rage.

10.1.3 Prepositional relative clauses

These are clauses like the one shown in (7)d., where the relative pronoun is connected to a preposition. The kind of connection depends on whether the preposition is part of a prepositional verb or the head of a prepositional phrase. In (7)d. the preposition forms a prepositional phrase with the relative pronoun: that is, the relative pronoun is the prepositional complement, and the phrase as a whole functions inside the relative clause as an adverbial. This is presented again in (9)a., but to make things clear, all the functions in the clause are now shown. In (9)b. the preposition is part of a prepositional verb, making the relative pronoun into a prepositional object (functionally a direct object like any other).

                            A   S   P-pass
(9) a. That is the house /**in which** my father was born/.
                          P_1 Od S P_1
    b. The opportunity /**for which** I had been waiting/ came along surprisingly quickly.

Notice that in (9)b. the preposition and relative pronoun have the same positions as those in (9)a., and appear to form a unit in the same way: however, this is not so. The preposition *for* is part of the prepositional verb *wait for*, and therefore part of the predicator, from which it is split off and placed before the relative pronoun. When one predicator is split like this, we mark each part as **P** and give it the same subscript numeral to indicate that the two parts belong together as one unit (see also 5.4.2).

This initial position in the relative clause is not the only possibility for prepositions. There is an alternative: **final** position, i.e. at the end of the clause. This counts for both prepositional verbs and prepositional phrases:

214   *The complex phrase (I)*

                                 A_1 S   P-pass A_1
(10) a. That is the house /**which** my father was born **in**/.
                 Od S   P
     b. The opportunity /**which** I had been waiting **for**/ came along surprisingly quickly.

In (10) we have a reversal of the situation in (9). A phrase-split has now occurred in the prepositional phrase in (9)a., whereas that in the verb phrase in (9)b. has been removed. In actual fact, this final position of the preposition in relative clauses is the preferred one in everyday language. The initial position is regarded as stylistically elevated.

Position of the preposition also affects the choice of relative pronoun. Only *which* and *whom* are permitted when the preposition is initial, as in (11)a. and b. When the preposition is final, as in (11)c. and d., all relative pronouns (including the **zero pronoun**) are possible:

                                   A   S   P-pass
(11) a. Mrs Quinn is the teacher /**to whom** the anonymous letters were **sent**/.
       (not *to who . . .)
                            A   S   A   P
     b. The bus stop /**at which** the children usually **wait**/ is by the station.
       (not *at that . . . , or *at ø . . .)
                                                        A_1 S
     c. Mrs Quinn is the teacher / **who** (**whom, that,** ø) the anonymous letters
       P-pass A_1
       were **sent to**/.
                          A_1 S   A   P A_1
     d. The bus stop /**that** (**which,** ø) the children usually **wait at** / is by the station.

10.1.4 The 'empty slot' phenomenon

Prepositional relative clauses underline a phenomenon that can be felt in all relative clauses: we will call this the '**empty slot**' phenomenon. Something has 'gone missing' at the end of the relative clause. In (11)a. and b., for example, where the preposition is initial, it is the whole prepositional phrase; in (11)c. and d., where the preposition is final, it is just the prepositional complement. The reason for this feeling is that these elements are parts of the verb complementation, and we expect them to follow the predicator, as they do in simple sentences. In relative clauses, however, these elements of verb complementation appear in initial position, where they are now represented by the relative pronoun. Going from simple sentence to relative clause therefore involves not only converting elements of complementation into relative pronouns, but also shifting them from final to initial position:

(12) a. Anonymous letters were sent **to Mrs Quinn**.

Mrs Quinn is the teacher /**to whom** anonymous letters were sent ~~to Mrs Quinn~~/.

b. Anonymous letters were sent **to Mrs Quinn**.

Mrs Quinn is the teacher /**whom** anonymous letters were sent to ~~Mrs Quinn~~/.

What we cannot do is keep the complementation elements in their original position **and** send them to initial position as well: *Mrs Quinn is the teacher to whom the anonymous letters were sent to Mrs Quinn*. Precisely this, however, is an error often found among EFL/ESL learners whose mother tongue deals differently with relative clauses from the way they have to be in English (e.g. in Hebrew or Korean, to name just two examples).

The 'empty slot' phenomenon is emphasised by prepositional relative clauses, in particular when the preposition is in final position. But the principle is the same for all relative clauses. The following are more general examples:

(13) a. We visited **a friend** in Bournemouth.

The friend /**that** we visited ~~the friend~~/ lives in Bournemouth.

b. Vincent has taken **a job** in a factory.

The job / ø Vincent has taken ~~a job~~/ is in a factory.

Relative clauses with the zero pronoun, as in (13)b., seem especially to provoke error as the **Od** is not overtly present in the sentence at all. The temptation to insert a 'false' personal pronoun (instead of simply repeating the full noun wrongly) is particularly prevalent, e.g. here *The job Vincent has taken it is in a factory*.

The 'empty slot' phenomenon is found also with other clause types, as we will see in Chapter 12.

10.1.5 The concept of restriction

Restriction was introduced in Chapter 4, 4.1.2.1 as being fundamental to all forms of postmodification, which show two basic kinds of meaning relation to the antecedent: restrictive and non-restrictive. The concept of restriction is particularly relevant to relative clauses, which is why it is taken up here again.

All the relative clause examples so far have been restrictive. This means that they identify the antecedent. Consider again:

(14) a. the car /which I am going to buy/
      b. the people /who we see most often socially/

The relative clauses here answer the question *Which one(s)?* Thus the 'car' meant in (14)a. is 'that one (and only that one) which I am going to buy'. Similarly, the particular 'people' referred to in (14)b. are 'those that we see most often socially' and no others. The antecedents alone could refer to any cars or people. The relative clause restricts the choice to the individual or group which fits the description. By contrast, a non-restrictive relative clause does not have this identifying or defining function. It simply gives added information. Consider (15)a. and (15)b. The only semantic difference between them is that the relative clause in the first is restrictive, whereas in the second it is non-restrictive (signalled here by the commas):

(15) a. The crew members who were still on the ship were rescued by helicopter.
      b. The crew members, who were still on the ship, were rescued by helicopter.

The version in (15)a. identifies which crew members were rescued by helicopter: that is, those (and only those) who were still on the ship. What is implied here is that other members of the crew were not rescued in this way (for example, because they had already escaped and were in safety): the restrictive relative clause here selects a particular group of crew members from the total number. In (15)b., however, **all** the crew members are meant. We can express this in the two sentences: *The crew members were still on the ship. They were (then) rescued by helicopter.*

If we do the same for (15)a., we have to say: **Some** *of the crew members were still on the ship. They were (then) rescued . . . .*

The non-restrictive relative clause in (15)b. is a kind of parenthesis, i.e. a clause conveying extra information not necessary to understand the antecedent. We can therefore take it out of the sentence (as we did just above) without altering the identity of the antecedent: *The crew members were still on the ship.* The parenthesis-character is shown by the commas. These also reflect pronunciation. Commas in writing usually signal pauses in speech. Here, slight pauses are made before and after the relative clause, and the clause itself has a separate intonation pattern:

(16) The crew members, who were still on the ship, were rescued by helicopter.

Restrictive relative clauses, by contrast, are pronounced with no pause and in the same breath as the rest of the noun phrase:

(17) The crew members who were still on the ship were rescued by helicopter.

In writing, the commas, as we have said, are an important signal of non-restrictiveness. However, if the intended non-restrictive meaning is clear from the context, the commas may occasionally be missing. This is found mainly when the non-restrictive clause ends the sentence: *Denise couldn't find her bicycle which she had left against the railings outside the park.* What is definitely not permissible is the reverse, so to speak: commas must **never** appear with restrictive clauses.

Restriction has certain consequences regarding the choice of relative pronoun:

- only *who(m)*, *which* and *whose* are possible in non-restrictive relative clauses;
- the use of *that* and the **zero pronoun** is confined to restrictive relative clauses.

Three final points: firstly, non-restrictive relative clauses are more common in formal rather than in informal language styles. Secondly, non-restrictive postmodification occurs more commonly with relative clauses than with most other postmodification types; it is therefore especially relevant to relative clauses. Thirdly, an analytical question: do restrictive and non-restrictive clauses have the same syntactic status? Phonologically and semantically, as we have seen, non-restrictive clauses are separate from their antecedent phrase. For this reason they could be regarded also as syntactically separate. They would then be clauses which are directly subordinated at sentence level (see SAGE, pp. 535f.). What speaks against this, however, is that the relative pronoun still has the head of a noun phrase as its antecedent (here: *crew members*), suggesting that the phrase relation is the same as in the restrictive case. This is what we will assume here also.

(16) is then analysed in the same way as (17):

(18) a. The crew members, /who were still on the ship/, were rescued by helicopter.
           S   S P A   A   P-pass   A

b. The crew members /who were still on the ship/ were rescued by helicopter.
           S   S P A   A   P-pass   A

10.1.6 The problem of indirect objects in relative clauses

Relative pronouns cannot function as indirect objects. These must always be paraphrased as prepositional phrases:

(19) a. *Marley is the person who I gave the money.
    b. Marley is the person **who** I gave the money **to**.

The normal requirement for indirect objects is that they should be positioned between the predicator and the direct object. With the relative pronoun as **Oi** this would not be possible, of course, as the relative pronoun has to introduce the clause. The only solution therefore lies in the prepositional phrase. A similar rule applies to interrogative pronouns (see 3.1.3).

10.1.7 Whose *and the* of-*genitive*

Whose, as we have said, is the genitive relative pronoun (see above 10.1.1). It is thought of as a pronoun because it represents the *s*-genitive of the antecedent noun. Within the relative clause, however, it functions syntactically as a determiner in a separate noun phrase:

(20) a. Mrs Simmons is the neighbour **whose car** was stolen.
    b. The person **whose money** I borrowed was Marley.

Whose is usually preferred only in reference to persons (not surprisingly, as it is the genitive of *who*). However, it is not completely ruled out with inanimate entities and sentences like the one in (21)a. below do occasionally occur, though mainly in colloquial language. Just as in the ordinary case the *of*-genitive is favoured for things, so we have a relative clause version in the form *of which*, as in (21)b. A problem here, though, is that the construction sounds a little awkward in the intonation pattern of a restrictive relative clause: *of*-genitives are therefore generally reserved for the non-restrictive case, as in (21)c. The most natural solution in the restrictive case is offered by the preposition *with*, together with a rephrasing of the sentence as shown in (21)d.

(21) a. The table whose legs were badly scratched cost far too much.
    b. The table of which the legs were badly scratched cost far too much.
    c. The table, of which the legs were badly scratched, cost far too much.
    d. The table with the badly scratched legs cost far too much.

In certain marked styles (e.g. elevated or emphatic) *of*-genitives can occur with person referents. The relative clause version is *of whom*, used like *of which* mainly in non-restrictive clauses. An often preferred syntactic variation with *of*-genitive relative clauses is to place the belonging noun before the *of*-genitive relative pronoun, as in (22)b. and (22)c.:

(22) a. Sissi Briggs, of whom the husband is unemployed, wants a divorce.
    b. Sissi Briggs, the husband of whom is unemployed, wants a divorce.
    c. The table, the legs of which were badly scratched, cost far too much.

Syntactically speaking, however, we no longer have relative clauses in (22)b. and c., but a kind of postmodification by noun phrase known as apposition. This is dealt with further below.

10.1.8 Relative adverbs

Sometimes the function of relative pronoun is taken over by the adverbs *when*, *where* and *why*, known in this case as **relative adverbs** (see also *SAGE*, pp. 539f.). Their function is adverbial, and the style a little informal. In more elevated language they are replaced by prepositional relative pronouns (in the following in brackets):

(23) a. Thursday afternoon is a time /**when** (**at which**) we are very busy in the office/.

b. There was a violent robbery yesterday in the street /**where** (**in which**) Rod works/.

c. I can´t think of a reason /**why** (**for which**) Jason should have been here yesterday/.

Why can also be omitted (i.e. replaced by the zero pronoun) in less formal English: *I can´t think of a reason Jason should have been here yesterday*. This does not generally apply to *when* and *where*, however.

10.1.9 Sentential relative clauses

This is a special case of a relative clause subordinated at clause level. **Sentential relative clauses** have the whole of the preceding clause as their antecedent, and are therefore not contained inside a phrase. They are always introduced by *which* and are only non-restrictive:

(24) a. She invited me to her party, / **which** was nice of her/.

b. Her husband whistles and hums in public, /**which** she finds embarrassing/.

The two-way arrow indicates that the whole clause is the antecedent.

10.1.10 Postponed relative clauses

In informal style relative clauses are sometimes separated from their antecedents, usually by adverbials belonging to the preceding clause. This postponement splits the noun phrase concerned:

220   *The complex phrase (I)*

```
            S   P   Od       A              A           S   P   Oi   Od
```
(25) a. Kay met **a friend** at the station yesterday /**who** gave her a lift home/.

```
         S    P              Od               A           A      Od  S      P
```
  b. I found several old photo albums in the attic last week /**that** I had not
```
     A
```
  seen before/.

Constructions like this are only permissible when there is semantically no doubt about what the antecedent is. A sentence like the following would probably be avoided:

(26) (?) Bennet married a girl from a midlands town that he wasn't exactly in love with.

This is not grammatically wrong, but humorously ambiguous: was it the girl or the town that Bennet was not in love with?

10.1.11 Further clauses inside the relative clause

Relative clauses can also contain further subordinate clauses. This is then ordinary clause-level subordination, with functional relations between any higher and lower clauses:

```
         S   P    Od  Od  S     P   A       S   P    A              A
```
(27) a. She married a man/ ø she had met [while she was on a cruise in the Caribbean]/.

```
         S    S      P     Od      S   P   Cs   A     S    P    Od
```
  b. A guest /who complained [that the steak was tough [after he had ordered it
```
         Co     P1-pass    A  P1-pass   Od  P1-pass
```
  well done]]/ was   later given his money back.

10.1.12 Secondary fronting

This also concerns further clauses inside the relative clause, but affects the syntactic status of the relative pronoun. Consider the following:

(28) a. An old friend that I had forgotten to contact phoned me the day after my wedding.
  b. Cleaning the flat is the task that I hate doing most.
  c. The woman who the police thought had committed the crime was arrested in Harlow.

The relative pronouns in these examples introduce relative clauses in the normal way. However, they have no functional relation within the main relative clause. They are syntactically part of a subordinate clause inside the relative clause. In (28)a., for instance, the relative pronoun *that* appears to be the direct object of *had forgotten*, but in fact it is the direct object of the infinitive sub-clause *to contact*. Similarly, *that* in (28)b. is the direct object of *doing*, not *hate*, while in (28)c. *who*, although apparently the direct object of *thought*, is actually not: it is in fact the subject of *had committed*. Analytically, this looks as follows:

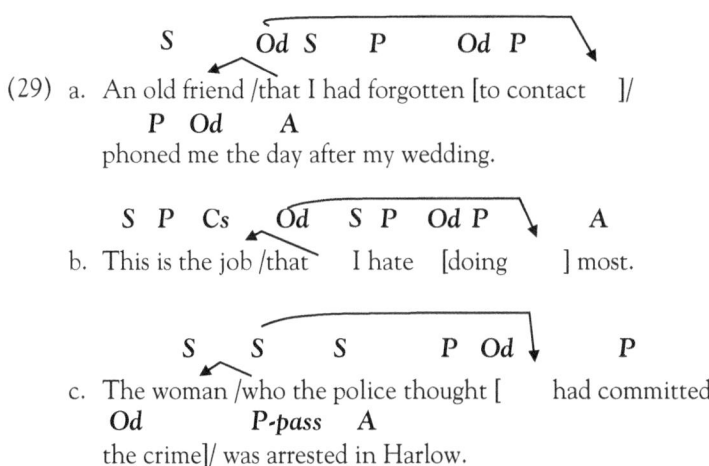

(29) a. An old friend /that I had forgotten [to contact]/ phoned me the day after my wedding.

b. This is the job /that I hate [doing] most.

c. The woman /who the police thought [had committed the crime]/ was arrested in Harlow.

We can consider this best in terms of the 'empty slot' idea introduced in 10.1.4 above. There we said that a phrase made into a relative pronoun is removed from a later position in the clause and leaves an empty slot there. In these cases, the empty slot is not left in the main relative clause, but in a sub-clause, indicated by the arrows in the examples. The fronted pronoun has been 'taken out' of that sub-clause. This phenomenon is what we call here **secondary fronting**. It is unknown in many other languages, and often strange to EFL learners. It is nevertheless very common in English, especially in speech and informal styles.

10.2 Postmodifiers: other structures as reduced relative clauses

What is expressed by a relative clause can often be conveyed more economically (in terms of syntax) by other structures. All three sentences in the following mean the same:

(30) a. The man **who is standing by the car** is my uncle.
  b. The man **standing by the car** is my uncle.
  c. The man **by the car** is my uncle.

222 The complex phrase (I)

The full relative clause in (30)a. is shortened to a present participle clause in (30)b., and reduced even further to just a prepositional phrase in (30)c. We will now look at these alternative structures in a little more detail, with particular focus on non-finite verb forms.

10.2.1 Participle clauses

Both present and past participles are common as postmodifiers. First, the present participle:

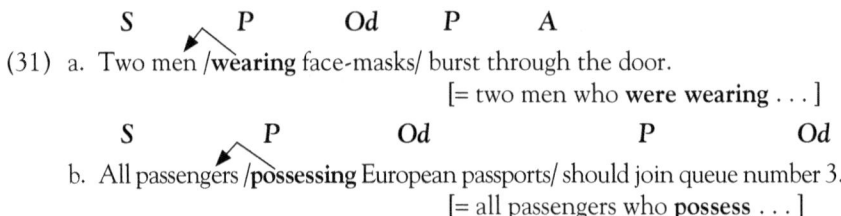

(31) a. Two men /**wearing** face-masks/ burst through the door.
                                         [= two men who **were wearing** . . .]

b. All passengers /**possessing** European passports/ should join queue number 3.
                                         [= all passengers who **possess** . . .]

The antecedent is always the implied subject of the present participle. As explained in Chapter 9.1.2, present participles have imperfective aspectual meaning and correspond to the finite progressive form. This is shown in the relative clause equivalent given for (31)a. With ordinary active (i.e. non-stative) verbs, a postmodifying present participle can have only this meaning. That is, it **cannot** generally replace a simple form in a relative clause. (32)b. is therefore not acceptable as an equivalent of (32)a.:

(32) a. I was introduced to a man who restores old furniture.
      b. *I was introduced to a man restoring old furniture.

Restores in (32)a. is clearly a general habit reference (see also SAGE, pp. 320f.). The participle form in (32)b., however, suggests an ongoing act (. . . *a man who was restoring* . . .). Things are different with stative verbs (see also 9.1.2.3). Here one does encounter present participle postmodification as an expression of the finite simple form. This is the case in (31)b. above. Other examples are:

(33) a word **meaning** 'rubbish' (= a word that **means** 'rubbish'); anyone *seeing* that picture for the first time (= anyone who *sees* . . .); a bottle **containing** colourless liquid (= a bottle which **contains** . . .).

Principally involved here are stative verbs that belong to the semantic categories of *possession* and *perception* (see also SAGE, p. 324).

Past participles in postmodification represent passive forms in the equivalent relative clauses:

```
           S     P         A              P    A    A
(34) a. The truck /parked across the street/ has been there for a week.
                          [past participle = the truck that has been parked . . . ]
         S  P  Od   P    A
     b. We ate beef /cooked in wine/.
                          [past participle = beef that had been cooked . . . ]
```

Here again the antecedent is always the implied subject of the participle.

10.2.2 Infinitive clauses

Infinitives also occur as postmodifiers, though in a restricted range of meanings, and under certain specific syntactic conditions:

```
              S      P      Cs       P    Od
(35) a. Christine was the only guest /to bring flowers/.
                          [antecedent implied subject = the only guest who
                          brought . . . ]
              S   P    Od      P        A
     b. Mr Creeley has a few words /to say on our new project/.
                          [antecedent implied direct object = a few words which
                          he would like to say . . . ]
```

These are rather different from participle postmodifiers. Infinitives are not a simple alternative to relative clauses in the way that participles are. There are two special semantic elements involved in (35):

- (35)a. is an example of a noun premodified by one of the following: *next*, *last*, *only*, or an ordinal number (*first*, *second*, *third*, etc.). This is one condition allowing infinitive postmodification of a relative clause type. As with the participles, the antecedent is the implied subject of the clause.
- (35)b., a more widespread type, shows the second condition: it has a modal meaning. In other words, a replacement relative clause here has to contain a modal verb. In cases like this, the antecedent is either the implied direct object of the infinitive (as here), or an implied prepositional complement, as in (36)b. below. The implied subject is the main clause subject in this example, but it may also be a generalised one, depending on context.

Here are more examples of what we call the **modal relative infinitive**:

224 *The complex phrase (I)*

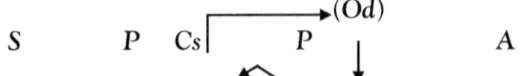
(36) a. Mrs Turner is the person /to see   for an appointment with the boss/.

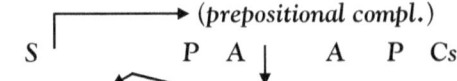
  b. The new store /to shop at   for shoes/ is Bryant's.

Modal relative infinitives are especially common with indefinite pronouns, such as *something, anything, everything*, etc.:

(37) a. I have nothing to do. (= . . . nothing that I should/must/can do)
  b. Is there anything more to add? (= . . . anything that I should/can add)
  c. Something to drink would be nice. (= something that I can/could drink)

10.2.3 Prepositional phrases

Prepositional phrases are not clausal postmodifiers as such, of course. But they have two clausal associations connected with noun phrases: firstly, most prepositional phrases that are potentially adverbial can be seen as reduced relative clauses:

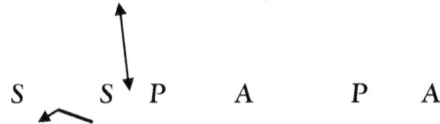
(38) a. The book on the table belongs to Carron.

  b. The book /which is on the table/ belongs to Carron.

Secondly, complex prepositional phrases quite often postmodify nouns:
  That's a cupboard for storing old files.
  We deal with complex prepositional phrases in the next chapter.

10.3 Postmodifiers: apposition

Apposition is the expression of the antecedent in other words. Traditionally, the standard case is where the postmodifier is itself a noun phrase. Again, this is not a clausal modifier, but we have good reasons for dealing with it here, as will become clear later:

(39) a. Have you met Mrs Stanmore, **our restaurant manager**?
  b. My brother, **an accomplished musician**, has joined the local chamber orchestra.
  c. This is the new maths teacher, **Tina Simms**.

Typically, as in (39)a. and (39)c., either the antecedent or the postmodifier is a proper noun, i.e. a name. The postmodifier gives extra information on who or what the antecedent is, or what it consists of. Naturally enough, this 'added information' element points to a non-restrictive role for the apposition noun. However, appositive nouns can equally have a 'narrowing down' function semantically: in specifying a particular member of a group, they are then restrictive:

(40) a. Tim´s sister **Beth** goes to Clongarth High School.
 b. I first met the maths teacher **Tina Simms** at a PTA meeting.

The implication in (40)a. would be that *Tim* has more than one sister, and in (40)b. that *Tina Simms* is not the only maths teacher at the school in question. Restrictive apposition commonly occurs when there is semantic focus on the appositive noun, and the antecedent characterises it by reference to category or type: *the actor Salvatore Caldero*; *the word 'sanctuary'*; *the herb oregano*; *the Greek letter sigma*.

Analytically, apposition should remain unmarked at sentence level, as it is not clausal and therefore has no internal sentence functions. However, in the case of non-restrictive apposition, there is a need for the sake of clarity to indicate that it is part of the preceding noun phrase. This will be done using the arrow convention showing the antecedent. With the restrictive type we will simply place the sentence function marker in such a way as to show that the postmodifying noun phrase is included. Here are three examples from above. All sentence functions are shown:

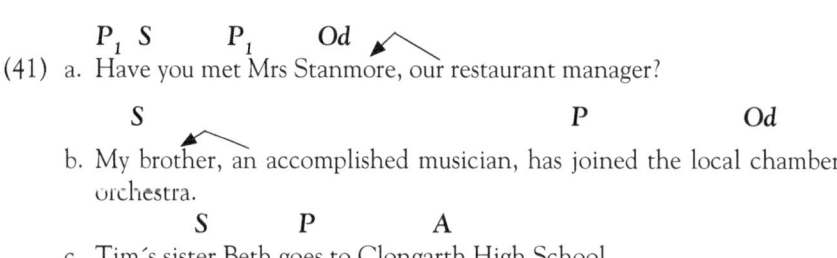

(41) a. Have you met Mrs Stanmore, our restaurant manager?

 b. My brother, an accomplished musician, has joined the local chamber orchestra.

 c. Tim´s sister Beth goes to Clongarth High School.

Apposition of the non-restrictive type shown in (41) has certain similarities to postmodification by relative clause. (41)b. could alternatively be expressed quite comfortably as *My brother, who is an accomplished musician, has joined the local chamber orchestra*. Nevertheless, apposition cannot generally be regarded as a reduced form of relative clause. Firstly, it is a plausible alternative only with the non-restrictive variety of apposition. Furthermore, the only permissible verb in the relative clause is *be* (not surprisingly, as the appositive relation is one of equivalence). Thirdly, relative clause replacement usually produces shifts of meaning:

(42) a. I saw the new maths teacher, Tina Simms, in town last Thursday.
 b. I saw the new maths teacher, who is Tina Simms, in town last Thursday.

The relative clause in (42)b. suggests that the listener or reader already knows the person *Tina Simms*, but the appositive version in (42)a. does not.

As no clausal element is involved, the kind of apposition discussed so far does not create a complex phrase. We will see below, however, that apposition can also include clauses, and indeed that particular types of apposition are entirely clausal.

10.3.1 Partitives

Apposition can also express just a part of the antecedent. The appositive noun is then often a numeral or quantifier used as a pronoun:

(43) a. Only about fifty delegates, **many fast asleep**, were present at the discussion.
   b. A whole troop of police, **some of them with dogs**, searched the train.

Here too, there is a semantic connection to the relative clause, and in fact a relative clause may be included in the appositive noun phrase: . . . *many of whom were fast asleep* . . . . Note in this case, though, that the relative clause postmodifies the appositive pronoun, and has no direct syntactic relation to the antecedent of the apposition. The same is true of participle clauses:

(44) a. Four young men, **two of them carrying knives**, were arrested yesterday after an affray outside La Dolce Vita coffee bar in Townley High Street.
   b. The three escaped convicts, **one of them considered very dangerous**, are still at large in the Manchester area.

Of course, clause structures introduced like this into the appositive noun phrase make it a complex postmodification of the antecedent noun.

Part relations are also involved when certain members of a group are specified or singled out as representatives. Focusing expressions, such as *for example, particularly, like*, etc., then usually accompany the apposition:

(45) a. Many low-income workers, **especially women in retail jobs**, are now suffering under the recession.
   b. The new trade restrictions will affect several important sections of the economy, **for example, car manufacture or chemical engineering**.

Here are two examples from above given full sentence analysis:

```
              S                P      Od    P-pass    A
(46) a. Four young men, two of them /carrying knives/, were arrested yesterday . . . .
```

       S   P₁ A
  b. Many low-income workers, especially women in retail jobs, are now
       P₁   A
     suffering under the recession.

Note that in (46)a. the participle clause is a second postmodification inside the first. As it is clausal, we place it in slants.

10.3.2 Appositive clauses

Postmodification by noun phrase is not the only form of apposition. Appositive postmodifiers can be entirely clausal. These **appositive clauses**, as they are called, typically postmodify abstract nouns, such as *idea, fact, plan, possibility, thought, wish, desire*, etc., and express the semantic content of the antecedent. The major finite type of appositive clause is the *that*-clause:

(47) a. I did not like the idea that we might run out of petrol in the middle of the desert.
     b. The fact that Fred has bought an expensive car reveals something about his income.

As with noun phrase postmodification, so also here the central characteristic of the appositive relation is that antecedent and postmodification are equivalent. With appositive clauses, this can be shown by inserting *be* between antecedent and postmodification and forming a separate sentence:
   *The idea **was** that we might run out of petrol . . . ; The fact **is** that Fred has bought . . . .*
   Note that in *that*-clauses the word *that* is a conjunction (in contrast to relative clauses, where it is a relative pronoun).
   Non-finite apposition is typically with an infinitive clause or *of* + gerund clause:

(48) a. Brian´s hopes of marrying Babsi came to nothing.
     b. Wendy´s intention to go to the beach was thwarted by bad weather.

Here again we can apply the equivalence test: *Brian´s hopes were of marrying Babsi; Wendy´s intention was to go to the beach.*
   Appositive clauses are usually restrictive, as in the examples. The most common non-restrictive type occurs with the gerund clause as direct postmodifier (i.e. without a preposition):

(49) a. Sadly, Ken´s great hobby, keeping bees, ended with the move to a flat.
     b. Caitlyn refused to give up her first love, painting landscapes.

Directly postmodifying gerund clauses are always non-restrictive.

10.3.3 Clauses as antecedents

We have already come across a similar phenomenon with the sentential relative clause (see 10.1.9 above). It is more common, though, with apposition. This is not surprising, as the equivalence factor provides a possibly firmer semantic base for comment and specification. It will also allow us simply to swap the roles of antecedent and postmodifier around. Applying this to (49) we get:

(50) a. Sadly, keeping bees, Ken's great hobby, ended when he had to move to a flat.
b. Caitlyn refused to give up painting landscapes, her first love.

This looks analytically as follows. Note again that the purpose of the two-way arrow is to show the whole clause as the antecedent:

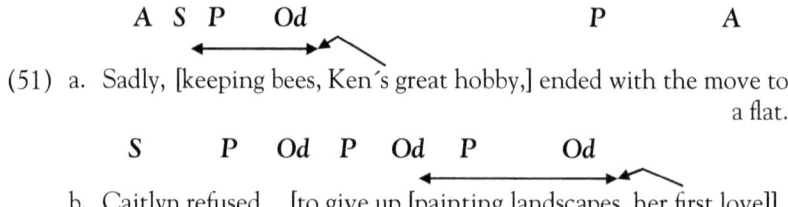

        A S P   Od   P   A

(51) a. Sadly, [keeping bees, Ken's great hobby,] ended with the move to a flat.

       S   P   Od P   Od P   Od

b. Caitlyn refused   [to give up [painting landscapes, her first love]].

Appositives postmodifying clauses are invariably non-restrictive, as the commas in the examples indicate. Antecedents can be other clause types, apart from the gerund:

(52) a. We had to make our escape in full moonlight, a problem nobody seemed to have envisaged.
b. Tommy said that he hadn't been informed, a complete lie actually.
c. To rehearse the whole play so early, the producer's first idea, would have been impossible.

Exercises

Exercise 1

Analyse the following sentences in terms of sentence functions:

1. We have never met the man who sold us this house.
2. The dog that my dad gave me for Christmas has run away.
3. Michael's wife doesn't like the present he bought her.
4. The person to whom we sent the letter has disappeared.
5. That is the child that I gave the money to.
6. The group we had booked the tickets for didn't turn up.
7. The pet names he calls his children are rather sentimental.

8 Mrs Bates is the neighbour whose son had the accident.
9 The town McGregor comes from is on the Scottish east coast.
10 Dave couldn´t find the socks June had knitted for him when he joined the army.
11 The man who stole the car Sandra got after she had passed her driving test has been arrested in Weymouth.
12 We have many students who don´t like the tests we set them.
13 The department head who turned down the offer the directors made him is Harry Benfield.
14 Violent films are the ones I hate watching most.
15 Unfortunately I have forgotten several important things about grammar that my teacher told me I should always remember.
16 The woman we imagined was his mother turned out to be his sister.
17 The meeting that Clarke had intended to arrange with the Italian CEO had now become unnecessary.

Exercise 2

Comment on the syntax of the -ing-forms in the following:

1 A man carrying a newspaper came out of the shop whistling the Welsh national anthem.
2 I remember Helen telling us to send her our manuscript on time.
3 After searching all the farm buildings, the police eventually found the shotgun standing against a tree in the garden.
4 Any person behaving suspiciously should be reported to Security immediately.
5 A bag containing dangerous chemicals was discovered lying under the sofa.

Exercise 3

State the differences in meaning between the a. and b. sentences in the following, and say how those differences arise. Provide possible contexts.

1 a. The spectators who were not standing under cover left because of the rain.
   b. The spectators, who were not standing under cover, left because of the rain.
2 a. The police-officer sitting on the bed examined Stacy´s diary.
   b. Sitting on the bed, the police officer examined Stacy´s diary.
3 a. Jenny found a meal cooking slowly in the oven.
   b. Jenny found a meal to cook slowly in the oven.
4 a. The conductor, Craig Lucas, is retiring.
   b. The conductor Craig Lucas is retiring.
5 a. I saw mail piled up on Steve´s desk.
   b. I saw mail piling up on Steve´s desk.

The complex phrase (I)

Exercise 4

In what way are the following sentences ambiguous, and why?

1   Masterson spoke to the workers in the factory.
2   Janice did not like the woman talking to her mother.
3   The motorcyclist turning right into Brunswick Road caused the accident.
4   The idea that he's preaching is awful.
5   The bus driver did not notice the car overtaking him.

11 The complex phrase (II)
Complex prepositional and adjective phrases

11.0 Complex prepositional and adjective phrases

The last chapter looked at clausal postmodification in the noun phrase. In this chapter we continue our examination of the complex phrase with an examination of clausal subordination in prepositional and adjective phrases, as exemplified in the following:

(1) a. **On sitting next to Jane** the man promptly spilt his coffee over her.
b. Jane was **sure that he did it on purpose**.

These examples echo those at the beginning of Chapter 10, with (1)a. slightly amended to fit the topic in this chapter. In the first case we have a gerund clause as the prepositional complement of *on*, and in the second a *that*-clause as adjectival complement of *sure*. Analytically we will deal with these at the sentence-function level in the same way as with the complex noun phrase, i.e. by putting the clausal phrase complements in slants (//). Functionally, the sentences in (1) then pan out as:

```
         A  P       A           S     A   P   Od    A
(2) a. On /sitting next to Jane/ the man promptly spilt his coffee over her.

       S   P   Cs        S   P   Od    A
   b. Jane was sure /that he did  it  on purpose/.
```

As shown in Chapter 10, the arrows indicate that the clauses in slants belong to the same phrase as the immediately preceding word, and that this is the head of the phrase. The sentence function shown above the head is the function of the phrase as a whole in the sentence concerned. In other words, *on sitting next to Jane* in (2)a. is a prepositional phrase functioning as **A** in the sentence as a whole, with *on* as the head and the gerund clause *sitting next to Jane* contained inside the phrase as prepositional complement. In (2)b. we have the adjective phrase *sure that he did it on purpose* functioning as **Cs** in the larger sentence, with *sure* as the head and the *that*-clause as adjectival complement. We will now look at such phrases individually and in detail.

232 *The complex phrase (II)*

11.1 The complex prepositional phrase

A clause inside the prepositional phrase occurs always as prepositional complement:

(3) Prepositional phrase

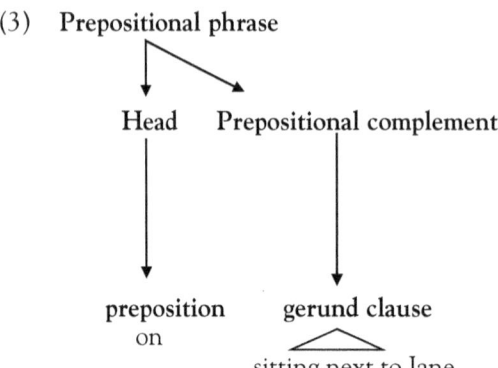

As pointed out in previous chapters, a triangle indicates that the particular unit (here the gerund clause) could be analysed further. (4) gives a more comprehensive breakdown of the phrases involved, together with the sentence functions, as shown already in (2)a.:

(4) Prepositional phrase

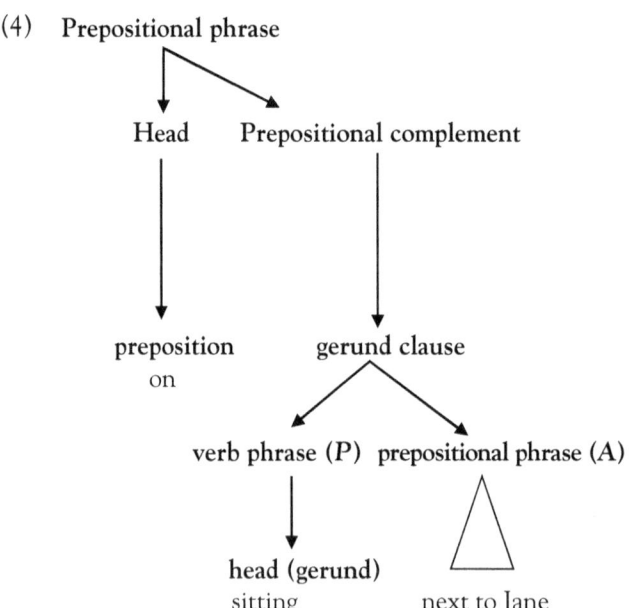

Gerund clauses, with their 'nominal character' (see Chapter 8), are particularly drawn to prepositions:

(5) Prepositional phrase

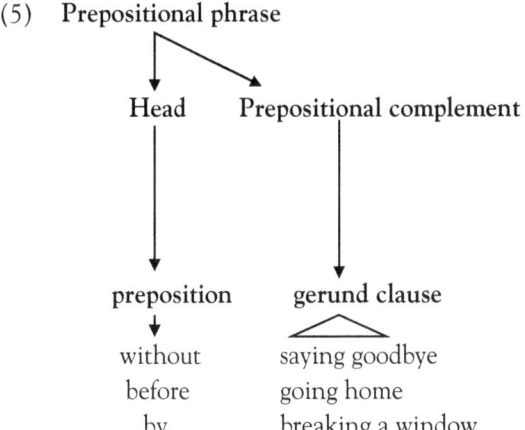

This is equally true, incidentally, when the preposition belongs to a prepositional verb. In this case the gerund clause is the direct object of the verb:

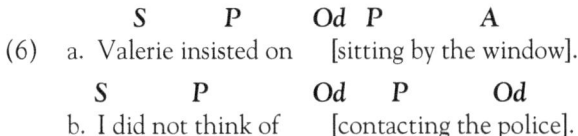

(6) a. Valerie insisted on [sitting by the window].
    b. I did not think of [contacting the police].

This is simply by way of reminder: clausal constructions with prepositions generally apply to both prepositional structures, i.e. to prepositional phrases and prepositional verbs. Prepositions can also be complemented by finite clauses. These are mainly confined to *wh*-clauses (discussed fully in the next chapter), and the prepositional phrase in such cases itself usually complements an adjective (see next section) or postmodifies a noun:

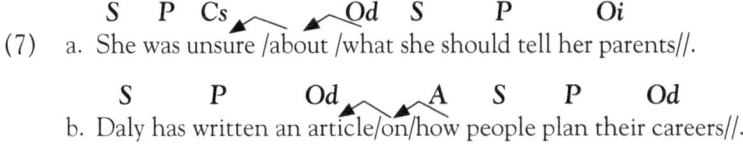

(7) a. She was unsure /about /what she should tell her parents//.
    b. Daly has written an article/on/how people plan their careers//.

11.2 The complex adjective phrase

Here, too, a clause inside the phrase occurs always as a complement, in this case, of course, as an adjectival complement:

(8) **Adjective phrase**

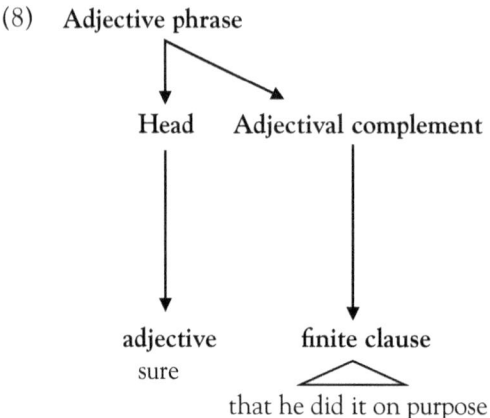

Semantically, there is some similarity here to noun-phrase postmodification: the adjectival complement tells us in what respect the adjective is to be understood, restricting its validity and relation to the content of the complement. Common complement types are *that*-clauses and infinitive clauses, and as briefly mentioned in the preceding section, also complex prepositional phrases. Adjectives of particular semantic kinds are followed by *wh*-clauses. Two special clause types occurring with adjectives are **comparative** and **consecutive** clauses, which we have not yet introduced. All this is explained in detail in the next sections below.

11.2.1 that-clauses

These particularly accompany adjectives that convey various mental states and attitudes, such as feelings, knowledge, prediction, etc.

(9) a. We are all **happy that Sanderson is leaving the firm.**
    b. He is **aware that people don´t like him.**

The *that*-clause expresses the semantic object of the attitude, i.e. what is perceived, known or thought, or what causes the emotion.

11.2.2 Complex prepositional phrases and wh-clauses

Prepositional phrases are a common form of adjectival complement (see Chapter 4, 4.3), and gerund clauses, as seen in 11.1, are a 'natural extension', so to speak:

(10) a. Yasmin is **good at helping other people**.
b. I felt **nervous about going to London for an interview**.

Indirect questions can follow adjectives relating to knowledge and awareness:

(11) a. I´m not **certain why you are asking me this question**.
b. Jamie was **unsure whether he should apply for the job**.

And as seen above in (7)a., prepositions can occur before the *wh*-clause, making it into a complement in a complex prepositional phrase:

(12) a. I´m not quite **clear on where we are going to meet**.
b. Are you **conscious of what this action might lead to**?

Wh-clauses are not always indirect questions. As we will see in the next chapter, they may also be nominal relative clauses, in particular with *what*, and sometimes also with *where*:

(13) a. Jill was generally not **interested in what her husband was writing**.
b. I was **shocked at where Sonya had to sleep**.

The difference between indirect questions and nominal relative clauses is not important at this point. It is explained fully in Chapter 12.

Sentence-analytical representation looks like this (taking just (10a.) and (12a.) as examples):

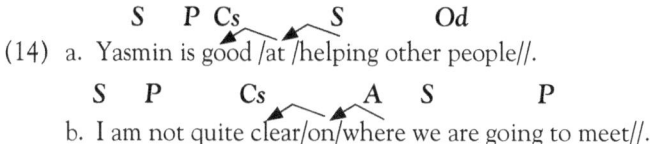

(14) a. Yasmin is good /at /helping other people//.

b. I am not quite clear/on/where we are going to meet//.

And in phrase terms, as in (15)a. and b.:

236 *The complex phrase (II)*

(15) a. **Adjective phrase**

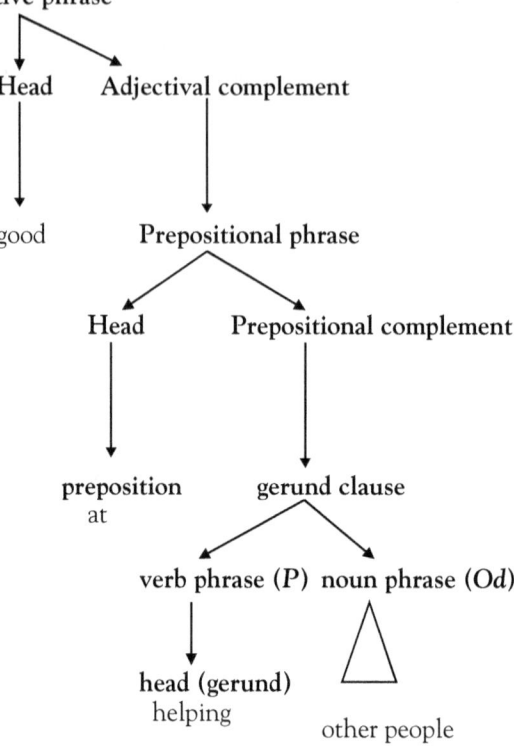

b. **Adjective phrase**

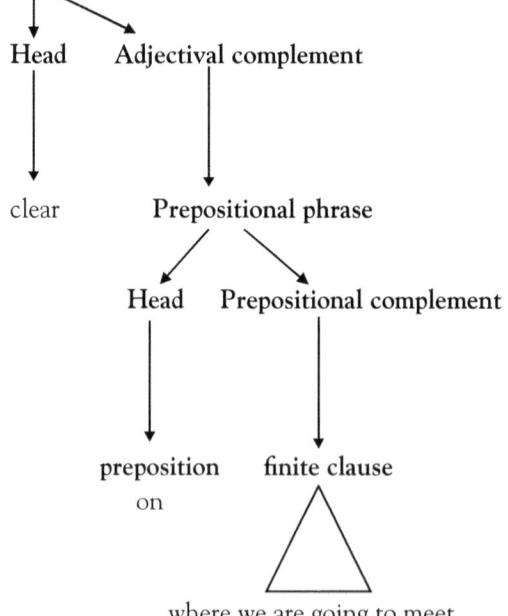

11.2.3 Comparative clauses

Comparative clauses and comparative phrases are used among other things in the comparison of adjectives (see also Chapter 4). As a basis for discussing the comparative clause, we will first give one or two words of reminder on the comparative phrase. This is introduced by *as* and *than*, known in this construction as comparative particles:

(16) a. June is taller **than Paul**.
b. Paul is not **as** tall **as June**.

The expression 'comparative particle' is a cover term for items belonging to various word-classes according to their position and function: *than* and *as* (when *as* follows the adjective) are prepositions (see also SAGE, pp. 166ff. or LGSWE, pp. 526f.). They introduce the comparative phrase, which is in general terms a prepositional phrase functioning as the adjectival complement. The **equative comparison**, shown in (16)b., needs another comparative particle (also *as*) to premodify the adjective. In this role, *as* is an adverb. With the '*as*. . .*as*-construction' (as it is often called informally), it is important, then, to identify premodifying *as* as an adverb (here: before *tall*), and complement *as* as a preposition (here: after *tall*).

We will now add a verb to the end of each sentence in (16):

(17) a. June is taller than Paul **is**.
b. Paul is not as tall as June **is**.

This does not change the meaning, but it does change the structural syntax. Instead of comparative phrases, we now have comparative clauses. Adding a verb, that is, has turned the phrase into a subordinate clause, which now requires internal analysis in terms of sentence functions. The comparative particle following the adjective has become a conjunction, as it now introduces a clause. The clause is still the adjective complement, but our simple adjective phrases in (16) have now in (17) become complex adjective phrases:

```
         S   P   Cs          S   P
(18) a. June is taller /than Paul is/.
         S   P      Cs        S   P
     b. Paul is not as tall /as June is/.
```

Internally the adjective phrases then look as follows:

(19) a.

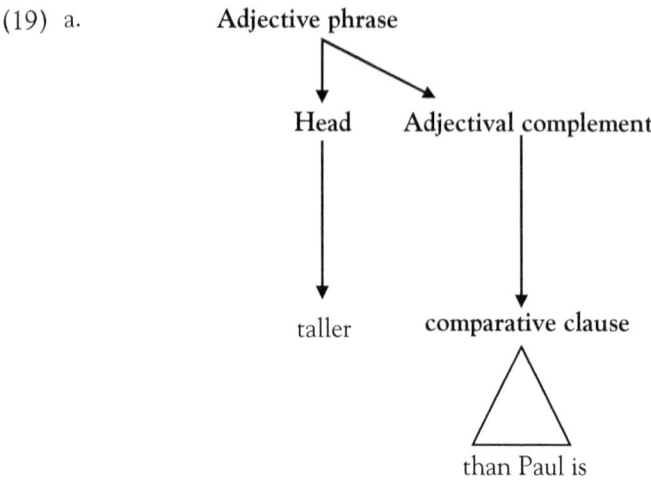

b.

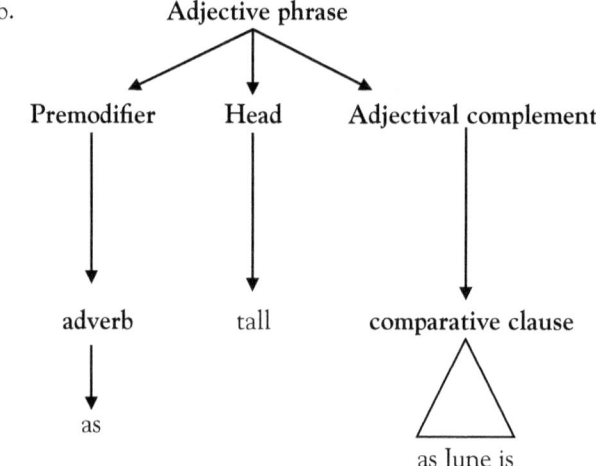

Comparative clauses are taken up again further below in connection with adverb and noun phrases.

11.2.4 Infinitive clauses

The infinitive occurs after adjectives in a variety of constructions and meanings. The exact nature of these is determined by the **lexical character** of the adjective (and/or certain modifying elements in the phrase). Depending on this, the infinitive action or state represents, in general semantic terms, one of the following:

- the cause of a reactive feeling: *Brian was glad to meet Penny again*;
- the object of a prior volitional attitude: *The couple were unwilling to sell their house*;

- the consequence of a condition present in a certain degree: *Harriet was too drunk to walk straight*;
- the specifier of a particular characteristic: *Tommy is quick to criticise others*;
- the possessor of a particular characteristic: *The book is easy to read*; *It is easy to read the book*.

In the sentences of the first four categories, the subject of the main verb is also the implied subject of the infinitive. Significantly, this is not the case with the two examples in the last category. As we will see further below, the infinitives here cannot be regarded as part of the adjective phrase at all. (The last example sentence is an extraposition, a structure we have already talked about to some extent in 7.5.1 and which we come back to below.)

Now for one or two more detailed considerations on the syntax and semantics of these adjective-infinitive relations.

11.2.4.1 Adjectives of emotion

Adjectives like *angry, delighted, glad, happy, sad, surprised*, etc., express emotional reactions to the event or state referred to by the infinitive. Notice that the event happens (totally, or at least in part) **before** the emotion occurs:

(20) a. Brian was glad to meet Penny again.
   (= Brian met Penny again. This made him glad.)
  b. Pia is delighted to win so much money.
   (= Pia has won so much money. This makes her delighted.)

The feeling, in other words, is the result of the action, as indicated by the paraphrases in brackets. In logical-semantic terms, the event reference is a **factive presupposition** of the emotion reference (see Chapter 8, 8.3.2.2): i.e. the sentences in (20) show the following presuppositional structure:

(21) a. X (Brian was glad to meet Penny)   » Y (Brian met Penny)
  b. X (Pia is delighted to win so much money)   » Y (Pia has won so much money)

11.2.4.2 Volitional adjectives

Adjectives of this type include *desperate, eager, hesitant, keen, prepared, ready, reluctant, willing*, etc. We said above that they refer to attitudes, but in a wider sense they also represent 'feelings', i.e. in the form of desire or willingness (= volition) for something to happen. The difference to the emotive adjectives in the previous section lies in the reversed time sequence of feeling and event. With volitional adjectives the emotion comes first: it is the wish for (or acceptance of) a later action:

(22) a. Brian was eager to meet Penny again.
       (= Brian had this attitude towards the future event *meet*.)
    b. Pia is reluctant to win so much money.
       (= Pia has this attitude towards the future event *win*.)

11.2.4.3 Consecutive clauses with the infinitive

Consecutive clauses state the consequences of having a particular characteristic in sufficient or excessive 'amounts'. They are mainly associated with the adverb modifiers *too, enough* and *so*:

(23) a. Colin is still too nervous to drive in heavy traffic.
       (= Colin is very nervous and as a result does not drive . . .).
    b. I did not feel strong enough to leave the house for long periods.
       (= I had too little strength and therefore did not leave the house . . .).
    c. He was so generous as to give all his money to charity.
       (As a result of his generosity, he gave all his money . . .).

As seen in (23)c., *so* requires the conjunction *as* to be placed before the infinitive clause.

Consecutive clauses do not occur just with the infinitive, nor indeed are they focused only on adjectives. This point is taken up again later in the chapter. A final note: adjective phrases containing consecutive infinitives create a systematic implicative relation to the infinitive act reference (see also Chapter 7, 7.6). That is, depending on the kind of modifier (*too, enough, so*), in combination with the positive or negative status of the main verb, the infinitive act is implied as either taking or not taking place:

(24) a. X (Colin is still too nervous to drive in heavy traffic.)
       → Y (Colin does **not** drive in heavy traffic.)
    b. X (He was so generous as to give all his money to charity.)
       → Y (He gave all his money to charity.)

Notice that for (24)a. (with *too*) a positive main verb implies that the infinitive act does **not** take place, i.e. X → not-Y. Negating the main verb, on the other hand, will imply that the infinitive act does take place, i.e. the implication is reversed: not-X → Y. For (24)b., with *so*, by contrast, the implication is positive-positive: X → Y. Negating the main verb here implies also negation of the infinitive act: not-X → not-Y. The same applies to sentences with *enough*, as in (23)b.

11.2.4.4 Points of analysis

To clarify: what we are discussing here is the infinitive clause as adjectival complement. Analysis of the examples here in 11.2.4 therefore looks on the sentence level as follows:

The complex phrase (II) 241

```
           S    P    Cs       P    Od    A
(25) a. Brian was glad (eager)/ to meet Penny again/.

        S   P  A      Cs       P         A
     b. Colin is still too nervous /to drive in heavy traffic/.
```

And the adjective phrases internally:

(26) a.

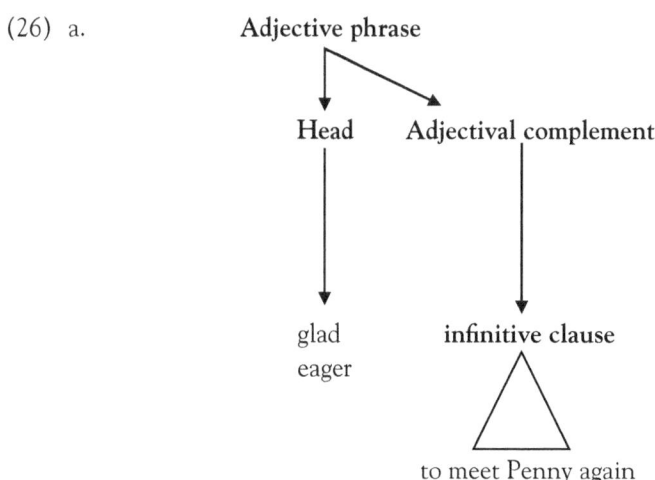

b.

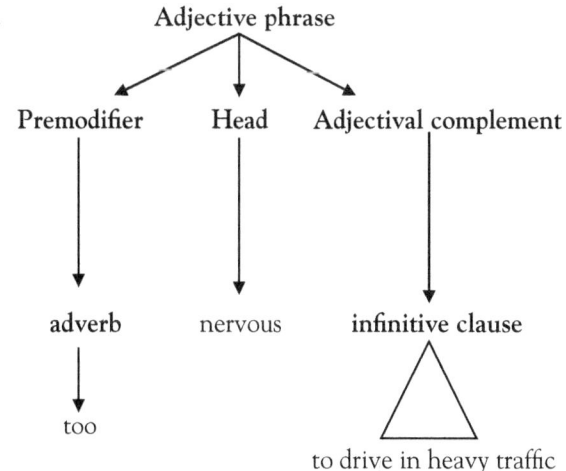

11.2.4.5 Infinitive clauses as specifiers

This relates to sentences of the type *Tommy is quick to criticise others* (given in the introduction to 11.2.4 above). At first glance the adjective phrase *quick to criticise . . .* may appear similar in its internal semantic and syntactic relations to the ones with a volitional adjective, such as *eager* or *ready*. A second glance, though, reveals differences. For one thing, *quick to criticise* creates an implicative relation, but there is none with volitional adjectives:

(27) a. X (Tommy is quick to criticise others).
→ Y (Tommy criticises others).
b. X (Brian was eager to meet Penny).
↛ Y (Brian met Penny).

Secondly, we can express X in (27)a. in alternative syntactic constructions that are not possible with volitional adjectives, for example, *Tommy criticises others quickly*; *Tommy is quick in criticising others*. These alternatives show that the adjective head (*quick*) in the original sentence is semantically rather like an adverb, i.e. it expresses a characteristic of the action; at the same time, of course, the adjective points to a characteristic of the subject, *Tommy*. The two directions – here Tommy and there the action – combine to tell us about the way in which the subject behaves. Volitional adjectives, by contrast, are just subject-centred, denoting, as we have said, the subject's attitude towards an anticipated event.

In the *quick-to-criticise* type, we call the infinitive clause a **specifier**, because it tells us in what sense the subject is 'quick', i.e. with regard to the stated action. This kind of head-complement relation is actually not very widespread. It is restricted mainly to the adjectives *quick* and *slow*.

11.2.4.6 Infinitive clauses as 'false complements'

The first of our last two examples in the introductory list in 11.2.4, *The book is easy to read*, shows a certain similarity to the *quick-to-criticise* type we have just been discussing. At first sight, that is, it appears to place the infinitive clause also in the role of specifier. The sentence as a whole, in other words, seems to attribute an adjective feature (*easy*) to the subject (*book*) and narrow it down to a particular domain of activity (*to read*). But consider now our final introductory example, *It is easy to read the book*. This is actually an alternative way of expressing the same sentence. (28)a. and (28)b., that is, are paraphrases of each other:

(28) a. The book is easy to read.
b. It is easy to read the book.

(28)b., as mentioned above already, is an example of the construction we call extraposition. There are two significant things about it in this connection. Firstly, we cannot apply it to the *quick-to-criticise* kind of sentence:

(29) a. Tommy is quick to criticise others.
   b. *It is quick to criticise others.
   c. *It is quick for Tommy to criticise others.

Neither (29)b. nor (29)c. make sense. Both are ungrammatical with the adjective *quick*. If we swap this for *easy*, of course, we do get grammatical sentences, as we have already seen in (28). Then, however, the pattern in (29)a. would not work, as shown in (30), which actually reverses the previous pattern of acceptability:

(30) a. *Tommy is easy to criticise others.
   b. It is easy to criticise others.
   c. It is easy (for Tommy) to criticise others.

The second important point about the extraposition version of (28)a. in (28)b. is this: it shows *the book* syntactically as the direct object of the infinitive. To re-cap on the sentence functions involved in extraposition (see also Chapter 7, 7.5.1), we will give a full function version of (28)b.:

	S-gramm.	P Cs	S-log.	P	Od
(31)	It	is easy	[	to read the book].	

We will not comment generally on the function pattern here (this is taken up again later in Chapter 12). What interests us now is *the book* as direct object of *read*. If (28)a. means the same, we have to account for the fact that here the same noun phrase (*the book*) appears as the subject of the sentence. The answer to the problem lies in recognising that this is a 'false' subject semantically. As we will see later, **false subject constructions** are a regular pattern in English, and require the following analysis:

(32)

	S-gramm.	P	Cs	S-log.	P	Od-log.
	The book	is	easy	[	to read	▼].

The infinitive clause itself is the 'real' or logical subject (**S-log.**), but is anticipated by a 'dummy' grammatical subject, as with extraposition. The difference to extraposition is that here the 'dummy' subject has a real function in the infinitive clause. 'Dummy' subjects help to avoid beginning the sentence with an infinitive clause, which is grammatically possible, but is usually regarded in communicative terms as undesirable (see also Chapter 7, 7.5). Extraposition and false subject constructions are discussed more fully in the next chapter, when we return from phrase- to sentence-level and consider the syntax and communicative purposes of these and other 'special' syntactic constructions.

The point to be made here, in the context of phrase syntax, is this: with extraposition and false subject constructions, the infinitive clause does **not** belong to the adjective phrase (see the use of square brackets). We are tempted to think that it does, when we read a word sequence such as *easy to read*: but it is a syntactic deception, a case of a 'false' complement. The infinitive clause, therefore, is not an adjectival complement at all, but a separate and independent part of the sentence.

With that we pass back to the sentence level. In the next chapter we will consider extraposition, false subject constructions and other special clausal forms in more detail.

Exercises

Exercise 1

Analyse the following sentences in terms of sentence functions:

1. The tourists left the café without paying for their drinks.
2. After settling in at your hotel you will receive a visit from our travel representative.
3. Carmen was not sure about what she should wear to the wedding.
4. Geoff was fined for driving too fast along Brighton promenade.
5. On returning to the camp-site, we were shocked to discover that our tent had been stolen.
6. Politically, Folthorpe never recovered from being defeated in the election.
7. Adam and Roberta had a big argument over where to go for their holidays.
8. The company is certain that it is going to be successful in developing this new far-eastern market.
9. The trainer was happy to see that his players were so confident about winning the next game.
10. Although she is keen to pass the exams, she has always been reluctant to work at improving her practical skills.
11. The town planners are angry at receiving so little public support for building the new shopping-centre.
12. As we were too exhausted to leave our hotel after arriving in London, we decided on having an early night.
13. My partner was more surprised to hear the result of the competition than I was.
14. Mother is just as relieved as I am that our new neighbours are much quieter than our old ones.
15. When it is necessary to have spare parts delivered immediately, Jones is slower to react than our other suppliers.

Exercise 2

Do complete phrase analyses of the following:

1. before boarding the plane.
2. excellent at solving problems.
3. surprised to see Madeleine.
4. anxious about leaving her mother alone.
5. too tired to eat any food.

Exercise 3

Using appropriate symbols, give the implicative meanings or presuppositions contained in the following:

1. Codd was too scared to jump.
2. We are sad to be leaving the island.
3. The family are wealthy enough to own four homes.
4. I am not prepared to pay the bill.
5. Julie is very upset to hear that the trip has been cancelled.
6. The dog wasn´t quick enough to catch the rabbit.
7. We weren´t unhappy to see them go.

12 Selected clause constructions

12.0 Return to sentence-level: particular clause constructions

We now want to examine common clause constructions of a slightly eccentric and individual kind, and to see how they fit into our functional scheme of things, adding where appropriate one or two observations on their usage. First point on the agenda is to give an overview of the two types we were talking about in Chapter 11 in connection with phrase syntax: extraposition and the false subject construction.

12.1 Extraposition

We have met extraposition so far with infinitive clauses (7.5.1, 11.2.4.6) and gerund clauses (8.1.2). It is also common with finite clauses (usually *that*-clauses, but occasionally other types that are mentioned further below). Here are some summarising examples, together with their common function pattern. Note that the **Cs** slot can also be filled by a noun phrase:

	S-gramm.	P	Cs	S-log.
(1) a.	It	is	dangerous	[to swim in this river].
b.	It	is	my intention	[to cross the mountains on foot].
c.	It	was	lovely	[lying by the pool in the sun].
d.	It	was	an insult	[saying that to Wanda].
e.	It	was	unfortunate	[that you could not attend the meeting].

The communicative purpose of extraposition is to create emphasis by placing the subject clause in final position. This is known as postponement. As we will see below, postponement is exemplified in other sentence types as well. Moving the clause from the real subject position at the beginning of the sentence leaves a 'gap' that must be filled by what we called in Chapter 11, 11.2.4.6 a 'dummy' subject. This is the grammatical subject (**S-gramm.**). With extraposition the **S-gramm.** is identical with the shifted clause, the logical subject (**S-log.**).

Extraposition is usual not only with infinitive clauses, as we have seen, but also with *that*-clauses in the subject function. In the case of gerunds, it is common in informal usage (see also Chapter 8, 8.1.2), although not generally regarded as necessary. Nevertheless, with gerunds accompanying certain adjectival expressions extraposition is either strongly preferred (e.g. with *no good* and *no use*) or mandatory (e.g. with *worth*): *It will be worth taking a taxi to the station* (**Taking a taxi to the station will be worth*).

12.1.1 Variations on verb and function

Extraposition is most commonly linked to the main verb *be*, but occurs with certain other verb types when the reference is general or impersonal. These are chiefly verbs which:

- denote mental/emotional reactions (*annoy, shock, surprise, worry*, etc.):
  It shocked us to see how poor the people were;
- refer in the passive to general or anonymous acts of thought or communication:
  It was assumed/thought/said that the firm was bankrupt;
- mean *seem, happen* or *become known* (e.g. *appear, chance, emerge, turn out*, etc.):
- *It appeared/turned out that suspect was innocent after all*;
- signify acts of perception and awareness (*occur, become clear, dawn on*, etc.):
  It suddenly occurred to me that I hadn´t paid the bill before leaving the café.

Extraposition can occur in complex transitive constructions with clauses that function as direct objects. The 'dummy' *it* is then the **Od-gramm.**, and the postponed clause the **Od-log.**:

	S	P	Od-gramm.	Co	Od-log.
(2) a.	Drayton	is finding	it	difficult	[to save money].
b.	Thick fog	made.	it	impossible	[to leave the harbour].

12.1.2 Attributive of

Infinitive clause extraposition is very common with **evaluative adjectives**, those that comment on people´s actions and behaviour. Here, the agent of the action (i.e. the implied subject of the infinitive verb), is usually specified by an *of*-phrase. Syntactically, this is then the adjectival complement:

	S-gramm.	P	Cs	S-log.
(3) a.	It	was	silly **of Robert**	[to park the car there].

	S	P	Od-gramm.	Co	Od-log.
b.	We	thought	it	kind **of Mrs Morley**	[to look after the children].

Semantically, this not only specifies the agent (*Robert* and *Mrs Morley* in the respective examples), but also allows the judgement on the action to reflect on the person as well.

248 *Selected clause constructions*

12.2 False subject constructions

This kind of construction was briefly introduced in Chapter 11, 11.2.4.6 in discussing infinitive clauses following certain types of adjective. The example given was (32) *The book is easy to read*, in which the apparent subject of the sentence (*the book*) is to be understood semantically as the direct object of the infinitive (*to read*), and it is then the infinitive clause as a whole, i.e. with the 'real' **Od** added (*to read the book*), which must be seen as the intended subject of the sentence. These 'real' functional relations behind the apparent syntax of the sentence were clarified in the paraphrase by extraposition (see example (28)). In fact we could also show these relations by quite simply placing the infinitive clause in initial position. The following three sentences then all mean the same, with the meaning of the first two shown at its clearest in (4)c. (this is not favoured stylistically, as we have said, but is still a grammatical sentence):

(4) a. The book is easy to read.   [false subject construction]
     b. It is easy to read the book.   [extraposition]
     c. To read the book is easy.

Like extraposition, the false subject construction is a way of manipulating sentence focus. However, in contrast to extraposition, which emphasises the whole sub-clause by postponing it, the false subject construction additionally profiles a particular phrase in the sub-clause by 'extracting' it from the clause, and placing it in initial sentence position (i.e. by fronting the phrase). This shifts the focus slightly. (4)b. and c. are about 'reading something', whereas (4)a. is about 'the book': here, the ease of reading it is named as one of its characteristics.

False subjects are not always infinitive clause objects. They can also be infinitive subjects or the **complement of a preposition** in the infinitive clause. We will now look at these cases in detail.

12.2.1 False subject: infinitive object

The following examples have the same hidden syntactic pattern of meaning as (4)a. That is, the subject of the sentence is to be understood as the direct object of the infinitive clause. It is the infinitive clause that is the real subject of the sentence. Extraposition equivalents are given in brackets:

(5) a. This camera is difficult to use.   [= It is difficult to use this camera.]
     b. My horse is great to ride.   [= It is great to ride my horse.]
     c. The film is good to watch   [= It is good to watch the film on a
        on a winter's evening.   winter's evening.]

Here is the analysis pattern again:

(6)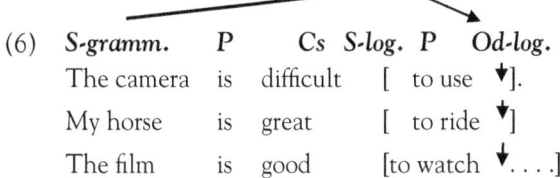
    S-gramm.   P   Cs S-log. P   Od-log.
    The camera is difficult [to use ▼].
    My horse   is great   [to ride ▼]
    The film   is good   [to watch ▼....]

False subject constructions can nearly always be paraphrased by extraposition. Note, however, that this is not true the other way round. Extraposition is possible with a much wider range of adjective types. With the adjectives in the following, for instance, only extraposition is permissible:

(7)   a. It is not polite to say things like that.   [*Things like that are not polite to say.]
      b. It is usual to give a dog bones.   [*Bones are usual to give a dog.]

Generally speaking, the kind of false subject construction discussed in this section occurs with evaluative adjectives (such as *bad, exciting, fantastic, good, great, lovely, nice, pleasant, wonderful,* etc.), and in particular with a sub-group that refers to levels of ease or difficulty (*awkward, hard, simple, impossible,* etc.). Ultimately, however, the precise syntactic possibilities have to be learnt in connection with the individual adjective.

12.2.2 False subject: prepositional complement

Going together with the same kinds of adjectives is a second and similar kind of false subject which stands for a missing prepositional complement at the end of the infinitive clause:

(8)   a. My old boss was awful to   [= It was awful to work for my old
         work for.   boss.]
      b. Henry is nice to talk to.   [= It is nice to talk to Henry.]
      c. The table is all right to look at   [= It is all right to look at the table,
         but bad to write on.   but bad to write on it.]

And the analysis pattern:

(9)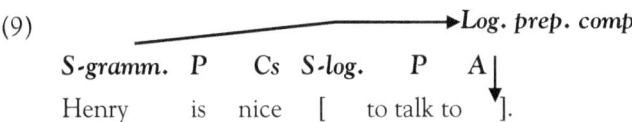
                                              ▶Log. prep. comp
    S-gramm. P   Cs S-log.   P   A
    Henry   is   nice [to talk to ▼].

In this and the preceding false subject pattern, noun phrases can also occur as subject complement, e.g.:

(10) a. My old boss was **an awful person** to work for.
　　b. This is **a difficult camera** to use.
　　c. Henry is **a pleasure** to talk to.

This alters the possibilities a little with regard to extraposition. If the noun itself expresses the evaluation or comment, as in (10)c., extraposition will work. In cases like (10)a. and b., where the adjective still expresses the evaluation and the noun is just a 'neutral' insertion, extraposition is **not** possible:

(11) a. *It was an awful person to work for my old boss.
　　b. *It is a difficult camera to use this.
　　c. It is a pleasure/a joy to talk to Henry.

Finally, there are certain types of adjectives within the broad evaluative range which cannot occur alone in false subject constructions, but are nevertheless acceptable if accompanied by a noun. (12)a. and c. are permissible because the evaluating adjectives premodify nouns. Without the nouns, however, as in (12)b. and d., the sentences are not acceptable:

(12) a. That was the wrong thing to say to Jill.
　　b. *That was wrong to say to Jill.
　　c. A field is a strange place to get married in.
　　d. *A field is strange to get married in.

The kinds of adjectives to which this applies are typically those expressing degrees of appropriateness and normality (*right, normal, strange, odd, peculiar*, etc.).

12.2.3 False subject: infinitive subject

With this third type of false subject construction, it is the implied subject of the infinitive clause that becomes the false subject of the main clause:

(13) a. Grandma was very generous to give you that money.
　　　(It was very generous of grandma to give you that money.)
　　b. You would be foolish to pay so much for a wooden bungalow.
　　　(It would be foolish of you to pay so much for a wooden bungalow.)
　　c. Dick was thoughtless to leave the dog without water.
　　　(It was thoughtless of Dick to leave the dog without water.)

At first glance this does not seem to be different from the ordinary **S + P + Cs** sequence with adjectives like *happy* or *keen*. After all, the main clause subject is generally understood as the subject of the infinitive if there is no further noun phrase in the main clause:

(14) a. Grandma was very happy to give you that money.
     b. Grandma was very keen to give you that money.
     c. Grandma was very generous to give you that money.

In all of these, 'Grandma' is the subject of the main clause and the implied subject of the infinitive, as we would expect also with catenative sentences such as *Grandma wanted to give you that money*. Insofar as this, (14)c. is a standard case, like (14)a. and b. However, there is a fundamental difference. The adjectives *keen* and *happy* relate entirely to the subject: they attribute characteristics to her. In (14)c., however, the adjective *generous* gives a value judgement on Grandma´s action. The difference is indicated once more by the paraphrase potential: extraposition, i.e. making the infinitive clause into the logical subject, can only be applied to (14)c. As it was Grandma´s action that was 'generous', and not her character or person, *Grandma* in (14)c. is a false subject, whereas in (14)a. and b. it is a genuine one. The analytical pattern in (13) is then the following:

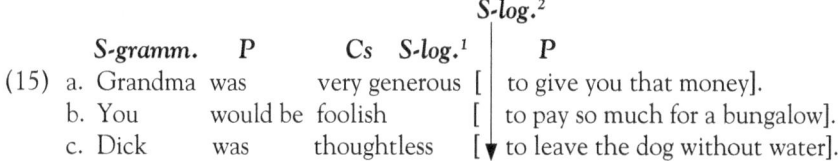

	S-gramm.	P	Cs	S-log.¹		P
(15) a.	Grandma	was	very generous	[		to give you that money].
b.	You	would be	foolish	[		to pay so much for a bungalow].
c.	Dick	was	thoughtless	[▼		to leave the dog without water].

(with S-log.² spanning over the bracketed infinitive clause)

Notice that we have two **S-log.** positions in this case: one for the main clause subject and one for the infinitive clause subject.

False subject constructions of this kind are very common with the **speculative** adjectives *bound, certain, likely, sure*:

(16) a. They are certain/likely/sure to arrive tomorrow.
        [= It is certain/likely/sure that they will arrive tomorrow.]
     b. Jonah is bound to get lost on the moors.
        [*It is bound . . .]

Two points are of note here. Firstly, extraposition is only possible with a *that*-clause. It does not work if the infinitive is kept, quite simply because we cannot then accommodate the infinitive subject in an *of*-phrase: *It is certain of them to arrive tomorrow*. Secondly, *bound* does not permit extraposition at all: *It is bound that Jonah will get lost on the moors*.

12.3 Existential sentences

Existential sentences are those that begin with *there*, which in this case has the role of an **existential pronoun** (and not an adverb!) (see also SAGE, pp. 574f., LGSWE, pp. 943ff.):

(17) a. **There** are many different varieties of apple.
 b. **There** were four books on the table.
 c. **There** is a train at 11am.
 d. **There** were three children playing outside the house.

As the term suggests, existential sentences state that an entity 'exists'. This can apply in a general way, as with (17)a., or in a more specific and defined sense, as in the rest of the examples: (17)b. refers to the existence of entities (*books*) in a certain local physical position; (17)d. does the same, but with additional reference to an activity which the entities named (*children*) are performing. Note that for these last two we can produce approximate paraphrases (or neutral equivalents) just by substituting main parts of the noun phrases for *there* in initial position:

(18) a. **Four books** were on the table.
 b. **Three children** were playing outside the house.

However, this depends for its success on the lexis and syntax of the individual elements involved. It will not work, for instance, for (17)a. or c.: **Many different varieties of apple are*; **A train is at 11am*. A unified solution, in accordance with our explanation above, is to assume that the literal meanings of the sentences in (17) should be represented in the following way:

(19) a. Many different varieties of apple **exist**.
 b. Four books on the table **existed**.
 c. A train at 11am **exists**.
 d. Three children playing outside the house **existed**.

This rather abstract semantic representation is made more concrete when we consider the communicative purpose behind saying that something 'exists'. It is essentially to introduce new information in the form of what is grammatically known as an **indefinite noun phrase**, i.e. one premodified by an indefinite article or an equivalent (such as a zero article or a numeral). Indefinite pronouns (*something, nothing, anybody*, etc.) also fall into this category. New information is often avoided in initial sentence position. It is generally preferred later in the sentence, where it gets more profile. The existential construction fulfils this purpose. It is a postponement device, similar in form and function to extraposition, giving end-profile to the main reference: a 'dummy' subject comes first, anticipating the real subject in its more stressed final position. The sequences following the head nouns in (17)b., c. and d. are postmodifications (italicised in the following for clarity):

	S-gramm.	P	S-log.
(20) a.	There	were	[four books *on the table*].
b.	There	is	[a train *at 11 am*].
c.	There	were	[three children /*playing on the village green*/].

Generally speaking, only *be* is acceptable as the main verb. Exceptions are certain catenatives expressing appearance (*seem*, *appear*) and 'chance' (*chance*, *happen*, *turn out*). However, *be* must then follow as the sub-clause infinitive. What would normally be the **Cs** of the sub-clause is then the **S-log.** of the main clause:

	S-gramm.	P	Cs	P	S-log.
(21) a.	There	seemed	[to	be	no alternative to the plan].
b.	There	happened	[to	be	a train at 11 am].

12.4 Cleft sentences

Cleft constructions are used for certain types of emphasis. As they always start with *It + be*, they might be confused at first sight with extraposition. In cleft sentences, however, the sub-clause is a relative clause. The emphasised element in the sentence is the antecedent:

(22) a. It was **the lorry driver** who caused the accident.
 b. It is **tomatoes** that I need for the recipe.

Analytically, this comes out as

```
        S  P        Cs         S    P      Od
(23) a. It was the lorry driver /who caused the accident/.
        S  P     Cs    Od   S    P       A
     b. It is  tomatoes /that  I   need   for the recipe/.
```

In contrast to the case with extraposition, there are no 'double functions' such as **S-gramm.** and **S-log.** involved here. The initial *it* is an impersonal pronoun. Though there is some type of postponing effect on the highlighted noun (especially in cases like (23)a.), the pronoun itself does not replace anything that comes later in the sentence. Syntactically, cleft sentences are emphasis-marking paraphrases of neutral, 'unmarked' sentences. A comparison of (23)a. and b. with their corresponding neutral versions shows what changes occur to produce the cleft variants:

(24) a. The lorry driver caused the accident.

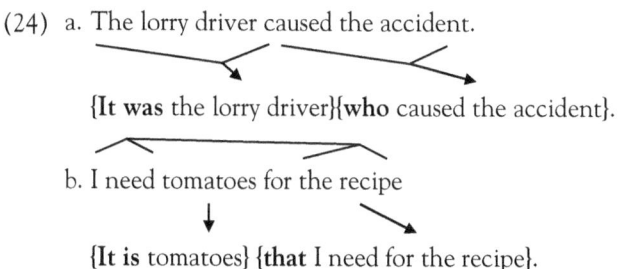

   {It was the lorry driver}{who caused the accident}.

 b. I need tomatoes for the recipe

   {It is tomatoes} {that I need for the recipe}.

Cleft means 'split'. The single clause of the original simple sentence is divided into two, as illustrated. The element to be profiled gets its 'own clause', so to speak, where it functions as **Cs** after *It + be*, a kind of semantic pointer unit with a communicative function that we might describe as 'highlighter'. The rest of the original neutral sentence becomes the postmodifier of the profiled element, i.e. it is subordinated inside the same phrase and thus relegated to a lower level in the clause hierarchy. This makes it less important syntactically, and underlines, by contrast, the prominence of the profiled element. The lower syntactic status of the relative clause also reflects the status of its information content: this is 'less important' as it is old information which is presupposed as known. The new information is the profiled element.

The profiled elements have different functions in the two original sentences: *the lorry driver* is **S**, and *tomatoes* is **Od**. Practically any functional element can be emphasised in this way, even adverbials. The following gives further illustration. (25)a. is the neutral sentence, and (25)b.–e. give different cleft versions profiling various elements of (25)a.:

(25) a. Jill was studying marine biology in Sydney last year.
   b. It was **Jill** who was studying marine biology in Sydney last year.
   c. It was **marine biology** that Jill was studying in Sydney last year.
   d. It was **in Sydney** that Jill was studying marine biology last year.
   e. It was **last year** that Jill was studying marine biology in Sydney.

Points to note:

- It is normally not possible to postmodify prepositional phrases like *in Sydney* in (25)d. by relative clauses. However, it is permissible, exceptionally, in cleft sentences. In this case, also exceptionally, we must diagnose the relative pronoun *that* as a functional adverbial in the meaning of *where*:

  S P   A   A   S   P   Od   A
  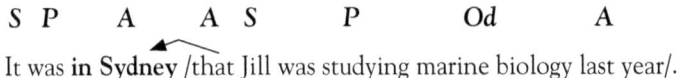
  It was **in Sydney** /that Jill was studying marine biology last year/.

- Everything said under the previous point applies also to *last year* in (25)e., with the relative pronoun standing here for *when*:

  S P   A   A   S   P   Od   A
  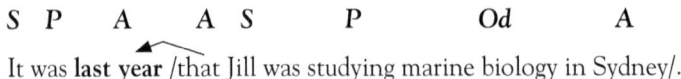
  It was **last year** /that Jill was studying marine biology in Sydney/.

- The following test will distinguish a cleft sentence from extraposition:

  Replace the *it* by the sub-clause. If this works, we have a case of extraposition, e.g.:

  It *was a disappointment* **that Tom cancelled his party**.

  ⟶ ***That Tom cancelled his party*** *was a disappointment*. (= Extraposition)

It was a disappointment **that made Tom cancel his party.**

⟶ **That made Tom cancel his party was a disappointment.* (= Cleft sentence)

Finally, let us come back for a moment to considerations of content already mentioned above: communicatively speaking, the profiled element in a cleft sentence conveys new information, while the relative clause usually expresses something known or presupposed. This becomes clear if we think of a cleft sentence as the answer to a *wh-*question, e.g. *Who caused the accident? What do you need for the recipe?* In communicative terms, therefore, the neutral sentence underlying a cleft sentence has an 'information gap'. If we call this X, we must say that (25)b. derives from *X was studying marine biology in Sydney last year*, (25)c. from *Jill was studying X in Sydney last year*, and (25)d. from *Jill was studying marine biology X last year*. In other words, X varies in position according to what the cleft sentence highlights. From this point of view (25)b.–e. derive, strictly speaking, from different sentences. These are all versions of (25)a., certainly, but with a different element missing in each case.

12.5 Nominal relative clauses

The classical nominal relative clause is one introduced by *what* in the role of nominal relative pronoun:

(26) a. Bobby didn´t like **what** we gave him for Christmas.
b. **What** you have said might interest the police.
c. **What** you become in adult life does not just depend on your upbringing.

Basically, the *what*-clause is a variant of a relative clause: *what* is a combination of antecedent and relative pronoun. Expressing these roles separately, we could paraphrase *what* in (26)a. by *the presents which . . .*, in (26)b. by *the things that . . .*, and in (26)c. by *the way that . . . . What* therefore stands for both a noun (i.e. it is 'nominal'), and the relative pronoun following the noun: hence the term nominal relative pronoun. Unlike regular relative clauses, the nominal relative clause is not part of a noun phrase: it is subordinated directly at sentence level and has sentence functions. This gives *what* the additional character of a conjunction. However, it is not one. Inside the clause it fills a sentence function, just like an ordinary relative pronoun:

```
              S      P      Od     Od  S   P   Oi       A
(27) a. Bobby didn´t like   [      what we gave him for Christmas].
           S  Od  S    P             P          Od
      b. [ What you have said] might interest the police.
           S Cs   S    P        A         P          Od      A
      c. [What you become in adult life] does not depend on your upbringing alone.
```

256 *Selected clause constructions*

Like ordinary relative pronouns, *what* can complement prepositions. The preposition is then always sent to the end of the clause:

            S A$_1$ S P   A$_1$ P   Cs

(28) a. Careful! [**What** you´re sitting **on**] doesn´t look very stable.

      S Cs$_1$ S P   Cs$_1$ P   Od

    b. [**What** I am interested **in**] doesn´t interest my husband.

A certain difficulty with nominal relative clauses arises in distinguishing them from interrogative clauses (i.e. indirect questions). We come back to this point below.

12.5.1 Other types of nominal relative clause

Where, *when* and words ending in *-ever* (*whoever*, *whatever*, *wherever*, *whenever*) can also introduce nominal relative clauses:

(29) a. Home is **where** the heart is.
    b. **Whoever** did this has made a big mistake.
    c. **Whenever** the plane lands counts as the arrival time.

Several of these are actually not pronouns, but adverbs: they function inside their clauses as adverbials, and are called **nominal relative adverbs**:

      S P Cs A   S   P

(30) a. Home is   [**where** the heart is].

      S A   S   P   P   Od

    b. [**Whenever** the plane lands] counts as the arrival time.

At first glance it may seem strange to have an adverb introducing a nominal relative clause. Nevertheless, clauses like this are also clearly 'nominal' in the sense that they fill the same functions as nouns, here **S** and **Cs**. Secondly, the adverbs themselves have the same combination meaning as we described above for *what*: that is, they stand for a noun antecedent + relative clause. What gives them their adverbial character is the fact that the relative pronoun equivalent must be combined with a preposition, i.e. *where* = *the place at which* and *whenever* = *any time at which*.

12.5.2 Pseudo-cleft sentences

A special variant in the usage of nominal relative clauses is in forming **pseudo-cleft sentences**. Here we are back again with the phenomena of **splitting** and postponement for purposes of emphasis (see 12.1, 12.4 above). In the following, a. and c. are the emphasis-neutral sentences, whereas b. and d. are the pseudo-cleft versions formed from them:

(31) a. Right now I need a good meal.
   b. **What I need right now** is a good meal.
   c. Phil's lack of professional experience worries me a little.
   d. **What worries me a little** is Phil's lack of professional experience.

Like its cleft counterpart, the pseudo-cleft variant splits a simple sentence into two clauses, one of which is subordinated as a relative clause: in this case the relative clause is a nominal relative clause, as shown in (31). The structural and functional pattern is as follows:

```
         S Od S P    A     P       Cs
(32) a. [What I need right now] is  a good meal.
         S  S    P  Od   A    P              Cs
     b. [What worries me a little] is Phil's lack of experience.
```

Postponement as an emphatic device is also involved here. This is most obvious with sentences like (31)d., where the subject of the neutral sentence (*Phil's lack of experience . . .*, (31)c.) is shifted into end-focus. It is less obvious in (31)b., where the profiled element is the direct object (*a good meal*) and is already in end-position in the neutral sentence (31)a. In this case postponement occurs in the sense that the sentence as a whole is **extended**, pushing the end slot of (31)a. even further to the right in (31)b. by the creation of a sub-clause in subject position. This extension effect counts equally for (31)d., of course, where it is added to the first kind of postponement (shift of original subject into end-position), creating what might be seen as a 'double effect'.

The order of clauses can be reversed, with the *what*-clause in second position:

(33) a. A good meal is **what I need right now**.
   b. Phil's lack of professional experience is **what worries me a little**.

This changes the emphasis. It is now the *what*-clause that is profiled, lending emphasis to the verb phrases *need* and *worries*, again through postponement into a later position.

Pseudo-cleft sentences are generally well suited to predicator profiling. Through the use of 'dummy *do*' in the *what*-clause (essentially an extended form of *do*-support) an action-reference is given end-focus. The usual emphasis through postponement is enhanced by the anticipation effect of *do*-support:

(34) a. **What Jim did then** was (to) get drunk.
   b. **What we're doing on Saturday** is decorating the bedroom.

Sentences like this tend to be confined to speech and informal language, probably because creating a second sub-clause to equate to the first (i.e. the *what*-clause) is felt to sound a little awkward:

258 *Selected clause constructions*

(35) a. [What Jim did then] was [(to) get drunk].
       S Od S P   A   P Cs P Cs

       S Od S P   A   P Cs P   Od
   b. [What we're doing on Saturday] is [decorating the bedroom].

Note that the verbs in the second sub-clause are non-finite: an infinitive is required as the equivalent of a simple aspect in the *what*-clause and a gerund as the equivalent of a progressive.

12.6 Interrogative clauses

These are indirect questions (see also Chapter 6, 6.4.1). We touch on them briefly again here because the *wh*-elements in them are sometimes difficult to distinguish from nominal relative pronouns and adverbs. We will confine ourselves to examples introduced by *what*.

(36) a. You know **what you must do next**.
    b. **What Jim did then** is a mystery.
    c. They had not told her **what was being discussed at the meeting**.

Here the *what*-clauses are interrogative clauses, and *what* itself is used as an interrogative pronoun. Unfortunately, a functional analysis will not help us tell the difference between interrogative and nominal relative clauses, as interrogative clauses are also 'nominal' in character and their pronouns and adverbs fill similar functions:

       S P   Od   Od S   P   A
(37) a. You know [what you must do next].

       S Od S P A   P Cs
   b. [What Jim did then] is a mystery.

       S   P   Oi Od Od   P-pass   A
   c. They had not told her [what was being discussed at the meeting].

The usual way of identifying an interrogative clause is to insert the phrase *the answer to the question* before *what*, and then to form a direct question from the indirect original. If this works syntactically and semantically then the clause is an interrogative one. Applying this test to (36), we get:

(38) a. You know **the answer to the question, 'What must I do next?'**
    b. **The answer to the question, 'What did Jim do then?'**, is a mystery.
    c. They had not told her **the answer to the question, 'What is being discussed at the meeting?'**.

The inserted phrases reflect the essential semantic role of an interrogative clause: it is referred to by elements in the main clause (e.g. verbs like *know* and *tell*) as representing a factor of knowledge to be possessed or communicated.

Selected clause constructions 259

Applying the test phrase to nominal relative clauses like those, for instance, in (26) above is clearly not possible:

(39) a. *Bobby didn't like the answer to the question, 'What did we give him for Christmas?'
 b. *The answer to the question 'What have you said?' might interest the police.
 c. *The answer to the question 'What do you become in adult life?' does not just depend on your upbringing.

Exercises

Exercise 1

Analyse the following sentences in terms of sentence functions, and name the type of sentence construction:

1 It annoys Myra that Grant always comes home late.
2 It was a cigarette-end that caused the fire.
3 The fire is certain to have been caused by a cigarette-end.
4 What caused the fire was a cigarette-end.
5 It was Jane's greatest wish to sail her yacht in the Caribbean.
6 They never discovered what caused the fire.
7 We found it nasty of Greg to say those things at the party.
8 It is not worth getting a bus into the village.
9 The mountain hut isn't easy to find in the dark.
10 There is no bus into the village before midday.
11 We were fools to believe such a ridiculous story.
12 There were about fifty students sitting in the chemistry lab.
13 Henderson is bound to find another job soon.
14 She's a lovely person to be with.
15 There is a huge lorry parked in front of my garage!

Exercise 2

Where possible, turn the following into false subject constructions. (Careful! You may have to add nouns in some cases!) If it is not possible at all, just leave the sentence as it is:

1 It was interesting to read the victim's diary.
2 It is not possible to contact Larry at home.
3 It was exciting to watch Real Madrid last season.
4 It is wrong to be in Cornwall at this time of year.
5 It is sure that McBride will turn up soon.
6 It is unusual to find them at home on Saturdays.
7 It was odd to ask Tracy that question.
8 It is surprising to have such luck.

Exercise 3

Make cleft sentences from the following in order to emphasise the underlined parts (one cleft sentence for each underlining):

1   Maisie works for a design studio.
2   The table was made in Shanghai.
3   We're going to the jazz concert next week.
4   Roger is on a study-trip at the weekend.
5   Sammy bought a horse from Cribbs Farm.

Bibliography

Biber, D., Johansson, S., Leech, G., Conrad, S. and Finegan, E. (1999) *The Longman Grammar of Spoken and Written English*. Harlow: Longman.
Fenn, P. (2010) *A Student Advanced Grammar of English*. Tübingen: Narr Francke Attempto.
Quirk, R., Greenbaum, S., Leech, G. and Svartvik, J. (1972) *A Grammar of Contemporary English*. London: Longman.
Quirk, R. and Greenbaum, S. (1973) *A University Grammar of English*. London: Longman.

Index

If not mentioned otherwise, terms are only indexed where they occur for the first time or when explained or defined in a more detailed way.

abbreviated forms 19
action nominal 184–6
active / active voice *see* voice
adjective 6, 20; evaluative adjectives 247, 249; gradability of adjectives 20; proper adjectives 20
adjective phrase *see* phrases
adverb 6, 21–3, 41; nominal relative adverbs 256; relative adverbs 219
adverbials 40–3
affirmative (positive) 35, 57
agent 8, 16, 36
agreement (concord) 35; person agreement 14; subject–verb agreement 16
anaphor / anaphora 12, 15, 24
antecedent 11, 15, 73, 210, 228
apposition 75, 218, 224
article / article word 23–5; definite articles 24–5; indefinite articles 24–5; zero article 25, 69;
aspect 17–18, 155, 157, 183; framework situation 192–3
attributive 21, 200
auxiliaries 17–18; auxiliary pro-forms 107; grammatical auxiliaries 18, 98; modal auxiliaries 18, 98; *see also* verbs

cataphor 24, 153
catenatives 102
causative constructions 204
clause 28, 30–1; absolute clauses 202; appositive clauses 227; comparative clauses 234, 237; conjunction clause 28, 122; consecutive clauses 234, 240; free clause 28, 122; gerund clause 162–3; infinitive clause 141–9; interrogative clause 258; main clause 132; nominal relative clause 138, 235, 255–9; participle clauses 189, 201, 222–3; postponed relative clauses 220–1; prepositional relative clause 213–14; reduced relative clauses 221; relative clause 211; sentential relative clauses 219; subordinated clause 127, 131; that-clauses 169, 234
cleft sentence 253–5
collocations 26, 89, 180
commands *see* imperatives
comparison 6, 20, 22, 84, 93; comparison of adjectives 237; comparison of adverbs 93; equative comparison 237; in flectional (forms) 84, 93; periphrastic (forms) 84, 93
complementation 19; adjectival complements 82–3; object complement 40; prepositional complement 79, 90, 115, 213, 231–2; subject complement 39; verb complementation 43, 143
complementation potential 43
composite lexical items *see* collocations
composition *see* phrases
concord *see* agreement
conjunction 27; complex conjunctions 28; co-ordinating conjunctions 123–4; correlative conjunctions 28; subordinating conjunctions 127, 130, 138; *see also* word-classes
co-ordination 122–6
countability (of nouns) 10, 77–8

declarative sentence 50
defining / non-defining *see* restriction
deixis 13
derivation 7

determiner 23–4; articles (definite / indefinite) 24–5; numerals 23, 66; possessive determiners 15, 25, 66; predeterminer 66–9; quantifiers 12, 20, 23, 25, 66
do-support 19, 51

ellipsis 123
'empty slot' phenomenon 214
enclitic *see* abbreviated forms
extraposition 153, 166, 246

function *see* phrase function or sentence function

genitive 12, 15; genitive noun 164; of-genitive 218; s-genitive 66
gerund 20, 71, 141, 161–2; base form of 181; perfect form of 181; perfect gerund 182; *see also* gerund clause
gradability *see* adjectives
grammar 3–8
grammatical function 34
grammatical independence 29
grammatical unit 16, 19, 34

head 9, 32; *see also* phrases

identification 66, 76, 130
idiomatic 26, 109
imperative 50, 60–1
implication 154–5, 176; factive meaning 176–7; implicative meaning 154, 175–6; implicative relation 154–5, 240, 242; negative implication 154–5
intransitive *see* transitive
inversion 19; auxiliary-inversion 51; subject–predicator inversion 50

lexical verbs *see* verbs

main verb *see* verbs
meaning 3–5, 8; *see also* semantics
modification 65–6; non-restrictive post-modification 75; premodification 65–6; post-modification 65, 72–3; restrictive post-modification 73–4
modifier 70
morphology 3–5

negation 19, 57–60, 103–4; phrase-focused negation 59; semantic negation (focus) 60
number (status) *see* countability

numerals 12, 20, 23, 77
noun 6–7; compound nouns 70, 162; genitive nouns 164; proper nouns 10, 20; *see also* word-classes

object 2, 13; direct object 4, 9, 37; grammatical direct object (Od-gramm.) 247; indirect object 37–9; infinitive object 248; logical direct object (Od-log.) 247; prepositional object 27, 109, 112, 163; *see also* sentence function
omission *see* ellipsis

patient 8, 37, 56
parenthesis 74, 216
participle 20, 71, 141, 188–9; base form of 198; past participle 18, 188, 201–2; perfect form of 198; perfect participle 198–9; present participle 161, 163, 188–9, 200–1
particle 26, 28; adverb particles 27, 90, 113; comparative particles 85, 237; negative particles 57, 103–5
partitive constructions 68, 226
passive / passive voice *see* voice
passivisation 56; complex transitive passivisation 57; ditransitive passivisation 56–7; monotransitive passivisation 55
patient 2, 8, 37
phonetics 3
phonology 3
phrase 8–9, 28–9, 31, 64; adjective phrases 9, 64, 82–4; adverb phrases 9, 64, 87–9; auxiliary phrases 100; comparative phrases 85, 93, 237; complex adjective phrases 234; complex noun phrases 209–10; complex phrases 209–10, 231; complex prepositional phrases 232, 235; composition of phrases 64; finite verb phrases 18, 98; head (of a) phrase 9, 32, 65, 85, 99; indefinite noun phrases 252; interrogative prepositional phrases 53; non-finite verb phrases 101; noun phrases 9, 64–5; phrase postponement 94, 105; prepositional phrases 9, 27, 53, 64, 79–81, 81, 224; verb phrases 9, 96–8
phrase function 64–5
phrase structure 64
postmodification 65, 72–3, 75, 210
postponement *see* phrases
pragmatic meaning 13

predicator 35–6
prepositional object 27, 109, 163
prepositions *see* word-classes
presupposition 168–9, 175–6, 239
progressive form 55, 155
pronoun 11–15; demonstrative pronouns 14–15, 23; existential pronouns 251; genitive relative pronouns 212, 218; indefinite pronouns 12–13, 252; interrogative pronouns 12, 14, 23, 51; nominal relative pronouns 138, 255; personal pronouns 13–14; possessive pronouns 14–15, 23; prop pronouns 14–15; reflexive pronouns 12–15; relative pronouns 14–15, 23, 138, 211–12; zero relative pronouns 212
proper adjectives *see* adjectives
proposition 16, 19
pseudo-cleft sentence 256–7

quantifiers 12, 20, 23
question 19, 50–4; direct questions 258; indirect questions 138, 256, 258; wh-questions 50–4; yes-no questions 50–1

receiver 38
recipient 145; *see also* receiver
restriction 73; 216; concept of restriction 216–17; non-restrictive 74, 216–17; non-restrictive postmodification 75; restrictive 73, 216–17; restrictive postmodification 73

secondary fronting 220–21
semantics 3, 5, 10–11, 15, 20–1, 26–7
sentence 28–9; affirmative sentence 35, 57; cleft sentence 253–5; complex sentence 128, 132, 134; compound sentence 123; declarative sentence 50; existential sentence 251–2; multiple sentence 31, 122; positive sentence 35, 57; pseudo-cleft sentence 256–7; simple sentence 31, 34–5
sentence fragments *see* ellipsis
sentence function 2, 35–43

specifier 90; infinitive clause 141–2
structure 6
subject 36–9; false subject constructions 248; grammatical subject 153, 243, 246; implied subject 146–7, 164; infinitive subject 250; logical subject 153, 243, 246; main-clause subject 147; *see also* sentence function
subject complement *see* complementation
subject divergence 165
subject relations 190
subject–verb agreement *see* agreement
subordination 127–9
syntax 3–4

tense 16–19, 156–7
transitive 37; complex transitive 40, 43; ditransitive 38, 43; intransitive 37, 43; monotransitive 38, 43
transitivity 43; *see also* transitive

verb 6, 10, 15–20; auxiliary verbs 17–18, 96; composite verb forms 17–18; complex prepositional verbs 111–13; complex transitive verbs 40, 43, 57; ditransitive verbs 38, 43; factive verbs 168, 176; finite verbs 17; implicative verbs 176; infinitive 18, 141; intransitive verbs 37, 44; lexical verbs 96; main verbs 96; monotransitive verbs 38; non-factive verbs 168 ; non-finite verbs 17, 139, 141; phrasal prepositional verbs 116–18; phrasal verbs 27, 113–16; point-telic verbs 195; prepositional verbs 26–7, 108–113; stative verbs 195; transitive verbs 37
verb complementation *see* complementation
verb phrase *see* phrases
voice 54–5, 158

weak forms *see* abbreviated forms
wh-word *see* interrogative pronoun
word-classes 6–7
word grammar *see* morphology
word order *see* syntax

For Product Safety Concerns and Information please contact our EU representative GPSR@taylorandfrancis.com
Taylor & Francis Verlag GmbH, Kaufingerstraße 24, 80331 München, Germany

www.ingramcontent.com/pod-product-compliance
Lightning Source LLC
Chambersburg PA
CBHW050531300426
44113CB00012B/2039